Warner Bros.

Warner Bros.

HOLLYWOOD'S ULTIMATE BACKLOT

STEVEN BINGEN

WITH MARC WANAMAKER, BISON ARCHIVES

TAYLOR TRADE PUBLISHING
Lanham · Boulder · New York · London

Published by Taylor Trade Publishing
An imprint of The Rowman & Littlefield Publishing Group, Inc.
4501 Forbes Boulevard, Suite 200, Lanham, Maryland 20706
www.rowman.com

16 Carlisle Street, London W1D 3BT, United Kingdom

Distributed by NATIONAL BOOK NETWORK

British Library Cataloguing in Publication Information Available

Library of Congress Cataloging-in-Publication Data
Bingen, Steven.
  Warner Bros. : Hollywood's ultimate backlot / Steven Bingen ; with Marc Wanamaker, Bison
Archives.
      pages cm
  Includes bibliographical references and index.
  ISBN 978-1-58979-961-5 (cloth : alk. paper) — ISBN 978-1-58979-962-2 (electronic)
1. Warner Bros—History. 2. Warner Bros. Pictures (1923–1967)—History. 3. Warner Bros.-
Seven Arts—History. 4. Warner Bros. Pictures (1969–)—History. 5. Motion picture studios—
California—Los Angeles—History. I. Wanamaker, Marc. II. Title.
  PN1999.W3B56 2014
  384'.80979494—dc23   2014007142

Printed in the United States of America

Contents

Foreword

WHEN I WAS working at Warner Bros., I was so busy I didn't realize what a fascinating place the studio itself really was. When I was invited to make a screen test in 1948, I wasn't really interested in being an actress at all, and working in film had never so much as crossed my mind. *Romance on the High Seas* had been written for Judy Garland, but the deal had fallen through. Betty Hutton was the next choice but had gotten pregnant. I was in Hollywood at the time, and my agent, Al Levy, talked me into performing a song at a party in Beverly Hills—which somehow led to an invitation to come to Warner Bros. for a screen test. I didn't know at the time that my life was about to change forever, that I would be on the lot for the next seven years, make seventeen pictures on its sets and backlots, record dozens of songs, and spend hundreds of hours working very hard in virtually every corner of the studio.

I learned much during my days at Warner Bros. When they first took me onto the *Romance on the High Seas* soundstage, I naïvely asked when we'd be leaving for the boat. Everyone laughed at me. But as I explored that film's intricate ocean liner settings, I realized that this soundstage and its dozens of sisters on the lot had actually been the place where hundreds of the movies I had watched growing up in Cincinnati had really been made. It astonished me that every location imaginable, from the high seas to tropical jungles could all be *created*, seemingly from scratch, in this remarkable place. Eventually it occurred to me that because most of what I thought I knew about ships or jungles, or about a thousand other places I'd never actually visited, actually came not from real life but from seeing these films. To this day I can't decide if Hollywood takes its visual cues from the real world, or if it is in fact, the other way around.

I'm afraid I took most of this for granted at the time, of course. But I'm proud to be able to say that I did learn very quickly to appreciate the very real talents of those I was fortunate enough to be able to work with. I was absolutely thrilled to be working with people like director Michael Curtiz and composer Ray Heindorf. It was great fun!

With this book we will all have a better appreciation of the studio lot and what went on there.

—Doris Day

Acknowledgments

A BOOK, LIKE a movie, or like a movie studio, is a collaborative project. The list of people who fed me anecdotes, information, or conjecture in putting together the story of *this* studio is a long one indeed. Although it occurs to me now, with some puzzlement, that the list of names included here is not so formidable as that for other books that I have been involved with. This puzzled me for a few minutes. After all, the book you now hold in your hands was at least as much work as anything I've ever attempted, and yet, when looking over the acknowledgments, it appears that I annoyed less people with my impertinent questions than I have in the past. How could this be?

The answer finally came to me. Warner Bros. Studios has been my backyard and my personal obsession for close to two decades. This is the story I was born to tell and have been writing, if only inside my head, for the last twenty years.

When I came to Hollywood, one of the first things I did was drive out to the Warner Bros. lot. I remember parking the car and just standing, transfixed, outside those tall walls. Because, like most tourists, I couldn't go inside, I had to settle for circling the fence line instead, peeking through the cracks in the walls, wanting to be on the other side.

Well, since then I *have* been on the other side. I've walked those same fence lines hundreds of times, only from the inside. I've shimmied up into the rafters above the soundstages. I've crawled through tunnels and underground passages. I've wandered through the vast warehouses of props and costumes, stood on the sets while the cameras were rolling, and marveled at postproduction wizardry. I've explored the backlots by moonlight and by flashlight. I've spent lonely hours in badly lit basements poring over studio records or trying to make sense of crumbling, curling blueprint rolls. I think it's safe for me to say that I know Warner Bros. Studios as well as anyone alive. Truth be told, much of the material between these covers I obtained, *absorbed*, on my own before I ever even knew I was writing a book.

That said, I've tried very hard not to make this story all about me. Certainly some sort of personal viewpoint is necessary in any endeavor. But I've tried very hard to let the story tell itself without slipping into first person. On occasion, however, I haven't been able to avoid telling the tale from my own perspective as an observer or a participant. I hope that the reader will forgive me these lapses—and blame me for any mistakes or omissions in the text and not the good people, alive and dead, whose names appear below.

Leith Adams, Angela Aleiss, Ron Barbagallo, Billy Blackburn, Eddie Bockser, Tina Brausam, Ned Comstock, Ben Cowitt, John Cox, Robby Cress, Linda Cummings-Whelen, Doris Day, Bill Elliott, Earl Hamner Jr., James Hampton, Amy Hilker, Yoko Honda, Janet Hoffmann, Sandra Joy Lee, Joan Leslie, Dick Mason, Geoff Murillo, Joe Musso, Camille O'Leary, Tom Ray, Ronald Charles Reeves, Dean Ricca, Lara Scheunemann, Nina Smith, David L. Snyder, Jim Stathacos, E. J. Stephens, Stan Taffel, Clint and Susan Walker, Cass Warner Sperling, and Fredd Wayne. Thank you, one and all.

I'd like to express my appreciation to Ben Burtt and Craig Barron for at least trying to explain the intricacies of old-school special effects and rear screen projection processes to me one afternoon in the Warner Bros. Research Library. Any mistakes in that chapter therefore indicate that they failed.

Jonathon Auxier, the curator of the USC Warner Bros. Archives, was always helpful and patient, even after years of digging up records and files for me to marvel over. Likewise, the staff of the Academy of Motion Pictures Arts and Sciences Margaret Herrick Library was there for me every time I needed them to be.

A special thanks to Robert Lane, as an architectural consultant and for painstakingly drafting for me the Warner Bros. studio lot map of my dreams, and to Mischa Hof, for answering a couple hundred questions about the Columbia-Warner Ranch and providing me with the perfect map of that fabled, mysterious property as well.

I'd like to thank the coauthors on my previous studio project, MGM: *Hollywood's Greatest Backlot*, Stephen X. Sylvester and Michael Troyan. And my agent Marilyn Allen, who understood what I was trying to do, even when I didn't.

And Marc Wanamaker and his amazing collection of photos from the amazing Bison Archives really, truly made it all possible.

And Beth Orsoff and Zoe Bingen, also known as my much-loved wife and daughter, for everything else.

Lastly, I'd like to thank all my friends who are still at Warner Bros. whom I failed to mention above. I hope that in the future I can still count on each of you for a drive-on pass. . . .

—Steven Bingen
Hollywood, CA

VISITING WARNER BROS. today, the studio feels like one of the few places in Hollywood, or anywhere, which, on the surface anyway, feels *exactly* the way a first-time visitor would have always imagined it to be.

First impressions, however, particularly in Hollywood, can deceive. It isn't until one has been to the lot—or, ideally, worked on the lot for a little while—that one starts to realize that some of those perceptions don't completely hold true.

First off is the much-venerated cliché about being discovered here and turned overnight into a star. Good luck with that one. And then there's the one about the glamour of moviemaking. After the first rush of excitement has passed, Warner Bros. doesn't feel glamorous at all. It probably never did. The place is more a well-greased factory than a decadent emperor's palace, more college campus than eccentric artists' colony.

Furthermore, and it's almost disappointing to admit it, but the people working in the offices on the lot seldom appear to be the cigar-smoking lunatics, megalomaniacs, tortured geniuses, sexual deviants, or preening, screaming mythmakers of legend either. Most of the people inside the studio gates are actually, at least to all outward appearances, happy.

There are, on any decent work day, five thousand people inside the compound. These industry insiders, from the talent to the lawyers, from the producers to the set painters, are, generally speaking, all proud to be at a point in their careers where they are working on the lot. A studio job is a symbol in the industry of success, an indication of being well paid, respected in their profession, and at Hollywood's very epicenter. The people at Warner Bros. are, generally speaking, proud to be working at, in, and for the studio at all—rather than looking into it from outside its gates. Which most people in the industry will admit to you that they have done early in their careers.

But most of those first impressions hold up, even after years spent on the lot. And the impression that the studio is best equipped to live up to is that, more than any other studio in the world, Warner Bros. *feels* like a movie studio is supposed to feel like.

What's more, it's hard to describe how wonderful it is for a visitor to see that this is true. So well does Warner Bros. embrace most of the surface clichés of film-making that the place almost feels like something designed by aliens who only knew about Hollywood by watching movies about the place. While other studios have continued to exist and continued to produce product, their physical facilities have been downsized, destroyed, marginalized, or outsourced. While other studios have seen their backlots mutate into theme parks or car parks and their production resources turned into carpeted office suites, Warner Bros. executives have continued to use their land and their resources exactly as they were designed to be used decades before anyone there today was born.

A day spent walking around Warner Bros. reveals, to a twenty-first-century visitor, many of the same sights and sounds that would have greeted a visitor twenty, or fifty, or seventy-five years ago; driving through the gates and cruising about the wide streets, past the commissary—where, sure enough, the actors playing cowboys sometimes really are seen eating outside with those portraying Indians—marveling at the wonders of the prop, costume, and makeup departments; and cruising wide-eyed between the rows of soundstages. And, finally, drifting onto the backlot, where fanciful architecture from a thousand worlds awaits its next close-up.

But, beyond the things that we recognize because these things are supposed to inhabit a Hollywood studio, the place feels familiar in a more subliminal way.

A footbridge connecting two postproduction buildings looks familiar enough when pointed out, but it takes on a somewhat haunted demeanor when we discover it was crossed by Judy Garland in *A Star Is Born*, played a sanitarium visited by Paul Newman in *The Helen Morgan Story* (1957), and, when decorated with barbed wire and plaster bricks, portrayed a prison wall breached by both Spencer Tracy in *20,000 Years in Sing Sing* (1932) and Superman in a much later television show.

A basement office under a crafts building looks like a basement office under a crafts building, until we recognize it as the wine cellar where a fistfight between James Dean and Rock Hudson was staged in *Giant*. It's hard not to hear the glass breaking and the cabinets splintering around the two stars when informed of this. Out on the backlot, a New York tenement street still has the fire escapes and alley-ways utilized in a hundred black-and-white gangster pictures, a dozen Technicolor musicals, and the cast of the TV show *Friends*.

The ghosts are all around. They may not be recognizable on a conscious level, but they and the places they haunt are, perhaps, just as recognizable to us as the homes and the hometowns where we actually grew up.

It should be emphasized before we journey onto the lot that our story is not about the people who made that lot what it is. That story has been told before, although some biographical prying into the personalities of the people who created Warner Bros. has been unavoidable. This book also is not about the business of producing movies, although once again the economics of Hollywood has often affected its physical development. And, lastly, this book is not about the films that the studio created, although . . . well, you get the idea.

What this book is, then, is the first-ever attempt to tell the story of Warner Bros. by documenting this remarkable 110-acre parcel of land. By going through the gates, behind the sets, and around the clichés, and exploring the most familiar yet least understood, and most photographed yet most paradoxically mysterious, property in the world.

ONE

Breaking Ground

S O HARDWIRED into our subconscious is Warner Bros. as a venerated American institution that it's somewhat hard to imagine that in the early years of the motion picture industry, Warner Bros., and most other film companies, were at one point not only considered disreputable, but their very existence was actually illegal.

In 1908 Thomas Edison organized the Motion Picture Patents Company, which attempted to force all producers to acquire a license from them in order to produce or exhibit motion pictures. In order to escape Edison's dictates and licensing fees, many pioneer film producers fled west, where the Edison trust was harder to enforce and easier to avoid. According to legend, "Director General" Cecil B. DeMille, who at this point in his career was neither a general nor a director, but instead had been eking out a living as a remarkably unsuccessful actor, was assigned the task of creating a western in Flagstaff, Arizona, for Jesse Lasky's Feature Play Company in 1913. Arizona had been selected for its authentic western locations and for its proximity to the Mexican border should Edison's agents make an appearance. According to this same legend, it was raining in Flagstaff when the train arrived there, so DeMille stayed on board that train and rode it all the way west to the end of the line, which was Hollywood, California.

Other fledgling filmmakers followed DeMille's example. Among these pioneers were the sons of Benjamin and Pearl Warner.

The name wasn't really Warner. For years, even members of the family didn't know what their actual name was. The only thing they were told was that Benjamin had emigrated from Poland (in 1883), so it was assumed that the name was probably "Varna" or "Verner." It wasn't until 2010 that his great-granddaughter Cass

There are very few photos of all four Warner brothers together. In fact, this is one of only two commonly used for business purposes. From left: Harry, Jack, Sam, and Albert. 1927.

discovered that the actual family name, not forgotten but rather suppressed in a rather touching attempt at sounding more "American," had actually been Wonksolaser—which would have been harder to spell out on marquees and on the side of the studio water tower than Warner.[1]

The Warner brothers (and there were actually seven of them, out of twelve children) who played a part in the development of the studio were Harry (1881–1958), Albert "Abe" (1884–1967), and Jack (1892–1978). A fourth brother, Sam (1888–1927), was vitally important to the destiny of the company, but died the year before the brothers acquired their Burbank lot.

Like most future movie moguls, the brothers drifted into the business almost by accident. First they were exhibiters, running other people's movies, and as new films became harder to acquire under Edison's repressive stewardship, they began to make their own product. The first picture they filmed themselves (in St. Louis, in 1912) was a two-reel western called *The Covered Wagon*, or *The Peril of the Plains*, depending on which city or which year you saw it in.

Success didn't come quickly, or easily, for the brothers. In 1917 Harry purchased the rights to James W. Gerard's inflammatory World War I memoir *My Four Years in Germany*, and the resultant film's success in 1918 went a long way toward giving them a degree of legitimacy in the booming young industry. The film itself carried many of the hallmarks that would later make the studio famous: a "ripped from the headlines" topic—in this case, alleged German atrocities—action, violence, and a marked political viewpoint, which was as rare in popular entertainment then as it is now.

In 1919, the brothers leased real estate on their first Hollywood studio lot—having previously rented production space in the Bronx in New York City, and, in California, in San Francisco, Edendale, and Santa Paula. This particular property was the Burston/Horsley Studio, located at 6050 Sunset Boulevard. According to historian Marc Wanamaker, during this period they also briefly leased space at yet another lot, nearby, on the corner of Santa Monica and Van Ness Boulevards.

The same year, the brothers shot the popular serial *Tiger's Claw* on this lot and at the Bostock/Selig Zoo. This period also found them, briefly, working out of yet another property at the corner of Washington and Ince Boulevards in nearby Culver City and downtown at the Horsley Park Studios. Near the end of the year, they could be found shooting Monty Banks comedies at Sunset and El Centro on a former Universal Studios facility as well. Each move, and each movie, brought them closer to mainstream success, and yet their breakthrough, the picture that would justify their years as relative bottom feeders, eluded them.

The Horsley Park Studio, seen here in 1915, would four years later become a temporary home for the fledgling company.

The future Warner Bros.–owned studio under construction. 1919.

In 1920, Sam convinced his brothers that in order to be successful, they would need to look successful first. He drove his skeptical siblings out to a massive (to them) 10-acre property, again on Sunset Boulevard. The cost of the lot was $25,000. But he emphasized to them how prestigious it would be to own the property out-right. He also played to their vanity by pointing out how good the name "Warner Brothers" would look when permanently mounted above the gate (the company name would not be finalized as "Bros.," as opposed to "Brothers," until incorpora-tion in 1923). Even the conservative Harry was eventually won over, and the deal was made. The company repeatedly missed making their monthly payments on the property for the first year, but somehow they held off eviction, convinced that their salvation was on the way.

It was. A banker with the wonderful name of Motley Flint, who had early on helped the brothers finance *Tiger's Claw*, again came to their rescue by working out a generous line of credit with Harry for a cool million dollars. Harry realized that the company would have to grow in order to survive. He used the money not to pay off debts or to retrench, but to secure other loans, often from shadowy loan sharks at staggering interest rates.

And Warner Studios *was* growing. But at the same time it was seldom more than a single missed payment away from financial ruin. The brothers' continuing inability to secure theaters in which to run their product kept their pictures from screening at all in many markets, and so returns on their production costs were often irregular or insufficient. Another problem was other studios that arranged that Warner films would be "delayed" by the film laboratories, the result being that what bookings their pictures did have were sometimes missed. Harry responded by putting Sam, always the most technical-minded of the brothers, in charge of building a three-story, 130-foot-long film laboratory from scratch on their lot. He did this in only ninety days.

Each brother had by now taken on the characteristic roles within the family, and consequently within the company, which they would play for the rest of their lives. Pragmatic Harry was the businessman. Even during this period, he increasingly spent most of his time in New York, arranging for financing from bankers and bootleggers to keep the fledgling studio afloat. Albert was the treasurer, although he usually deferred to Harry over where exactly these finances would come from and how they would be used. Sam, the middle brother, was both the technical expert and a mediating force between the older, more conservative half of the family, Harry

"Welcome Exchange Executives to Warner Bros. Pictures Convention" shouts a banner in front of the Warner Sunset Studio. The bus in the foreground is pulling a portable generator to illuminate the gala affair. 1925.

and Abe, and the youngest brother, Jack. Jack L., or J.L. Warner, as he liked to be called—although the "L," at least at first, stood for precisely nothing—was the one who usually selected the scripts, hired the talent, and assured that the product actually got made.

On April 4, 1923, Warner Bros. was incorporated in Delaware—then as now, a business-friendly state. Most of Hollywood's future giants were originally family-run businesses. Harry and Jack Cohn were the actual creators of Columbia Studios, and Walt and Roy Disney built an empire that they originally called "Disney Brothers." Yet the Warners were the first ones, ultimately the only ones, to make it official and part of the company's name and logo. Warner Brothers—and Warner Bros., it would be from then on.

The corporate landscape of Hollywood was already largely in place, or would be by the end of the decade. Hollywood's seven major studios—the other six being MGM, 20th Century Fox, Columbia, Paramount, Universal, and RKO, the last of which would be displaced as a major in the late 1950s by the Walt Disney Company—continue to dominate the industry to the present day. These organizations are often referred to collectively, perhaps romantically, perhaps sarcastically, as the "Seven Sisters." But that phrase itself, with its odd, lingering echoes of Greek myth, was in actuality borrowed from the name of a particularly luminous star cluster known to set in the West, the land where mythological heroes always journey in search of their destinies.

As the Warner Company gestated and then expanded, so too did their lot on Sunset Boulevard. The property had been used as a studio for only a year before the brothers purchased the lot, so most of the construction and improvements had been up to them. An impressive administration building with Greek-style columns rose in front of Sunset Boulevard in 1923. Pedestrians on the sidewalk in front could not have realized that this administration building was mostly a façade. The only offices in the building were behind the windows and behind those columns facing the street. Very few employees worked in offices at all during this period. Most "administration" at the studio was conducted on the stages, the largest of which was in the same building, behind those tiny, nearly unnecessary offices. In fact the building itself, much like a backlot, was constructed almost entirely of wood. Only the ornate fronting facing the street suggested the solidity and respectability that the brothers, and their industry, were striving for at the time.

Six additional stages of assorted sizes eventually encircled the plant, which the brothers kept busy grinding out serials, westerns, and melodramas during this period. The most successful of these pictures starred a German shepherd and World War I veteran named Rin Tin Tin. Sam Warner's remarkable laboratory was just south and slightly east of the administration-building-shooting stage, sandwiched between a property room and the mill, where sets and props were constructed. A water tower, a symbol of corporate filmmaking then as now, stood behind a lumber yard and was

Jack Warner, left, takes to the KFWB microphone like he was born with it in his hand. Brother Harry, right, isn't so sure. 1925.

visible from nearby Van Ness Avenue. There was no designated backlot, although exterior sets were constructed, or torn down, as needed.

In 1925, the brothers got into radio when they constructed twin transmission towers at the studio with the letters "KFWB" in glowing lights printed on each of them. Those call letters, which allegedly stood for "Keep filming Warner Bros.," were actually a happy accident, randomly assigned by the U.S. Department of Commerce when Sam applied for a license. KFWB would continue to be affiliated with, and provide advertising for, the studio until 1950, although the station would be moved to the Warner Theatre on Hollywood Boulevard when it was discovered that its broadcasting was somehow interfering with the sound being recorded in the stages below.

In April 1925, Sam talked his brothers into acquiring an experimental sound system called Vitaphone, which had been developed at a laboratory in Manhattan. Other systems for combining sound and cinema had existed, at least in theory, for years. But the problem had always been how to amplify the audio (despite the existence of technology for doing so, which itself went back as far as 1913) and how to play back that amplified sound in synchronization with a projected picture.

Considering the financial straits the brothers still found themselves in during this period, and even considering the steady, remarkable popularity of Rin Tin Tin, their faith in this untried system is rather remarkable. In fact, Sam had to purchase some of the Vitaphone patents personally when his brothers initially refused

A Vitaphone projector, even simplified for public consumption, as in this 1927 press photo, illustrated all too well just how complicated and convoluted synchronizing audio and visual media really was in the 1920s.

to participate. At one point he threatened to take the process to Paramount before Harry agreed to let Warner Bros., yet again, risk everything on what could have been another mad scheme.

The first Vitaphone shorts were produced under Sam's supervision at the Vitagraph Studios in Brooklyn, New York. Vitagraph was a long-established production company that Harry had recently arranged to purchase, and from which the name "Vitaphone" had been created. The tests were not encouraging, and the resultant shorts were reportedly not well received by audiences at the two theaters, which had been initially and expensively wired to accommodate the process.

Undaunted, the brothers decided that audiences accustomed to silent films would have to be "educated" to appreciate talking cinema. Consequently, these early efforts continued music and effects and songs—but no actual dialogue.

The first feature film selected by the brothers to utilize the Vitaphone process was *Don Juan* (1926), which even without the expensive sound system would have been a most unusual Warner Bros. picture. The film was a period piece with

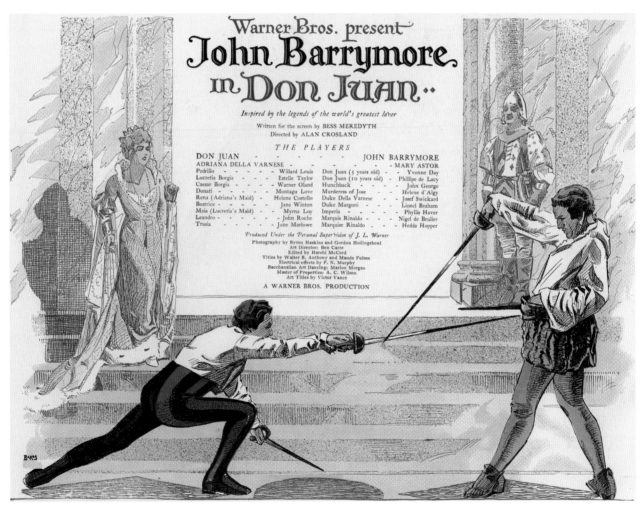

Publicity materials for *Don Juan* were forced to deemphasize the films' most marketable asset, its soundtrack, in markets where a theater equipped to project Vitaphone had not yet been installed. 1926.

expensive costumes and settings, and it headlined a non-canine star, the very prestigious (and very expensive) John Barrymore.

Ultimately, *Don Juan* was well received. But once again, the very limited number of theaters where the picture could be projected insured that it would not be a moneymaker. What's more, although the film had music and sound effects, the lack of dialogue made the result virtually indistinguishable from any silent picture from the same era—which of course would have been projected in the big cities with a (live) symphonic score, anyway.

It was obvious that the next Vitaphone release would have to be a sensation if the process, and if Warner Bros., was to survive. *The Jazz Singer* (1927) had been written as a Broadway vehicle for headliner Al Jolson, who, ironically, had then passed on it. Not only was Jolson signed to act and sing in the film version, but ultimately his adlibbed dialogue, "Wait a minute, wait a minute, you ain't heard nothin' yet. Wait a minute I tell ya, you ain't heard nothing," would be the first words of dialogue ever spoken in a commercial feature film.

The film was shot in Stages 1 and 6 on the Sunset lot. Certain sequences were done in New York and at the Vitagraph lot in East Hollywood as well, which the brothers had acquired as part of the purchase of that company. The technical details were daunting, and everyone on the set looked to Sam for the answers. A concrete bunker in the middle of the studio was designated the "recording stage." Inside, Sam and his crew sweated over the large black discs on which the sound would be recorded. The sound itself was transported from the set via 6-inch thick black cables that serpentined out from the stage doors and across the lot into this booth.

Furthermore, once the sound had been captured it was discovered that editing these discs was an impossibility. The sound could only be altered by dubbing the resultant disk, selectively, onto yet another disk, and into the desired sequence, and by dealing with the resultant loss of quality each time this was attempted. What's more, because the film and the disk were separate, any alternation of either one would cause the sound on the rest of that disk to be out of synchronization with the film on the rest of that reel! Nathan Levinson, a musician, eventually figured out a way to dub multiple recordings onto a "master" and was promoted to "sound engineer," a newly invented title, for his trouble.

There were hundreds of resultant aesthetic problems as well. The language of sound movies had yet to be worked out; indeed, it had to be invented during those long hours inside that dark little room. If, for example, Jolson was seen singing by the camera at the very back of a theater, would the resultant sound volume need to be lower than if the camera were positioned closer to the stage? And if the angle changed during the song to that closer angle, would the sound volume then need to be adjusted as well?

The Jazz Singer premiered on October 6, 1927, in New York City's Times Square. The film was a sensation, but none of the brothers were there for the greatest moment of their lives. Sam had died of a cerebral hemorrhage the day before.

Original artwork for the "Warner Bros. supreme triumph," *The Jazz Singer*. 1927.

Hollywood had created its first talking picture, and talking pictures had created their first martyr.

The success of *The Jazz Singer* was immediate and irreversible. It has been estimated that *The Jazz Singer* made as much as $5 million at U.S. box offices. Within a year, more than 400 theaters would be wired to project sound movies—although in early 1930, the brothers caved in to pressure from theater owners and started using Fox's competing, and less cumbersome, "sound on film" process to allow beleaguered theater owners to pay for a single and universal format. This had been a battle Harry had lost in spite of being there first.

The frenzied New York premiere of *The Jazz Singer*. None of the brothers were there. October 6, 1927.

Never again would Warner Bros. be a poverty row studio scrounging for theaters and audiences. In September 1928, Harry purchased the Stanley Theater Corporation, which owned 250 theaters in seven states, in order to solve the company's continuing distribution problems. He also gobbled up a music-publishing conglomerate, and in the following month he purchased two-thirds of First National Pictures, a major producer-distributer. In 1929 Harry bought the company outright.

First National had been founded in 1917 by Thomas Tally and James Williams, and was composed of a syndicate of theater owners both hungry for product and with the financial resources to produce that product themselves. In 1918, they had signed superstar Charlie Chaplin to a million-dollar contract, probably one of the first times in American business that a single individual was so well compensated.

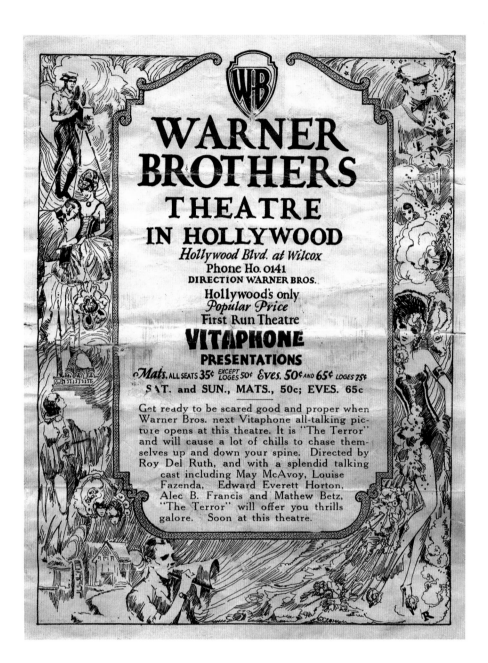

WARNER
BROTHERS
THEATRE
IN HOLLYWOOD
Hollywood Blvd. at Wilcox
Phone Ho. 0141
DIRECTION WARNER BROS.
Hollywood's only
Popular Price
First Run Theatre
VITAPHONE
PRESENTATIONS
Mats. ALL SEATS 35¢ EXCEPT LOGES 50¢ Eves. 50¢ AND 65¢ LOGES 75¢
SAT. and SUN., MATS., 50c; EVES. 65c

Get ready to be scared good and proper when Warner Bros. next Vitaphone all-talking picture opens at this theatre. It is "The Terror" and will cause a lot of chills to chase themselves up and down your spine. Directed by Roy Del Ruth, and with a splendid talking cast including May McAvoy, Louise Fazenda, Edward Everett Horton, Alec B. Francis and Mathew Betz, "The Terror" will offer you thrills galore. Soon at this theatre.

1926 window bill heralding upcoming Warner Bros. Vitaphone talkies, including the first sound horror film, *The Terror*.

But battles with other producers-distributers, notably with archrival Paramount, had made First National vulnerable and perhaps more inclined to listen to Harry's offer. An interesting tenet of the final agreement was an arrangement with Warner Bros. to keep the name First National "alive" even after the final sale had been completed. In fact, the words "A First National Picture" would open many Warner Bros. films until as late as 1958! In 1929 alone, Warner Bros. produced a head-scratching 86 feature films, 45 of which were released under the First National banner.

This puzzling arrangement was not just a sentimental or contractual one, however. At the time, the name and logo for First National equaled higher rentals from theaters than did Warner Bros. So the Warners used both names, hoping that the WB titles would someday obtain rentals equal to those of First National—which eventually happened. In fact, in Great Britain and other overseas territories, Warner

Vintage postcard depicting the Sunset Boulevard Studio as it appeared in 1932. Note the KFWB transmittal towers.

Bros. for several years used the First National logo almost exclusively because the WB shield still meant nothing in Europe.

The primary reasoning for purchasing First National had been, again, for the company's name and for its theater chain. But there was another benefit to the buy-out as well. It was a benefit probably not immediately apparent to the brothers, but one that would ultimately become more entwined with the Warner Bros. identity than any other single asset in their history.

TWO

....

Burbank

D AVID BURBANK was a prosperous New Hampshire–born dentist who purchased almost four thousand acres of farmland in the southeast San Fernando Valley in 1867. Much of the land had originally been part of the vast Rancho Providencia tract, which ran along the Los Angeles River to the base of the Hollywood hills. In fact Mount Lee, eventually home of the infamous Hollywood sign, is just above the current studio and just behind the adjacent Disney lot, but is not visible from either studio because it is located on the opposite side of the mountain. The actual Hollywood district, with separate zip and area codes, now officially stops just beyond both studios' back gates. The current Warner Bros. lot is quite literally close enough to touch Hollywood, but not quite close enough to see it.

Management and production at First National Pictures on the west coast were at the time based at the Brunton Studios on Melrose Avenue, now the home of their one-time rival Paramount Pictures. Although the industry was more than a decade old in 1926, there had never to that time been a purpose-built studio constructed from a preexisting plan designed according to a single architectural theme or motif. Existing studio lots had been converted from army barracks or warehouses, or had been designed piecemeal, with some sections opulently designed and expensively realized and other structures on the same lot thrown up on the cheap, depending on the current fortunes of management.

But First National decided to do things differently. They purchased sixty-eight acres of this Burbank farmland from a farmer named Howard G. Martin (who had lived on the property since 1908) on February 17, 1926. This property included

Howard Martin's ranch house continued to stand on the property even after it was absorbed by First National, and in fact it was occasionally used as a set until 1952.

Dr. Burbank's original farmhouse, probably the oldest structure in the city, which would survive on the property near the current corner of Warner Boulevard and Avon Street until 1952.

For the first time at a movie studio, architectural models were carefully designed and plans were drawn up detailing every building and street. Even more impressively, the lot was consciously designed using elements that would be carried over from building to building, tying the sprawl of the property together and giving it an architectural unity unique among industrial sites of any period.

At the time, Spanish Revival was the preeminent design style in California. This motif is still reflected on the lot by the terra cotta tiled rooftops on many of the buildings and the rancho-style stucco walls and vaguely Moorish detailing. Surprisingly, this look was carried over to the later bungalows and soundstages as well, the rooftops of which were even painted red in the 1930s in order to mimic, backlot-like, the tiled rooftops on the earlier structures.

The Austin Company, which conveniently had offices in Los Angeles, was selected to design the new studio. The original plans called for thirty-six buildings, including eight stages. The budget for phase one on this project was set at $2.5 million.

Construction at the new studio would begin on March 28, 1926. Surviving photographs of the process, taken by official chronicler Cary Wilson, show a very

View of the studio looking north into the San Fernando Valley, with simulated red tile roofs visible on top of many of the stages. Circa 1950s.

muddy construction site populated by dozens of offices, four crafts buildings, and four shooting stages, all going up in a very orderly fashion seemingly at the same time and at the same speed—and teams of efficient-looking workers in white (if necessarily mud-soiled) coveralls, smiling into the camera at us from the other side of the soon-to-be site of a million movies.

The first of those movies, astonishingly, would begin principal photography on the lot a scant three months later, when, on June 25, cinematographer-turned-director Silvano Balboni yelled "action" to his leading lady, the beautiful Anna Q. Nilsson, from across a muddy set constructed for a film to be titled *The Masked Woman*. Decades later, Nilsson would bookend her rather tragic Hollywood career with a cameo appearance in Billy Wilder's brilliant and acidic *Sunset Boulevard* (1950). But on this morning anyway, all things were in ascendance.

When the new studio fell into the Warners' collective laps almost inadvertently, Jack Warner, the brother with the most sense of place about his soon-to-be empire, toured the vast new factory, and immediately saw past the mud and the wet cement and instead saw a place to build his own personal empire. The Burbank Airport was already up the road, a problem for sound recording, and for period pictures to be sure (a 1940 memo suggesting floating balloons to keep air traffic away was largely ignored, and the problem continues to this day), but overall the property was perfect for realizing every dream that Jack had ever had.

One thing that the new studio did not contain was a sound department, or facilities for recording sound. When the Warners acquired the property, this was the

Stages 4 and 2 are on the right above Dressing Room 3. The building in the foreground on the left was a suite of editing rooms—and still is. June 19, 1926.

first situation that needed to be remedied. An ingenious jury rigging by the overworked sound people in Hollywood allowed the audio to be transmitted via phone lines across the Hollywood hills to Sunset Boulevard, where it was recorded in the same airless booth as pictures shot in the stages on that lot. The sound occupied so much bandwidth when transmitted through telephone cables that only one movie could be made at a time, and only at night.

The first picture made at the studio by Warner Bros. was a Richard Barthelmess vehicle entitled *Weary River* (1929). In November 1930, Jack decided to move all of the company's remaining production facilities and his personal office to the new lot in Burbank. Previous to this date, J.L. had been forced to keep his office on the Hollywood lot as part of an agreement with the U.S. Justice Department about keeping the two companies "separate." Even after the official move, the original Warner Sunset studio, like the Vitagraph lots in East Hollywood and Brooklyn, New York, would continue as annex properties, but the power behind the throne, and the throne itself, would thereafter be found in Burbank.

The first Warner-dictated addition to the new studio was the so-called Warner Building, which was the first home of the Music Department, which had been created as a result of Harry's 1928 purchase of M. Witmark and Sons music publishers. The building is still used today and contains a large screening room (211 seats) and suites of offices.

September 15, 1928. Stages 4 and 5 under construction. At the time, there were no provisions for soundproofing these stages—an expensive mistake.

By 1930, the lot contained seven stages (newly and expensively soundproofed at $13,000 each), an administration complex that consisted of four separate but adjacent buildings, a complex of dressing rooms, and, of course, sound and sound-recording suites. The backlot, or rather the area set aside for the construction of exterior sets, was at the time located on the eastern, or back part, of the lot, just south of where the Burbank family farmhouse at the time still stood. Movie studios of this era had yet to fully realize that these sets, recreations of architectural styles that were not available naturally in Los Angeles, could be used, with the assistance of new signage and camera angles, for subsequent films set in similar locations. Eventually, however, these outdoor sets became more elaborate and more substantial as their usefulness became apparent.

The first *permanent* backlot set at Warner Bros. (that is, if one can use such a word anywhere inside a Hollywood studio) was a "Brownstone Street," which was constructed in the late 1920s to run from the junction of the commissary and a suite of recording stages to the rest of the (largely undeveloped) backlot. Originally the set was, as was the tradition at the time, only two single-sided façades facing each other for roughly the length of a single city block. But this New York City–inspired boulevard proved so versatile, and so lucrative, that it eventually, as production demanded, became what it originally had been designed only to portray;

Rare snowfall in Burbank was the occasion for this photograph looking southeast across Olive Avenue at Stages 2, 4, 6, and 8. 1932.

an actual row of city buildings outfitted with electricity, staircases, landings, and interior apartments. The set is still in use, and as of this writing it is probably being photographed for something at this very minute. The following year, a legendary "New York Street" rose at the lip of the Brownstone district. The backlot expanded east from there.

On December 4, 1934, a fire started inside a machine shop near an outdoor mine set for the Michael Curtiz picture *Black Fury*—currently, the corner of Warner Boulevard and Avon Street. Curtiz rallied his crew of approximately seventy to battle the flames and was quickly aided by other employees and the staffs of the nearby Burbank, Los Angeles, and Hollywood Fire Departments, as well as the on-lot Fire Department commanded by its sixty-five-year-old chief, Albert Rounder. According to the *Los Angeles Times*, nearby Toluca Lake resident Bing Crosby and Warner Bros. stars Dick Powell, Warren Williams, Helen Morgan, and Kay Francis helped man the fire line. Ultimately, the blaze took out most of the standing backlot east of New York Street, as well as the studio's crafts departments, a property warehouse, and eight tractors just purchased as props for an upcoming Joe E. Brown comedy, *Earthworm Tractor*.

The aftermath of the December 4, 1934, fire that burned most of the backlot.

More tragically still, the fire also snuffed out the film vaults, where priceless negatives from many early Vitagraph and First National films were stored, and ended the life of Chief Rounder, who as the fire was brought under control sat down on the ground complaining of pains in his chest that turned out to be a heart attack. His last words were reported to be "We licked it, didn't we?"[1]

Jack Warner, however, was not licked. "We have ample facilities at our Sunset Boulevard Studio to take care of all of our immediate mechanical and constructional requirements. Shops that have been destroyed will be rebuilt as quickly as the ground can be cleared of debris. The loss is fully covered by insurance," he told the press.[2]

Those losses were estimated to be between $250,000 and $500,000. Fourteen acres of largely brand-new studio real estate had been leveled. But, unlike even a few years earlier, Jack's optimism could no longer be dismissed as mere bravado. In the year the studio was being rebuilt, he also found time to produce fifty-four feature-length motion pictures.

Physically, the studio continued to expand as well, with the original sixty-eight First National acres eventually expanding to over a hundred. In 1929, Harry started

After the 1934 fire, the backlot was quickly rebuilt.

purchasing the land that would eventually become the Warner Ranch as well. At the same time, the studio also apparently purchased or leased property near Cordova Street in Burbank, which was usually referred to internally as "30 Acres" or "the North 40."

In 1931, they also purchased the Teddington Studios in London for the purpose of producing "British" product to fulfill legal quotas that needed to be met before Hollywood films could appear in English cinemas.

Another popular location for Warner productions during this era and beyond, constantly leased by the studio but never purchased, was the Providencia Ranch, which in fact was across the street from the back of the studio. The property was, at the time, sometimes still referred to as the old Universal Ranch, and in fact had been part of that studio's original development. In 1915 D. W. Griffith had filmed battle scenes for his landmark *The Birth of a Nation* on the property. *Black Legion* (1937), *Jezebel* (1938), *Sergeant York* (1941), *Objective Burma* (1945), and *Night and Day* (1946) are among the pictures that filmed sequences on this hillside property, which today is the permanent home of the Forest Lawn Memorial Park Cemetery, where many of the studio's late and legendary stars rest.

Warner Bros. was the first studio to take a stand against Nazism with *Confessions of a Nazi Spy* (1939) and was the first American studio to pull their offices, and films, out of Germany. In 1944, a German buzz bomb struck a studio rooftop at the Teddington lot in England and destroyed the primary shooting stage, the administration building, and several other structures. It also took the life of the studio manager, Anenda Max "Doc" Salomon, who was Jack Warner's wife's cousin and one of his most loyal employees. So grieved was Jack by his old friend's killing that he

"30 Acres," a backlot property the studio operated near Cordova Street in Burbank, as it looked in 1947.

ordered a plaque put up on the wall facing the lawn in his office in Burbank. For the rest of his life, Jack would always point it out to acquaintances while walking across the lot. The plaque is no longer there, sadly (Jack Warner Jr. once mentioned that his sister Barbara kept it), although Jack transcribed what it said and even had it printed in his own autobiography: "In Memory of A. M. 'Doc' Salomon, who served Warner Bros. faithfully and well for 30 years, and who gave his life in line of duty during the robot bombing of England on July 5, 1944."[3]

The war ended with the studio still making unprecedented profits. In 1947 they ended the fiscal year $22 million in the black, their biggest profit ever. At the time, 3500 employees entered the gates of the Burbank studio every work day. But an era was ending at the same moment that it was peaking, and things would never be the same. In May 1948, the U.S. Supreme Court ruled that the studio's control of production, distribution, and exhibition constituted a monopoly, and so the Warners and Hollywood's other aging moguls would have to sell off their theater chains, which had been the reason for the purchase of the Burbank property to begin with.

An aerial view of the Warner lot and south Burbank from 1939. Note the "30 Acres" backlot property slightly northeast of the studio proper, and, beyond that, the future Walt Disney Studio lot, under construction.

Originally, the Warners had hoped that they could avoid the new regulations by having two brothers own production and distribution and letting a third own all the theaters separately—a sly idea, indeed, but one that their lawyers nixed. Of the four hundred theaters in their circuit, the brothers probably particularly hated to give up the prestigious Warner Bros. Hollywood Theater on the corner of Broadway and 51st Street in New York City—because it was lit by the largest electric sign in the world, a fact that they seldom failed to mention in publicity releases.

The loss of income from the theaters was something that none of the Seven Sisters were ever able to fully recover from. Although smaller studios, such as Columbia and Universal, neither of which had ever owned a significant number of screens, ultimately fared better. In 1952, the Warner Bros.' financial record indicated $87,548,158 in assets from land holdings. The following year, the first year without the theaters, the number was only $11,038,336, although the sale of the theaters did add considerably to the company's reported profits for that particular year.

The backlot Bonnyfeather Street in flames in the May 16, 1952, studio fire.

The disastrous Supreme Court ruling was bad enough. But it was coupled with an inevitable aging of talent on both sides of the camera in Hollywood. By the 1950s, the major studios were all at least thirty years old and had become a part of the very establishment they had once craved admittance to. This made those studios' movies, in general, less vibrant and less challenging than they had been in previous, less complacent decades. James Dean, the most interesting Warner Bros. leading man of this period, was an exception, but his tragic death in an auto accident in 1955 probably shoved the company backward into its previous, apathetic state. A growing and unexpected indifference by audiences, perhaps sensing all of this and lured away by television, as well as the flight of middle-class audiences away from urban areas and urban theaters and into the suburbs, were probably additional causes for a drop in movie attendance in the 1950s.

The bad luck continued. On May 16, 1952, a fire broke out in an unused corner of New York Street. The flames quickly engulfed the nearby Stage 21, the largest on the lot, and burned it to the ground along with much of the backlot. As in 1934, the studio's executives and stars, including Kathryn Grayson, Burt Lancaster, and Ray Bolger, pitched in to help out. Exploding incandescent bulbs kept both professional and amateur firefighters' nerves on edge by popping incessantly and unexpectedly as everyone worked to extinguish the blaze, which ultimately consumed about $1.5 million of the studio's assets and history.

On July 9 of the same year yet another fire began, this time east of the setting of the first blaze near a ships' dock setting beside the ruined Stage 21, which had yet to be fully cleared away. Forestry lookouts up to eighty miles away reported seeing the flames, which this time consumed twenty-five acres of real estate valued at nearly $5 million. Also destroyed was the original Burbank farmhouse, which was the only "real" structure on the backlot. Initially arson was suspected: a *Los Angeles Times* article speculated that investigators were on the lookout for an unidentified "fire happy person," but eventually it was ruled that both fires were, in fact, accidental.[4]

In the wake of the two fires, J.L. surprised no one when in 1953 he announced that he was "tapering off" film production for as much as ninety days to concentrate on rebuilding and restructuring the company.[5] Truthfully, however, J.L. was probably wondering most what to do about his brother Harry.

The second 1952 fire, on July 9, 1952, destroyed most of the sets from the bottom of the backlot Tenement Street to the Los Angeles River.

The relationship between Harry and Jack, always somewhat confrontational, had been disintegrating since Sam's death in 1927. Sam, as a middle brother, had been a moderating force between the loud, brash Jack and his unsmiling (and usually unapproving) older brother. By the 1950s, Albert was largely out of the picture industry and in retirement in Florida. That left Jack and Harry to battle over the studio, which they did.

In 1956, the three brothers agreed to sell all of their stock to an outside investment group for just over $20 million. Immediately after the sale, however, it was announced that Jack had bought back that same stock and was now staying with the company as president, a title that had been Harry's for decades.

Harry never recovered from this betrayal. He suffered a massive stroke from which he never recovered, either, and he refused to ever speak to Jack again. He died on July 27, 1956. J.L. was at a casino in the south of France at the time and did not attend the service.

Four days after Harry's funeral, on August 4, 1956, Jack crashed his 1947 Alfa Romeo into a coal truck after a long night at the baccarat tables. Badly injured, he was unable to return to his studio for nearly four months. When he did come back to work, he was touched to see that "Welcome Back Jack" banners had been spread across all the gates. He entered the lot by driving under one of them, which included a picture of his own smiling face.

THREE

Front Lot Studio Tour

WITH THE ARRIVAL of the 1960s, while Jack Warner was moving into his fifth decade as a movie mogul, the studio he created continued to move forward as well. But, like Warner himself, Warner Bros. Studio now seemed increasingly scared and oblivious to the world outside the gates. There would be very little new construction during this period, and very little would be modified or updated on the lot either. Consequently, many buildings still looked the same as they had in the 1920s when they had been constructed. So in the 1960s, these buildings, and to a certain degree the property itself, had a dated, wax museum quality about it. Ugly, faded carpets, even by the standards of the 1960s; ancient, wheezing air conditioners; and posters on the walls heralding long-forgotten films were, during this period, the standard in nearly every office and hallway in nearly every building.

The employees working in these buildings, many of whom had been with the company for decades by the 1960s, were, like the lot itself, out of touch, graying at the temples, and perhaps a little reticent regarding new ideas and new blood. As hard as it is to believe now, during the 1960s there were almost no young people working in Hollywood. The unions had made it virtually impossible for anyone from the outside to get employment on a California movie set. And so the same loyal staffers who had been at the studio during World War II, or their offspring, were still toiling on the lot in the 1960s.

Even the talent *in front* of the camera was elderly during this period. Vintage, beloved stars like John Wayne, who had made his first Warner Bros. film in 1932, and Doris Day, who had started her career on the lot in the late 1940s, were still topping the box office charts during this period, although less people were going to

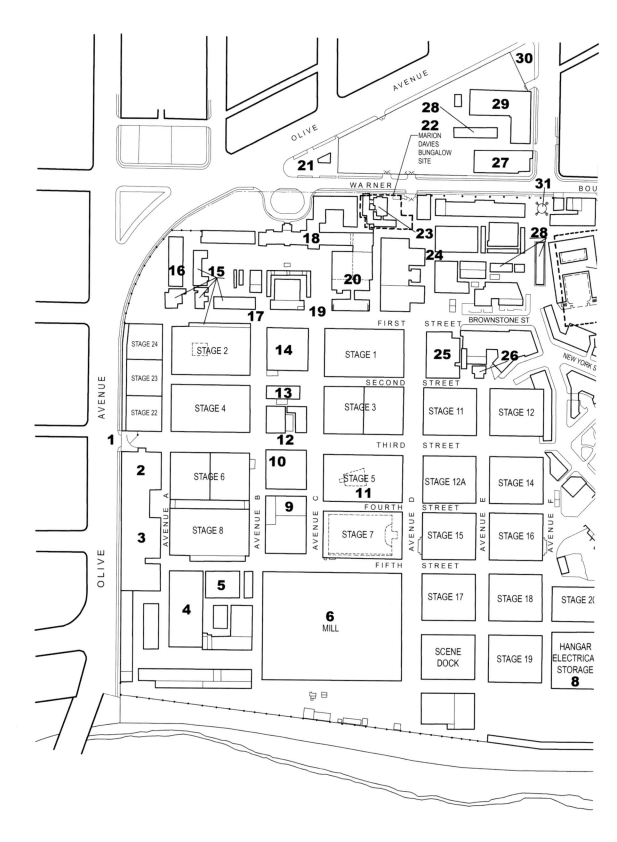

Studio map, circa 1967, with numbers corresponding to the sections in this chapter. Courtesy of Robert Lane.

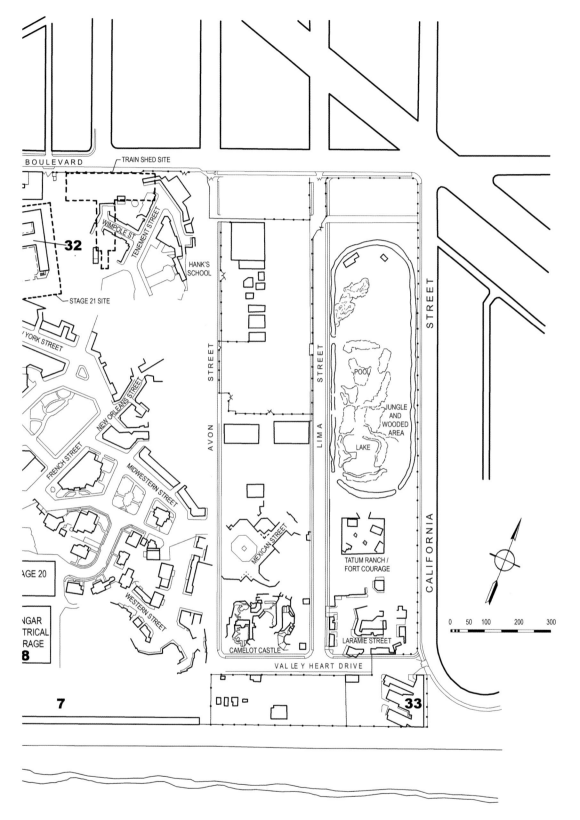

KEY:

1. Front Gate
2. Security Department
3. Property Building
4. Transportation
5. Electrical Fixtures Department
6. Mill
7. Scene Docks
8. Set Lighting
9. Mail Room
10. First Aid
11. "Stage 5" Departments
12. Fire Department and Power Plant
13. Camera Department
14. Makeup and Still Portrait Building
15. Dressing Rooms
16. Writers Building
17. Casting Department
18. Administration Complex
19. War Memorial
20. Costume Department
21. Drug Store
22. Marion Davies Bungalow (Site)
23. Frank Sinatra Office
24. Postproduction Complex
25. Commissary
26. Schoolhouse
27. Warner Records
28. Film Vaults
29. Film Lab
30. Tiger's Den Club
31. Water Tower
32. Television Building
33. Cartoon Department

BOULEVARD

TRAIN SHED SITE

WIMPOLE ST

TENEMENT STREET

32

HANK'S SCHOOL

STAGE 21 SITE

Y YORK STREET

NEW ORLEANS STREET

FRENCH STREET

MIDWESTERN STREET

AGE 20

NGAR TRICAL RAGE

8

WESTERN STREET

AVON STREET

LIMA STREET

MEXICAN STREET

CAMELOT CASTLE

POOL

JUNGLE AND WOODED AREA

LAKE

TATUM RANCH / FORT COURAGE

LARAMIE STREET

STREET

CALIFORNIA

VALLEY HEART DRIVE

7

33

0 50 100 200 300

the movies, and the audiences who did frequent cinemas were themselves predominantly older. These audiences apparently took comfort in seeing their familiar idols enact familiar situations amid an increasingly unfamiliar world.

With the eventual passing of the original studio heads, the other original studios had changed as well. RKO had effectively ceased to exist in 1957. Most of the 20th Century Fox lot was bulldozed in the early 1960s to construct Century City, a shopping and business complex, and MGM's fabled backlot would also be sold and demolished within a few years. The Columbia lot on Sunset Boulevard would soon be sold off as well. Universal survived by transforming their lot into a theme park, and Paramount, having been purchased by Gulf + Western in 1966, floundered badly for most of the decade. Only Warner Bros., and the last actual Warner brother, continued to operate as they always had, even while production diminished and the world moved on outside their gates.

Inside those gates, in the 1960s, the studio may have no longer been the vibrant and aggressive entity it once was, but because there was so little change the place had become a veritable attic of Hollywood history, made physical and laid out in inexplicable and wondrous patterns over 110 acres. And there is value in this as well. In the 1960s, Warner Bros. Studio was wondrous and bizarre, half museum, half industrial site—and perhaps something of a surrealist's dreamland, with recognizable objects from hundreds of movies cluttering the shelves in the property department, or rotting in the scene docks, or parked along the studio streets, waiting for a next assignment, which would probably never come.

Filmmaker George Lucas, who came to the lot in 1967, said that "it was great. It was an interesting time, because I don't know if it'll ever happen again, where you can sort of be in this great old movie studio, and not have anything going on. And have the streets all empty and the offices all empty. There were a few people there, but not very many. It was really an amazing time. It was very romantic, in a kind of funny way."[1]

It is, then, during this lonely, haunted, and romantic year of 1967 that we will explore the studio. Construction and demolition and amendments and subtractions during earlier and later periods will be noted when necessary, but primarily it is this era, and this year, when feudal old Hollywood was giving way to the corporate industry that survives today, and when the lot was already reflecting some of each dynasty, which we will explore in detail.

A detailed lot map is provided with the following departments numbered both here and on that map. The gates are swinging open.

1. Front Gate

The original front gate, the outsider's bridge into the six miles of paved roads inside the Warner lot, was first known as the "First National Gate," then the "Cosmopolitan Gate," and finally the "North Gate." It faced Rowland Avenue, which in 1955

The spacious art deco–inspired Olive Avenue gate became the main artery in and out of the studio in the 1930s—which it remains today. 1933.

was renamed Warner Boulevard. Increased auto traffic made this small and attractive entrance impractical, and so slowly the majority of the attention shifted over to a wider and more centrally located venue on Olive Avenue. Originally known as the "Auto Gate," and then as "Gate 2," a title that it still carries, this portal eventually took on a status comparable, if not quite equal, to Paramount's famous arched entrance on Melrose Avenue.

In one regard, however, the Warner gate was more versatile than Paramount's more famous entrance. While Paramount's gate was so recognizable that on camera it could only play the main gate at Paramount, and in fact would look hopelessly phony with any other name on it, the Warner gate looks like a movie studio gate—but it could be a movie studio gate at *any* studio. Therefore this entrance, with the proper signage, could play the Oliver Niles Studio in *A Star Is Born* (1954), Swan Studios in *Inside Daisy Clover* (1965), and the unidentified movie lots of *Boy, Did I Get a Wrong Number!* (1966); *The Way We Were* (1973); *Ed Wood* (1994); *Bowfinger* (1999); and *The Backlot Murders* (2010). Oddly enough, when Mel Brooks came to the lot in 1974 to film *Blazing Saddles*, he was disappointed to discover that the

The Front Gate used as a set in *Blazing Saddles*. The Warner Bros. sign on the guard shack was a prop, as the studio was actually the called The Burbank Studios during this period. 1974.

signage on this gate had recently been replaced with a generic placard that read, "The Burbank Studios." He ordered this sign taken down and replaced with a prop Warner Bros. sign and shield for that picture's riotous climax in which fighting cowboys break out of the gate and end up in a fistfight that climaxes on nearby Hollywood Boulevard.

In the 1960s the entrance here had a metal gate, a guard shack, and a beautiful art deco "Employee's Entrance" sign, all of which are visible in many of the above movies. Both the sign and the hinged gate itself were taken down in the 1990s. In 1991 actress Sean Young tried to crash this gate wearing a vinyl cat suit—that's right, a vinyl cat suit—in an apparently spontaneous audition for director Tim Burton, who was casting the role of Catwoman for *Batman Returns* (1992) on the lot at the time. Security escorted both Young and her outfit off the lot, although she would return to the studio, much humbled and apparently much more appropriately dressed, to guest star in an episode of the TV series *ER* in 2007.

Today, there is no gate "at" gate 2 at all. Consequently, the guard shack is monitored twenty-four hours a day. It is estimated that more than six thousand vehicles per eight-hour shift enter through this entrance, one of seven current ways to crash the studio.

2. Security Department

Blayney F. Matthews took the job of security chief of Warner Bros. in 1934 after a career with the Bureau of Investigation in the Los Angeles District Attorney's office. Most other members of the WB security staff were former policemen, investigators, security personnel from other studios and other industries, and, occasionally, would-be actors as well.

Matthews' staff was expected to be the public face of Warner Bros., and they were often the only actual face associated with Warner Bros. that would-be visitors

Warner Bros. Security Officer Duke le Due issues (presumably) a speeding ticket to bicycling starlet June Travis. 1935.

Close-up of a Warner security officer's badge. 1959.

and tourists would ever see. It has been calculated that more than three thousand visitors to the studio, not counting employees, enter, or try to enter, the lot daily; and each of these, from the obscure to the celebrated, would have to be cleared and given a pass to do so. How many of these people would be ultimately turned away at these gates, disappointed and disillusioned, is unknowable.

Matthews' and his successors' responsibilities did not stop at the gates, either. He and his staff, itself larger than sixty percent of the municipal police forces in California, were expected to provide security at premieres, at studio events, and on off-lot locations as well.

The Security Department was based in a small office at the Auto Gate in a corner of the property building. For many years, they shared this space with the payroll and timekeeping offices. Today, they have the space to themselves.

3. Property Building

Just to the right of the main gate is the massive labyrinth known as the Property Building. The building was constructed in early 1937, when the property department was expanded from its original location in a much smaller building that would later be used for the makeup and still departments. The Property Building consists of three floors and a basement, with floor space encompassing 247,000 square feet of the world's most peculiar real estate.

Millions of individual items of all shapes and descriptions are stored and maintained by this department. In 1943, the Property Department clocked 11,385 pieces going out their doors for one scene in one film: a street market sequence in *Saratoga Trunk* (1945). This inventory included everything from wooden pushcarts to replicas of food, such as the plaster watermelons that would have spoiled on the set had they been real. These numbers were apparently typical.

All of the pieces housed here are either property ("props"), meaning items to be used onscreen by an actor, or set dressing ("set dec," short for "set decoration"), a

A massive *Gold Diggers of 1935* hotel set. Dressed courtesy of the Warner Bros. Property Department. 1935.

term that refers to items seen in the background but not actually touched or handled by the talent. There is much confusion even within the industry as to what constitutes a prop, what constitutes set dec, and even what is considered a costume. A sword, for example, is a costume if an actor wears it. But if that actor pulls the sword out of its scabbard and pokes someone with it, the sword becomes a prop. If he never touches it, but it is seen hanging on a coat rack next to his suit of armor, the same sword is now considered set decoration, as are the coat rack and the suit of armor, for that matter.

Many of the pieces housed here are genuine antiques, including torchieres that once adorned Tsar Nicholas of Russia's palace (and, unlike the tsar himself, survived the Russian Revolution), furniture imported from Europe before World War II, and antiques that survived the 1906 San Francisco earthquake. The Warner family used to justify trips to Europe in the 1930s as "prop-buying" expeditions, which would have been fine except the props that they shipped back to the studio were, more often than not, pianos. Actually, pianos were difficult to store, and difficult to use at a studio like Warners, where screen characters were more inclined to reach for a gun than for a song. The department ended up with so many of the instruments that as late as 2008, it was still trying to sell off antique pianos in their annual lot sales.

People outside of Hollywood would be surprised, and perhaps shocked, to know that an actual antique is not more desirable to a set decorator or a property master than a reproduction. In fact, many an item original to the period would be less desirable than a pasted-together copy, due to the original item's age or fragility, or its inability to photograph dramatically.

Photographable artwork presented a particular problem. Even today a visitor perusing a row of busts of Mark Antony, for example, might admire their presumed authenticity until noticing that they actually depict Charlton Heston *as* Mark Antony. In 1939, department head A. C. Wilson claimed, "If a Rembrandt or a Corot is wanted, the studio has an artist who can paint a better one." He went on to elaborate that "real Rembrandts have dark backgrounds. Black, blue or brown, and these do not fit our camera purposes. Real Rembrandts are also too shiny. We have our own man paint a good copy which will have no halation. And which will look better in a camera reproduction, than the real Rembrandt would."[2]

Therefore, while roaming the endless hallways in the building, it isn't surprising to discover priceless antiques stored next to knockoffs that would be worthless anywhere else, and to learn that both items would be rented to studio productions for the same amount of money. This visitor might also be surprised to discover that pieces with a historic place in film history, meaning items handled by a star or used in a classic picture, are not more valuable to the next picture that uses them; in fact, the famous and memorable props are actually less likely to rent to future productions because there is a danger of these pieces being recognized by, and therefore being distracting to, their audience.

Simulated masterpieces, and a few real ones too, all competing for wall space in the Property Building. Circa 1930s.

In 1947, set decorator Jack McConaghy noted wryly that a single bedframe, notable because of its distinctive tufted green headboard and recently used by Cecil Kellaway in *Always Together* (1947), had previously been inhabited by Bette Davis in *Deception* (1946) and *The Private Lives of Elizabeth and Essex* (1939); Charles Boyer in *All This, and Heaven Too* (1940); Ronald Reagan in *Kings Row* (1942); Ingrid Bergman in *Saratoga Trunk* (1945); and Paul Muni in *The Story of Louis Pasteur* (1936). "Pretty good for a piece of furniture which probably cost about $89 when it was new," he reflected.[3]

The classic example of a prop becoming *too* famous for its own good is to be found in the odd and mysterious tale of the most famous movie prop in history. Dashiell Hammett's *The Maltese Falcon* was published in 1930. Warner Bros. purchased the rights and filmed the story under that title in 1931. In this version Ricardo Cortez, not Humphrey Bogart, played private eye Sam Spade on the trail of a priceless falcon statue. For this picture the Prop Department either found or constructed an ineffectual, peacock-looking falcon, which inadvertently undermined the serious nature of the story. This gooney bird survived long enough to bizarrely cameo in a John Wayne western made the following year, *Haunted Gold*

(1932)—but has since, mercifully, disappeared. In 1936 the story, if not the bird prop, was recycled as *Satan Met a Lady*, with the delightfully oily actor Warren Williams playing a Sam Spade surrogate, and a ram's horn, of all things, standing in for the black bird statue.

In 1941, screenwriter John Huston talked the studio into letting him make his directorial debut with yet a third version of Hammett's story. Apparently the original 1931 falcon prop could no longer be located, which was probably for the better. So in June 1941, "clips of falcons and similar birds" were obtained from the Research Department for reference. A falcon statue, measuring 11.5 inches tall from head to tail feathers and standing on a 3-inch base, was designed by the Art Department. In the studio Staff Shop, molds were made under the direction of department head Harry Platt, and at least two formidable-looking falcons were created out of poured lead and then painted black to be photographed on screen.

It has long been speculated that at least one plaster of Paris or resin falcon was made from the same molds as well. This has never been proven. The line item in the picture's budget for the prop falcon(s) allegedly specified construction costs of $683.60, but does not elaborate on how many statues were actually commissioned or created.

Humphrey Bogart, who was now playing the screen's third, and most memorable, Sam Spade, apparently dropped one of the statues on his foot during production, and as the statue—which was cast from lead, remember—weighed forty-seven pounds, the actor had to go to First Aid for treatment. The bird itself suffered a case of misaligned tail feathers, which some viewers claim are visible in the film.

When the movie wrapped, the falcons, however many there were at this point, went back to the Property Department from where, occasionally, they were cast in other films. *Illegal* (1955), for example, features the black bird rather prominently on view in actor Edward Platt's law office. *Frankenstein 1970*, a 1958 Boris Karloff vehicle, gave it screen time as well, as did John Ford's *Cheyenne Autumn* (1964), in which it can be spotted in set photos on Karl Malden's mantle.

About this time, William Conrad, an actor (later famous on television for *Cannon* and *Jake and the Fat Man*) who was then directing horror movies at the studio, claimed that Jack Warner *gave* him one of these lead falcons, presumably as a joke. Apparently neither one of them thought that a bird statue from an old movie could be anything more than a forty-seven-pound paperweight.

Also about that time, however, something strange started to happen. Humphrey Bogart had died in 1956, but in April 1957, the Brattle Theatre near Harvard University rather arbitrarily began scheduling old Bogart movies. By the early 1960s, young people, for whose parents Bogie had been a hero, found themselves responding to the actor's characteristic cynicism and distrust of authority—a stance that must have seemed cutting edge indeed to the increasingly disillusioned students of the period—and a "Bogart cult" was born.

Subsequently, key Bogart films were rereleased to other theaters and to television; they were viewed by his young fans, sometimes dozens of times each, with these fans sometimes even quoting the dialogue back at screenings. Woody Allen, then another key figure with college audiences, even made a movie on the subject, *Play It Again, Sam* (1972).

Among these newly revered films was, of course, *The Maltese Falcon*. The bird statue itself, which in the film is finally exposed as a fake, came to represent to these students all of those values that society and their parents and their government seemed to want them to personify at any cost. But this later generation was the first to worry that, like the falcon itself, these very values could turn out to be ersatz, valuable only, as Sam Spade had said, as "the stuff that dreams are made of."

Because of the black bird's newfound, or rather refound, notoriety, it became impossible for the Property Department back at the studio to place their Maltese falcon statue(s?) in a bookcase or on top of a fireplace mantle in any other movie, because an audience in the 1960s would have immediately recognized it. Movie props, as mentioned, are most valuable when they are anonymous. Therefore, a straight-back chair is liable to work more often as a prop than an ornate throne is, because audiences would be more likely to recognize the throne from other movies than they would the chair. The falcon, it seems, had by the 1960s become the movie's most recognized throne.

In 1975, Columbia Pictures released a *Maltese Falcon* spoof called *The Black Bird*. To publicize the film, 250 new plaster birds were created by the Warner Bros. Staff Shop. Many of these falcons have since been represented by their owners, either intentionally or innocently, as having come from the original film. In fact, several of these second-generation birds have been sold or auctioned off for considerable coin as having come from the earlier movie. They didn't, although there is, of course, still a slim chance that there may be an authentic plaster bird out there, somewhere. Incidentally, Columbia added to the confusion by using a different, larger falcon statue onscreen for *The Black Bird*. One of *these* falcons still lives on a shelf in the Warner Bros. Hand Prop Room.

When William Conrad died in 1994, his family agreed to auction off his falcon as well. It ended up selling for $398,500, an astonishing price, at the time, for a movie prop. (Christie's, the auction house handling the item, had estimated the bird's worth at $30,000–50,000.) The "Conrad bird" seems to have vanished since then, although it was reportedly on display in Orlando, Florida, in the 1990s. Recently, rumors have surfaced that it is in Jordan, of all places.

The other lead falcon, the one with the bent tail feathers, vanished from the studio, and its whereabouts were unknown for many years. When it reappeared, as mysteriously as it had vanished, it was purchased by Dr. Gary Milan, who occasionally was kind enough to loan his bird to the studio for display in the Warner Bros. Museum. In November 2013, Bonhams, in association with Turner Classic Movies, auctioned off this falcon for an astonishing $4,085,000. As befitting the mysterious nature of the statue's entire strange saga, the identity of the winning bidder has not been disclosed.

The Property Department is divided into sections where a standing inventory of some six million items is maintained. The Hand Prop Room on the ground floor contains pieces that are generally handled by the talent. It is in this room where many half-familiar objects from half-remembered films make their home and where roaming the vast isles is reminiscent of both exploring a lonely museum and shopping at a shabby, multifamily garage sale.

Items ranging from tables and chairs to Chinese rickshaws and Roman chariots inhabit the other floors and the basement. Some of the odder and more surreal rooms or collections on these floors include a "Polynesian Room" adorned with South Seas–inspired Tikis, as well as fisherman's nets, rubber sharks, and plastic lobsters. Nearby was the so-called Road-Kill Room, which is no longer there but was largely made up of dead, taxidermied animals, presumably designed to be laid out alongside a Texas highway.

Much of the second floor is taken up by the Drapery Department, which moved with Property to its current location in 1937. The Drapery Department was created in 1924, when a production called *Lady Windemere's Fan* called A. C. Wilson at the Sunset Studio lot requesting curtains—which the department did not carry. Wilson hired upholsterer Fred Gilroy for the job, and it was Gilroy and future Drapery Department head Mac Mulcahy who expanded the department's responsibilities to include not only window treatments but upholstery and flooring as well. The department still exists in this same location. Many of the staff have been in the department for more than twenty years. One storied employee can boast of being there for forty—and he had a father who worked there before him.

The machinery, the shelves, the cutting tables, and the vast racks of curtains (enough to allegedly drape the entire *Queen Mary* twice), including one used by Jolson in *The Jazz Singer*, all have the same odd sense of permanence about them as the staff. The glass on the windows facing the studio street below has turned yellow with age, giving the department a timeless, sepia quality, which somehow is not at all at odds with the rest of twenty-first-century Hollywood, which can be seen moving on outside.

4. Transportation

The Transportation garage was designed in 1930 by Transportation Department head Art Klein. Before that, the studio garage had been near the commissary. The new building covered 25,000 square feet and could warehouse one hundred vehicles at one time. Five bays with underground pits kept the studio's rolling fleet on the move. The building and its annexes also contained an oil and grease rack, a paint shop, a wash rack, fuel pumps, battery and machine shops, and showers and offices for the staff. Transportation sheds for oversized vehicles were in the same area, although many of the vehicles were parked next to the scene docks along the river as well, or stored in a two-acre shed at the studio ranch in Calabasas.

These vehicles were, and are, arguably the oddest assortment of production-related trucks, vans, cranes, trailers, insert cars, generators, sound trucks, fire engines, and automobiles of every imaginable variety in the world. This was especially true when the studio's collection of bought and rented picture cars—vehicles that appeared onscreen as props—was factored in. In 1932, it was estimated that the company owned and maintained some seventy-five vehicles. So rapidly did the studio and the department grow that, ten years later, the Warner Bros. fleet consisted of 365 production vehicles and some three dozen picture cars. Art Klein would stay at his post until his death in 1955. In the twenty-first century, the studio's Transportation Department, still operating out of the same building, reportedly had five hundred pieces garaged on the lot.

A Transportation Museum, constructed for the benefit of the Tour Department on that building's northern end, routinely sets aside whatever picture cars are not

Part of the Transportation Department's fleet of rolling stock in the 1940s.

working at the moment for the enjoyment of the guests. Consequently, Batmobiles routinely share floor space with Clint Eastwood's *Gran Torino* (2008), the General Lee from *The Dukes of Hazzard* (1979–1985), Austin Powers' Shag-Mobile, and whatever else there may be room to show off.

5. Electrical Fixtures Department

Constructed in 1926, this building was unassuming and unimpressive from the outside. Walking inside the double doors, however, was an entirely different situation. From the cement floor all the way into the rafters could be found hundreds of practical lighting fixtures—lamps of every imaginable variety. Each was designed not to light a set, but to be photographed as part of one. From chandeliers to single bare light bulb receptacles, from streetlights to stoplights, anything used to illuminate anything else lived here.

The department was organized at the Sunset Boulevard Studio by Robert D. Martin, who talked J.L. into buying him a tool chest after he was hired for three days to assemble some decorative lighting fixtures in 1923. Martin was a World War I veteran who had previously worked as an electrician, stunt driver, boxer, and special effects man. He enjoyed telling his family about how he also doubled for Boris Karloff on *The Walking Dead* (1936), when the star was too timid to lay down in a mad scientist's laboratory set next to one of Martin's crackling electrical gizmos. Martin also invented a machine that could manufacture "cobwebs" by spinning a rubberized compound through the blades of a fan—still in use, incidentally, industry-wide today. During World War II, he briefly left the studio and enlisted in the U.S. Army Air Force's First Motion Picture Unit (FMPU), which had been organized by his old employer, Jack Warner.

The most famous single fixture in the department has always been "Big Bertha," a room-sized chandelier that sparkles through the reflected light of 36,000 illuminated pieces of Czech crystal. Bertha's story is as murky as that of the Maltese Falcon. One tale holds that she was purchased from a movie theater on Hollywood Boulevard in 1963 for *My Fair Lady*. This is doubtful, because although she is plainly visible in the Embassy Ball sequence in that film, she is also visible in a great many pictures made before that.

Employees of the department who probably were not there will also tell you that *My Fair Lady* was shooting under the chandelier on November 22, 1963, when the unit received the news that President John F. Kennedy had been assassinated. The story goes on to state that star Audrey Hepburn gathered the entire crew under the light to inform them of the tragedy when director George Cukor was unable to do so. This story, touching though it is, is as hard to verify as Bertha's origins, however. And, speaking of origins, Bob Martin's family has always claimed that he told them that Bertha is one of the pieces that came from the tsar's palace in St. Petersburg, Russia.

The inventory of the electrical Fixtures Department, including the legendary "Big Bertha," right. 1940.

Other recognizable units to be found inside the department include *Daily Planet* ceiling lights from the *Superman* pictures; medieval candelabra (retrofitted with electric bulbs) from Errol Flynn's last great swashbuckler, *The Adventures of Don Juan* (1948); and a Texas-sized chandelier from Reata, the million-acre cattle ranch in *Giant* (1956). One of the oddest pieces, which always elicits questions from guests, is a lamp made of a giant tortoise shell, which apparently can only boast of one credit, the Richard Pryor vehicle *Jo Jo Dancer, Your Life Is Calling* (1986).

In 2011, after more than eighty years, the Electrical Fixtures building was torn down in order to construct an on-lot office complex. The inventory, however, was all folded into the Property Department, and so the thousands of storied illumination devices inside, including Big Bertha and all her conflicting origin stories, were carefully moved down the road to their new home in the Property Building, where they reside today.

6. Mill

The construction complex at Warner Bros. is the largest in the entire motion picture industry. The Mill, as it has always been called, was created from the ashes of the 1934 fire that destroyed most of the construction and labor buildings on the lot

Dick Powell, Glenda Farrell, Lola Lane, Hugh Hubert, Rosemary Lane, and Ted Healy in a scene from *Hollywood Hotel*. Note the exotic torchiere in the center of the set, which, like Big Bertha, was rescued from the tsar's palace in Russia. 1937.

at that time. It was decided, when the time came to rebuild these departments, that it would be safer to construct all of them under one enormous all-encompassing roof than in separate, much smaller units, an idea that has never been replicated on this scale anywhere else.

When the building was completed in 1936, the studio was not shy about trumpeting the pyramid-like dimensions of their new behemoth. The ground floor alone covers more than five acres of real estate and almost 130,000 square feet of construction space. The second floor offers another 67,890 square feet, and the basement yet another 66,080 square feet of workable real estate. A press release produced when the building opened boasted, "It is now possible to start a big set at one end of the building with merely a blueprint and a pile of lumber at the beginning and have it emerge at the other end complete in every detail, ready for the actors to step into it and start to work as soon as it is moved onto one of the large sound-stages." Another ultimate benefit is that sets no longer needed to be constructed on those stages themselves, as had been the custom in the past, thus freeing those stages for additional shooting days during the construction period.

Most of the building is used for this sort of set construction. Someone with too much time on their hands once figured that in an average year (1973, in this case),

The southern side of the 227,000-square-foot studio crafts building "Mill"—the largest such structure in the world. Circa 1940.

the Mill chewed through fifteen miles of lumber and nineteen and a half tons of nails.[4] The building's Mechanical Department, which includes the Machine Shop, the Foundry, the Tin Shop, and the Mechanical Drawing Room, occupies the next largest area under the giant roof. The Machine Shop alone takes up some 10,000 square feet.

Smaller, but no less important, are the Carpenter Shop, the Furniture Repair Shop, the Bicycle Repair Shop, a ladder storage house, an Electrical Equipment Repair Shop, a Tool Sharpening and Die-Casting Department, a lumber room, a tool room, a Property Construction Shop where items not found in the Property Building are created, an Upholstery Shop, a Sheet Metal Shop, a Plumbing Shop, a shop where process screens are made, a Glass Construction Shop, a Welding Shop, a Tin Shop, a Sign Shop, a Paint Shop, a Neon Shop, a gunpowder room, a Key Shop ("Errol Flynn is notoriously careless with his dressing room key and duplicates are always available here," Lloyd Bacon [no relation to the director of that name], who was in charge of that tiny department, groused at one time),[5] and a foundry.

Near the center of the complex is the Staff Shop. An uncountable number of architectural molds—some place the number at more than sixty thousand—are stored on the walls and in a shed outside. These plaster or gypsum molds represent

Harry Warner allegedly liked to walk through this set assembly area in the Mill and pick nails off of the floor to give to workers for "recycling." His employees considered giving him a cane with a magnet on the tip to make it easier for him to do so, but ultimately decided such a gift would only embarrass the company president. Circa 1940.

the sum total of the world's architecture. From these pieces can be created reproductions that ornament sets and create the illusion that the setting is ancient Rome, or the decks of the *Queen Elizabeth*, or the Oval Office. The Staff Shop's most popular product is the "brick walls" that populate the sets for most pictures and that here are turned out by the acre every year. In fact, the same industrious tabulator who gave us the above figures once estimated that if a year's moldings were to inexplicably be laid out 4 feet wide, the trail of these curious pieces would run unbroken for sixty-five miles. Believe it or not.

Yet another department, Scenic Arts, is on the second floor. A metal staircase carries a visitor to a fireproof steel door with counterweights that are pulled up a chain when the door is opened. Inside is a high, narrow room lit by sunlight that streams in through paint- and grime-spattered glass windows. On either wall are immense wooden paint frames, each 30 feet long and 100 feet high. The frames can be raised and lowered into a slot in the floor that goes down to the first floor. Just

Artists apply their talents to recreating a religious tableau in the Mill's Scenic Arts Department. Circa 1980.

looking down into these slots is a precarious sight, and in fact at least one worker has been killed by falling into them. These open rectangular pits enable an artist to work at any spot on a scenic backdrop from the same position, rather than having to use scaffolding, as Michelangelo and other inferior, non-Hollywood-based artists were uncomfortably forced to do.

In fact, the old scaffolding-based process is exactly how the backings were being painted in 1931 when Vern Strang organized the department (Vern's son Ron, and grandson Ed, would later follow in his footsteps in the department). At the time, the frames were strung along the wall of a soundstage (Stages 6 and 7), and an artist was given scaffolding, paint, and ladders and told to hang on and be careful. In 1937, any still-surviving artists from this precarious early process were relocated to this new room.

What these artists paint is anything seen in the background or through a window in one of the studio's pictures. From cloudscapes to starscapes, from plantations to pyramids, the job of the artists here is to create photographic reality, or rather reality designed to look real *when* photographed. The detail on these backdrops, which usually seem to be created while the artist is talking or drinking a coke or absentmindedly doing something else, is nearly photographic. For cityscapes, the reality is enhanced even more by leaving windows in "office buildings" almost unpainted, so that light, usually powerful 5000-watt "skypans," can shine through them. For seascapes, individual strands of tinsel are glued to the front, which are invisible but pick up light nonetheless, adding a shimmering effect to the "waters."

This is an art form that changed very little over the decades, at least until 2001, when large-format graphic printers, which can enlarge an actual photograph hundreds of times, started to gain prominence. High-definition digital cameras were allegedly the reason for these printers supplementing hand-drawn backdrops on American film sets, as some complained these new cameras were capable of exposing painted backdrops as just that.

Nevertheless, there remain applications where a painted background is still preferable, so the scenic backdrop painting room survives and is still used, although this is perhaps due to the uniqueness of the room itself more than to any significant amount of business. After all, what else could this curious place be used *for*?

The Mill basement in the 1940s was, along with the laboratory building on the other side of the lot, intended to be used as a bomb shelter, should the need ever arise

Author Steven Bingen risks danger and discipline for exploring sealed-off underground tunnels beneath the Mill and adjacent soundstages. 1996.

for one. Fortunately, it didn't, so the Warner Bros. print shop, photo lab, and stock footage library ended up occupying much of the real estate. Numerous tunnels, most of which have been closed off, also spider web out from this building to the sound-stages and into the basements of other buildings. Some of these tunnels were probably designed for Vitaphone recording, but now they are silent, closed off, and forgotten except by the ghosts and rats and other dark occupants who still reside there.

The mill has, not surprisingly, been used as a set many times over the decades. When production is faced with the dilemma of building or renting a location to play a factory or industrial site, or shooting this one, it really has never been a decision at all. Consequently, parts of the building can be seen onscreen in *Black Legion* (1937; Bogart's character worked there), *A Streetcar Named Desire* (1951; Karl Malden's character worked there), and *Swing Shift* (1984; Goldie Hawn's character worked there). The Mill was also an auto plant in *The Great Race* (1965) and *Dave* (1993), an aircraft plant in *The Spirit of St. Louis* (1957), a construction plant in *Each Dawn I Die* (1939), a textiles mill in *Pajama Game* (1957), a hospital in *The Steel Jungle* (1962), a laboratory in *The Omega Man* (1971), a hotel basement in *Giant* (1956), and a theater basement in *Damn Yankees* (1958).

In 2002 Clint Eastwood investigated a murder in back of the Mill in *Bloodwork*, which unwittingly harkened back to the building's long service in crime films, usually as a prison. In both *Angels with Dirty Faces* (1938) and *White Heat* (1949), James Cagney did hard time here. In fact, decades later for the TV series *The F.B.I.* (1965–1974), the building was still playing a penitentiary. As late as the 1990s, next to the staircase going up to the Scenic Arts shop, there existed a stenciled-on statute quoting from an Illinois penal code, added as set dressing for that series. No one seemed to question why it was there. It had by that time been there longer than most of the actual employees and was seldom remarked upon, a silent testimony both to the building's long and schizophrenic history, and to how seldom anyone during that period bothered to paint the walls.

7. Scene Docks

They have been called Hollywood's graveyards. Scene docks are large, often open areas where walls, and flats, staircases, and oversized props from completed productions are hauled off in the hope that they can be recycled and reused in other productions. The studio's largest indoor scene dock was constructed in 1936. Yet even at 21,000 square feet, and with a fourteen-thousand-foot annex added in 1960, it could never hope to hold all of the sets that all of the Warner Bros. movies shooting on the lot had utilized and discarded. A 1941 article mentioned "750 columns, 900 miniature buildings, 235 jail units, 125 church pews, 3500 wooden balusters, 700 doors."[6]

There were so many pieces that hundreds of them inevitably ended up rotting away in the sun, spilling south, lining the banks of the Los Angeles River, and running parallel along the base of the lot's southern border.

An aerial view of the studio, looking north across the vast open scene docks, where the sets from hundreds of movies went to die. The Quonset hut–styled Set Lighting Hanger is visible as well, lower left. Circa 1975.

If I may speak personally for a moment, long before I ever worked at the studio, in the late 1980s I came out to California with the goal of seeing the inside of Warner Bros. for the first time. I eventually succeeded because my brother was friends with someone at Warner Records who promised to get us inside the lot. And, true to her word, she did, although I don't think she understood why this was so important to me.

I remember a lot of things about that day. But one of my most vivid memories of the whole experience was wandering down into the rear of the studio and seeing the Scene Dock area. I remember thinking how much fun it would have been to be a kid and to be able to play in a magical place like this. Years later, I was told that for many years, the gigantic plaster redwoods from *Valley of the Giants* (1938) and the giant mechanical ants from the science fiction classic *Them!* (1954) had rotted away like silent sentinels in this area. I didn't see any giant ants, or redwoods, but there were a lot of other curious artifacts there to capture my imagination. Part of the fun was the vague familiarity I felt with some of the items. I'd never been to the studio before, yet many of the pieces seemed just beyond my memory's ability to identify them. That spiral staircase corkscrewing up into the sun. Where had I seen it? The frontier fortress gates; what were they from? The olive-colored helicopter fuselage, the adobe well, the swinging salon doors—where had I seen them before? Where, and how many times?

Some items I *could* definitely identify. One of the alien spaceships from the TV Series V (1984–1985) was sitting on a metal armature. I hoisted myself up into the cockpit and was delighted and astonished to note that the vessel's interior was entirely dressed. The cabin contained elaborate wiring and lights and switches and controls to make the thing look like it could really work, and perhaps even be used to conquer the earth. I was unable to attempt anything so ambitious, however, because the labels on the control panels, unfortunately, were all in the language of the alien "visitors."

In one aisle was a fairy-tale carriage, made of some sort of highly varnished, but aging, reddened wood, covered with gold gilt and ornate scrollwork, and with matching velvet upholstery inside. Years later I asked someone where this most unusual object had come from, and was told that Jack Warner had purchased it from some European principality for the purpose of his personal transportation to some movie premiere or another. I have no idea if this story is true, or any way of verifying it one way or another. I do know, however, that some years later, the carriage was rented, or perhaps purchased outright, by Disney for their 1997 *Cinderella* remake. I still wonder what happened to that magic carriage after that, because it never did come back to the studio.

Nearby I was amused to find a full-size lifeboat. Ominously painted in black lettering near the bow on each side were the words "R.M.S. Titanic." At the time I remember thinking this label grimly amusing, even whimsical. But I've spent the decades since occasionally wondering what project this prop could possibly have come from, as neither Warner Bros. nor Columbia Pictures, which was sharing the property at the time, has ever been associated with a picture about the sinking of the Titanic. So how, exactly, *did* the thing get out there?

Unfortunately, most of these pieces are gone now. When Warner Bros. rededicated their lot in 1990, a great deal of money was expended repainting and cleaning up the physical property after years of comparative neglect. The acres of flats and walls and props and furniture rotting away along the river, always an eyesore to those not inclined to see the magic, were cleaned out, except for the pieces used most often, which would thereafter be stored inside a new scene dock, to be constructed efficiently and economically out of corrugated metal and chain link fencing. The old, original enclosed scene dock was turned over to the Grip Department for storage of their equipment. In 2008 it was removed as well, and Stage 23 was ultimately constructed on the site.

8. Set Lighting

Each soundstage routinely utilized an average of 240 lighting units, ranging in size from tiny 200-watt "Inkies" and smaller, to the aptly named, 10,000-watt "Big Eye Tener Solarspots." The studio also maintained a fleet of arc light units, which simulated the color temperature (approximately 5600 degrees Kelvin) of the sun, and so were useful for generating fill light outdoors, or for shooting interiors inside a soundstage. Much of this equipment was stored here in this gray, Quonset hut–style, corrugated metal shed, constructed here in the late 1940s. Many of the cumbersome arc lighting units, and later the more compact HMIs (hydrargyrum medium-arc iodide) that replaced them, were also warehoused inside storage units behind the Brownstone and New York Street sets.

The building, which occasionally doubled as an aircraft hangar on camera, was removed in 1998. Stage 29 now occupies the site.

9. Mail Room

The Mail Room was organized in 1934. Before that there were "couriers" used for delivery, and before that the mail was presumably dropped at the gate and left to fend for itself. Fifteen local boys were hired. Six years later the staff had increased to twenty-eight. In the 1940s, the department acquired its more or less permanent home here in a corner of a building it shared with the Grip and Printing departments. John Frederick Pappmeier was the department head. Pappmeier was a former backlot laborer, hired in 1933, who spoke with a stutter and was obsessed with bowling. He was suspicious of the boys who were under his care. Rightly so, because most of them had obtained their positions through nepotism, and all of them thought of the job, with its constant physical labor and demeaning green uniforms, as the bottom rung on a ladder to better things.

The "better things" legend is probably true, to a point. No less than Darryl F. Zanuck, who rose to a position of power at Warners and later founded 20th Century (Fox) Pictures, was allegedly once a "courier" for Jack Warner. Even today, many an executive from his carpeted office suite will fondly tell you about his freewheeling days in the Mail Room—although often those Mail Room days would in truth have to be followed by college, law or business school, and two or three positions at other studios or networks before returning in triumph to bigger salary and more prestige back at their old alma mater.

Pappmeier divided the lot into a grid consisting of six mail routes, circumvented every twenty minutes. At its peak, the department handled about fifteen thousand pieces a day. The staffers walked or bicycled an estimated fifteen miles a day. They also filled in for the receptionists and secretaries and gave tours of the studio to guests for executives.

In the 1960s, the department was moved to the former schoolhouse, and later to a bungalow near the administration complex. In 1995, the Mail Room offices

Bette Davis "helping" the crew light a scene with a Mole-Richardson brute arc during the filming of *The Cabin in the Cotton*. Note that the lighting unit still has the First National name and logo stenciled onto it. 1932.

were moved again to the new Bridge Building on the backlot. Studio couriers and messengers, a different department today with different responsibilities, now operate out of a building near the Transportation Department.

10. First Aid

In 1939, the Publicity Department released a statement proclaiming that Paul M. "Doc" MacWilliams would go "down in Hollywood history as the man who brought modern first aid and accident prevention methods to the studios." It must have been a slow news week, but the claim isn't far off the mark.

Although he apparently had no formal medical training and was, perhaps not too surprisingly, actually an actor, MacWilliams' adlibbed skills as a medic came in handy from the very beginning. He created the position of on-set medic for no less than D. W. Griffith, on no less than *The Birth of a Nation* (1915). Later, actor Jean Hersholt credited "Doc" with saving him from death by sunstroke on the Death Valley location of Erich Von Stroheim's *Greed* (1925).

MacWilliams created the first on-lot First Aid department at Brunton (later Paramount) Studios and moved to Warners in 1930. Warner Bros. claimed that his department reduced accident and illness among employees by 78 percent. "I figure that's worth more than acting," MacWilliams liked to say.[7]

The department is still of vital importance today. A typical example of its literal life-saving importance occurred on March 6, 1981, when director William Friedkin had a heart attack on the way to his office on the lot. He managed to drive through the gate and asked to be taken to First Aid. While being treated in their infirmary, he allegedly "died." "I was moving through darkness, as though on an escalator to a light," he remembered later, after he was revived.[8]

The First Aid Department has had several homes over the decades. The most recent has been this corner of Stage 5 (now Stage 15). 2012.

"I guess," he said about his recovery, "God didn't want the guy who directed *The Exorcist.*"[9]

When this building, which the department had inhabited since 1946, was destroyed in the 1994 Northridge earthquake, the department moved to the western corner of Stage 15, where it remains today.

11. "Stage 5" Departments

"Stage 5" was the umbrella name on the lot for the assorted special effects and design departments that cohabitated in a honeycomb of offices nestled in the walls of one of the studio's busiest soundstages—and for the stage itself, unlike any other on the lot, where their efforts were realized.

Byron Haskin, who was later a notable director but started off designing special effects in Stage 5 and later ran that division, said that "almost every department in the studio had its counterpart in the special effects unit. We had our own designers, art directors, set building facilities and our own camera and electrical crews. The

Stage 5 was the only stage on the lot that included offices and departments. The corner offices now house the First Aid Department, the General Store, and offices for the series *Conan* (2010–). Circa 1935.

department also had its own film laboratory, cutting facilities, business office and even its own writers."[10]

Fredd Wayne, who started out in the Mail Room and went on to a long career as an actor, remembered walking onto this stage in 1942 when *Air Force* was shooting miniatures there.

Part of the stage, from one end to the other was covered in tiny green replicas of jungle foliage: trees, plants, bushes, vines and peasant's huts made to represent Wake Island and the area surrounding Clark Field in the Philippines. When hidden smoke pots among the miniatures were lit, the camera very high on a swivel crane attached to a camera dolly on tracks started rolling and the crane swooped down as two dolly grips rapidly pushed the dolly forward. But when the action appeared on screen you were with the crew in that crippled plane, hurtling through smoke and flames.[11]

Don Siegel, another noted director, started out in Stage 5 designing and directing montage sequences. Late in his career, he described his first impressions of the place: "It was full of activity, with a number of units working on the large stage. We passed Bette Davis, sitting in car in front of what appeared to be a transparent

Miniature ships were a big part of the Stage 5 technician's special effects arsenal, especially during the World War II era.

screen. A wind machine was blowing at her. Two men, on opposite sides of the car were jerking two-by-fours vigorously under the car, making it bounce up and down. I wondered if Miss Davis would get car sick."[12]

What Siegel was watching was one of the oldest tricks in the movies, the simulation of an actual exterior location achieved by projecting a previously shot sequence of that location onto a screen in front of which the talent reacts while being filmed. Many of these sequences were done on this stage, and since virtually every Warner Bros. movie had scenes achieved in this way, it's fair to say that almost every Warner Bros. movie made between 1930 and 1960 was partially filmed on this very stage.

The process of creating process shots is almost impossibly detailed and complex. And perhaps the most surprising aspect of its continued usage was that it never became an assembly line affair, as new challenges and problems tended to crop up almost every time. The primary difficulty in achieving convincing process shots was the elimination of "hot spots" on the process screen—that is, places where the light from the rear projector on the rear screen was brighter than others. This was solved by placing that projector progressively farther back from the screen it was projecting onto until the hot spots were no longer visible. Sometimes Stage 5, even at 22,660 square feet, was not big enough to eliminate the hot spot. Occasionally, the projector would have to be placed *outside* the stage, and would need to shoot through a tented, darkened cone from across the street and into the stage door, then across the 206-foot length of the stage and onto a screen in the opposite corner in front of which the actor was performing. The motor on this far-flung projector would also have to be synchronized with the motor on the camera recording the actor reacting to whatever was being projected, so as to avoid the flutter that would have resulted from the shutter on one machine not being in perfect synchronization with the shutter on the other. Remember that some pictures contained dozens of sequences involving this process.

Sometimes the melding of two pieces of film, or a piece of film and a painting, was done optically, rather than "live." Stationary mattes were achieved by exposing only part of a piece of film, backwinding the camera, exposing only the previously unexposed part of the frame while shooting a second sequence, and hopefully blending the two disparate scenes into one single "take." Traveling mattes involved masking selected parts of the frame, such as a dinosaur walking across a cityscape, by filming the reptile stomping in front of a screen (usually blue or green) and optically melding that image with a background of say, New York City, which is insensitive to that color, so that only the dinosaur and the separately shot cityscape are ultimately visible.

In those predigital days, this was a painstaking trial-and-error process. A basement in the corner of the stage contained a miniature film laboratory, where a few test frames from the composited sequence could be processed and checked to see what needed to be adjusted.

The actual matte paintings used in these techniques got much larger and more difficult to photograph properly with the advent of Cinemascope and other

The Special Effects Department tries to create convincing "at sea" sequences, using a prop boat and a process screen, for *Too Much, Too Soon*. 1958.

widescreen processes in the 1950s. Consequently, in 1957 the Matte Department moved to a new building where the Camera Department had long been based in order to meet these new, and very wide, challenges.

Mechanical special effects, those tricks not involving opticals at all, were created in a next-door building that survived until the 1994 Northridge quake. In 1997, another new building, opposite the Mill, inherited the Mechanical Special Effects Department. Optical effects are now farmed out to outside contractors, such as George Lucas' Industrial Light and Magic, and are no longer composited on lot.

Elsewhere at Stage 5, most of the offices on the second and third floor were taken up by the studio's sixty-three-person Art Department, which was responsible for the physical look of every film that came out of the studio, equaling as many as twenty-three hundred sets a year, as well as the design and construction of the physical studio and the backlot. A successful art director at Warner Bros. had to have theatrical, historical, artistic, architectural, modeling, budgeting, and drafting

Every set in every Warner Bros. movie came out of Art Department offices such as this one. Note the models on the shelves labeled according to assorted backlot locations. Circa 1930s.

experience in order to conceive and design everything that would appear onscreen, as well as motion picture engineering experience in order to be able to physically render those ideas for the camera, and to ensure that no more set was constructed than would be required by the director, all within budget and on time.

If there ever was a Warner Bros. "house style," it was probably through the 1930s work of Polish-born Anton Grot, who often collaborated with director Michael Curtiz and whose somewhat expressionistic sets worked particularly well for Curtiz's grand sea epics like *Captain Blood* (1935) and *The Sea Hawk* (1940). Without Curtiz, Grot also made valuable contributions to the gangster classic *Little Caesar* (1931), the horror movie *The Mystery of the Wax Museum* (1933), and the very stylized Shakespearean romp *A Midsummer Night's Dream* (1935), among many others. Grot retired in 1950.

Sharing the upstairs offices with the Art Department was the studio's Research Library. The library was created in 1927 as an on-lot source for fact checking historical, cultural, and geographic details as needed by production. To this end, a surprisingly small (never more than fourteen) but undoubtedly diligent staff eventually collected something approaching the sum total of the world's knowledge. By the early 1940s, the department could boast of some seven thousand books, bound magazine runs going back as far as 1842, hundreds of research "bibles" of accumulated facts and photos, and an amazing collection of clipping files, which got larger and larger as the decades ticked by. These files contained photos variously taken from location trips and clipped from the world's press by the diligent staff on every subject imaginable.

For example, if one were to go to the file cabinet drawer heading for "Reptiles," one would see different files for every serpent and lizard imaginable. A search for the section labeled "Reptiles—Turtles" would yield yet more files, at least one for each species or variety of turtle, each file getting progressively more specialized than the one before it. At the very end of the "Reptiles—Turtles" drawer (or drawers), the heading would splinter yet again into "Reptiles—Turtles—Misc," where could be found anything that did not fit in any of the earlier files. In this spot in this drawer, there even existed a file intriguingly headed "Reptiles—Turtles—Misc—Freak." Inside this file one would find newspaper and magazine photos of albino, oversized, and two-headed turtles. At the Warner Research Library, one just never knew when a two-headed turtle might come in handy.

Carl Milliken was, for decades, the library's biggest champion. A naval World War II veteran who started at the studio in 1935, he returned after VJ day and eventually ended up heading the department. He continued to work with and to compulsively add to the collection, and was probably the only person alive who knew all of its secrets. By the 1970s, he boasted of collecting over twenty thousand books for the company. He stayed with the collection and with the studio even in 1973, when his services in providing research and clearances were made available to outside productions. In 1975, however, his bosses donated the entire unwieldy collection to the Burbank Public Library. Warner Bros. board chairman Frank Wells made a statement to the press about how the move would "assure the collection[']s continuation and growth in the hands of a professional staff."[13] Milliken, separated from what had become his life's work and apparently not considered "professional staff," went home.

In 1992, after many years in outside hands, the Warner Research library was returned to the care of Warner Bros. itself. The company had by this time again taken an interest in managing the library for profit by servicing outside productions as well as internal ones. Warners had, in 1988, acquired the equally formidable MGM Research Library through their purchase of Lorimar Telepictures, and was eager to combine the two collections into the largest library of its type in the world, which they did. Today the Warner Research Library, sistered with MGM's collection as well as the Hanna-Barbera Research Library (acquired through WB's purchase of Turner Entertainment), is intact—including the file on freak turtles— and happily is available to filmmakers and historians.

An aerial view of the Warner lot in 1933 with the word "Mines" clearly visible on the top of Stage 5, center. A reference to "Mines Field"—later Los Angeles International Airport, 14 miles away. 1933.

In the 1930s, Soundstage 5 had an arrow on its roof pointing southwest with the word "Mines" painted on top. This was a reference to Mines Field, which would, in 1949, become the Los Angeles International Airport. Apparently this was in response to a perceived danger that near-sighted aviators would think that the soundstages were airplane hangars and try to land.

There is, however, apparently no truth to the rumor that Jack Warner had the roof repainted to say "Lockheed" with the arrow pointing to the nearby defense plant in order to keep away the Japanese Air Force during World War II.

12. Fire Department and Power Plant

The on-lot power plant was part of the original studio construction. The original six generators were capable of carrying a load of 35,000 amps at 110 volts, roughly the equivalent of a power station for a city of twenty-five thousand people. One hundred miles of underground cable were buried to service the entire lot. With the coming of sound and early color film stocks (which by themselves necessitated the tripling of the lights on a set), the need for stable current increased disproportionally. Portable, diesel-powered generators were brought in to fulfill additional needs.

The studio power plant, left, and the WB Fire Department, right. Circa 1930s.

Even today, with a second powerhouse behind this one, generators do a lot of the heavy lifting on stages; on the backlot, where power is not always readily available; and on location.

Next door is the studio firehouse. Constructed in 1936 after the fire that took the life of Albert Rounder, the department and the building survive to this day. George Kitchen succeeded Chief Rounder as fire chief and stayed on the job through the 1952 fires, retiring in 1956.

13. Camera Department

Located south of the Makeup and Still Departments Building, the Camera Department was originally north of that same building. Its longtime home here was described in 1940 as a "squat one story building in the center of the lot."[14] During the studio era, a standing inventory of ten Mitchell cameras, as well as accessories, cranes, and dollies, were maintained and managed out of this department under the supervision of E. B. "Mike" McGreal, who also nominally, at least, was in charge of the Still Department next door. Magazines were loaded and unloaded in a lightproof booth at the back of the building with 1,000-foot spools of 35 mm film each representing about ten minutes onscreen. Any camera working on any stage would have been checked out of this building and was McGreal's responsibility.

A bevy of beautiful extras, on the lot for the musical *Colleen*, wave at the camera from the studio fire truck. 1936.

When Technicolor film was introduced as a viable process in the 1930s, part of the contract any studio had to sign in order to shoot a color film using the process was that Technicolor would supply the cameras, which used a cumbersome beam-splitter process to expose three strips of 35 mm film at the same time. Originally, the effects of this agreement on the Camera Department were minimal, as comparatively few Technicolor pictures were being made. But with the introduction of Eastman color in 1952, which allowed color film to be shot in a conventional 35 mm camera, studios' accountants of the 1950s discovered they rather liked the idea of renting cameras, and avoiding the expensive overhead entailed by owning their own. Consequently, by the 1950s, this building was being used by the Matte Department, and the nominal "Camera Department" only handled magazines and accessories for cameras, which usually came from outside manufacturer Arriflex. In fact, the first Hollywood motion picture shot on an Arriflex camera was the 1947 Warner Bros. feature *Dark Passage*.

With the introduction of the Panniflex camera in 1972, Panavision became the supplier to Hollywood for most of their camera needs. Even today, Panavision is the industry standard for filmmakers, even those shooting digitally.

Inside the Camera Department, technicians had to keep their fleet of Mitchell cameras and camera support equipment ready for near-constant usage. 1938.

Panavision has always insisted on owning their cameras and accessories outright, making a camera department in modern Hollywood a quaint and barely remembered thing of the past.

14. Makeup and Still Portrait Building

This building, originally the home of the Property Department, was snapped up by Perc Westmore in 1935 when the Property Department moved to their new quarters. Westmore had to convince his bosses that he needed such a spacious building (29,500 square feet), as originally the "Hair and Make-up Department" had consisted of a corner in the dressing room complex. They needn't have worried; by 1940, Westmore was commanding a staff of thirty-five and was complaining that the new building was also too small.

Perc was one of six sons of George Westmore. So influential had been the elder Westmore as a makeup and hair designer in early Hollywood, a profession he virtually invented, that eventually four of the Seven Sisters would have a Westmore family member in charge of their respective makeup departments.

Perc was particularly proud of his laboratory, which contained vats and ovens where plaster life-masks of actors were created, and with which he could experiment with prosthetic noses and chins and hairpieces. A sign in the corner of the laboratory ominously, and somewhat mysteriously, contained only the cryptic words "dry guillotine"—a phrase that Perc seemed to find more amusing than any of his clientele did.

Westmore was usually too busy to apply the makeup himself, although when he did, his favorite makeup chair was to be found in room 3. His private office contained assorted preset lighting setups to simulate black and white, Technicolor, exterior light, and even ultraviolet rays to reveal hidden pigments or blotches on his beloved life masks, which presumably could later be replicated on the star's actual faces.

Westmore would remain at his post until 1950, although he would return to the studio occasionally for special assignments. Like most longtime Warner Bros. employees, however, he never completely escaped the long shadow cast by the WB shield. In 1955 he was hired to re-create the startling Queen Elizabeth I makeup that he had designed for Bette Davis in *The Private Lives of Elizabeth and Essex* (1939) on a much older Davis, for the Fox picture *The Virgin Queen*. His last WB credit was for the western *There Was a Crooked Man* (1970). After that, he packed his makeup case and colored lights and went home, where he died the same year.

The Westmore legacy continues in Hollywood to this day. Marvin G. Westmore, Perc's nephew, got started at the studio for *My Fair Lady* (1964) and continued to work out of the department his uncle started through *Blade Runner* (1982) and the TV series *V* (1984–1985). It's not known if he ever used the chair in room 3.

The Makeup Department continued to operate out of this structure until the late 1960s, when it was moved to the adjacent Camera Department building so that Data Processing could occupy the space. By this time, most makeups were applied in trailers, rented for the occasion and parked outside the soundstages anyway. Early in the twenty-first century, the department was phased out altogether in favor of the more economical method of using freelance artists and equipment instead.

Upstairs in the same building was the Still Photography Department, which was reached by entering from the northern side doorway and climbing an interior staircase past Westmore's laboratory.

The job of this department was somewhat unique in that, unlike virtually any other craft department on the lot, still photography actually contributed virtually nothing to the filmmaking process. A project could work its way across the lot from script to preproduction to distribution without ever climbing these stairs. And yet yard for yard, more Hollywood glamour came out of the second floor of this building than anywhere else on the lot. Arguably, it's possible to suggest that stars were born in this building and under the lights of its loving still cameras rather than under the

Audrey Hepburn, modeling one of her signature gamine looks, outside the Makeup Department. 1967.

larger, hotter lights and moving cameras of the soundstages outside. Before an actor was ever filmed, he or she was photographed here first as a prerequisite, as part of an early search to discover the mysterious, elusive qualities necessary for stardom. And it was the thousands of sexy, intoxicating, silvery photographs that came out of this building, which were fed to fan magazines and mailed out to the public by the thousands, that truly kept an established star on people's minds. During World War II, when GIs were overseas and could not actually see Hollywood's product, they still knew who Ann Sheridan was and worshiped her from her still photographs alone, which, truth be told, sometimes told better stories than her movies did. Today, more people remember Marilyn Monroe, although they may not know it, from her ambiguous still photos, reproduced on everything from expensive art books to T-shirts, than from her movies, which comparably few people bother to watch anymore.

The most well-known Warner Bros. still photographer, and perhaps the most famous Hollywood still man of all time, was George Hurrell. In point of fact, Hurrell was only at Warner Bros. for a short time, from 1938 to 1940. Although Hurrell joined the company with a great deal of fanfare, the association apparently was not a happy one, although many Warner stars certainly benefitted from his idealized, nearly godlike treatments of their faces and figures.

The Warner Bros. still photographers responsible for creating the more familiar, and longer lasting, house style, and whose dramatic but less glamorous work perhaps better reflected the more realistic but still idealized patina of the studio's movies, included Scotty Welbourne, Bert Six, Schuyler Crail, Elmer Fryer, and Buddy Longworth.

The Still Photography Department also processed and distributed their own product, via an in-house lab. Interestingly, today Warner Bros. is the only studio in Hollywood that still has a photo lab—today housed in the basement of the studio Mill and that, like its predecessor, provides both photography and lab services. The current department is managed by Greg Dyro, an accomplished photographer himself.

The building where all of this happened also once included a shoeshine shop, and it briefly housed a drama school for studio actors. Today, the studio Credit Union shares the space with production offices, currently for the television series *Ellen* (2003–).

15. Dressing Rooms

Scattered behind the administration complex are several clusters of buildings of various sizes and shapes. Some of them look like multistoried office complexes. Some look like nothing so much as 1930s-era California bungalows. All of them, collectively and individually, have an interesting story to tell us, but retain many secrets. These buildings are all part of the Warner Bros. Dressing Room complex.

For many years, as a Warners archivist, I was often asked by many of the current residences of these buildings who occupied their particular offices before they moved in. For some reason, everyone wanted to be told that their rooms once housed either Errol Flynn or Bette Davis. No one ever imagined anyone but Davis or Flynn as occupying their particular space. Producers and their staffs—neither of whom, conceivably, had ever seen a Davis or Flynn picture—were still inexplicably hungry, desperate even, to be told that one or perhaps both stars had occupied their particular offices in earlier decades (no one ever suggested that they were in the same dressing room as the same time, but it could still happen, I suppose). Occasionally, someone would call and ask if Marilyn Monroe had once slept in their office, but as Monroe made only one movie for the studio, *The Prince and the Showgirl* (1957), shot in England, I usually dissuaded them of this notion right away, which usually led them to then hopefully ask about Davis and Flynn instead.

A half-dozen scandalously attired pretty starlets frolic in front of the Dressing Room complex to promote *Footlight Parade*. 1933.

Unfortunately, the name inscribed on inner office correspondence and envelopes directing people or parcels to those stars' dressing rooms always seemed to generically say "Miss Davis's dressing room." Nothing else was needed because everyone on the lot would have *known* where that was. And so the actual building and room have proven elusive.

There were several dressing room complexes, both freestanding bungalows and apartment-shaped units, all clustered in this area. Two of the oldest are in the extreme northwest corner of the studio and still stood in the 1960s, although, then as now, they were no longer used as dressing rooms.

The first one was built as part of the original studio construction as digs for Corinne Griffith, who was one of the most popular and beautiful actresses of the late 1920s. In an irony that no one seemed to notice at the time, Miss Griffith would much later write the novel *Papa's Delicate Condition*, which would be filmed here on her old lot in 1963. The building would eventually be divided in two sections. On the western side, J.L. created a veritable Ali-Baba's cave of a trophy room where he delighted in showing off the studio's and his own personal medals, military citations, and Academy Awards to guests and dignitaries. On the other side of the building was both a steam room and the executive dining room, where those same visitors, having presumably been dazzled by all the awards, would then be wined and dined

Bette Davis' dressing room. A location for this suite proved to be difficult to obtain. 1943.

and steamed by the mogul. Superstar George Clooney's Smokehouse Productions would occupy the building in the early twenty-first century.

Next door to the Griffith dressing room is a similar suite built in 1926 for actress Colleen Moore, who at the time was married to First National producer John McCormick. Miss Moore fled the studio and her marriage in 1930, but the building continued to be used as both a dressing room and as production offices for talent. Dolores Costello, who at the time was involved in a very volatile marriage to John Barrymore, was the second tenant, although talking pictures had already stalled her career, which never quite recovered.

In the late 1930s, the same building became the west coast office for company president Harry Warner, who was spending more time in Hollywood during this period "in order to keep an eye on Jack." Geographically, the office is as far away from Jack's own office suite as it was possible to be, while still being near the Administration Complex. Briefly, in the 1960s, superstar Steve McQueen's Solar Productions

The freestanding dressing room on the left was built in 1926 for actress Colleen Moore. It later housed Dolores Costello. 1946.

also occupied this building, although he would soon move across the lot to a larger suite where he retrofitted an underground bowling alley into a personal shooting gallery, a touch that earlier, less macho tenants of this building never thought of. In the early 1970s, producer George Pal occupied the space. In 1975, superstar Clint Eastwood moved his Malpaso Productions over from Universal (where he had shot the first *Dirty Harry* picture, even though it was a WB film). He has been on the lot and in the same building ever since.

Nearby are four more dressing room buildings. Three of them were constructed in 1926, and the fourth was built a couple years later along the wall of what was then Stage 2 (and which today is Stages 4 and 11). This last is the only one that looks the same today. As it is not used as dressing rooms anymore, tenants and guests there are always surprised to find that the offices in this building include showers! Two of these buildings were removed early on as part of an expansion of the Costume Department and the third, which once was the home of the Casting Department, is now production offices.

Built in 1931, the "Star Dressing Room" is, by virtue of its name, the most intriguing dressing room of them all. The building, which was rebuilt into deluxe studio office space in 2012, has two floors and once boasted a striking view of the studio tennis courts.

J.L. started to keep this court locked when it was discovered that anyone who felt like it was wandering onto the court for some practice. Warner used to give keys to stars and executives who were in his favor, and send a minion to retrieve that key from an employee who was on his way down. This latter moment was probably most often experienced near the end of one's career at Warner Bros.

Dick Mason, a longtime employee of the studio, who started out in the Mail Room and ended up working in Jack Warner's office, and who later managed the Tour Department, used to tell an intriguing story that may contain a clue about the great Flynn-Davis mystery. Mason claimed that Murray Hamilton, later a noted character actor—his credits would include *The Graduate* (1967) and *Jaws* (1975)—mentioned to him that he himself had worked in the WB Mail Room in the 1940s. Hamilton claimed that it had been his job to keep the charismatic but often besotted Flynn sober by routinely searching the star's dressing room and removing the often hidden alcohol bottles he always found there. One day, Hamilton remembered finding four bottles hidden among the actor's effects, yet Flynn inexplicably turned up drunk that day anyway! With nothing else to do, the company was dismissed, and Flynn was literally carried out of the soundstage to sleep it off. While being escorted away, Flynn's drunken eyes had briefly focused on him, and smiling he had said to Hamilton, "You found four bottles kid, but I hid five!"[15] When Mason told me this story, I asked him if Hamilton had mentioned where that dressing room was. Dick smiled, knowing what I wanted to know. "Sure. He told me it was over there somewhere." And then he had pointed, vaguely, over at the Star Dressing Room Building. So maybe . . .

After nearly a decade of listening to stories like this and digging through studio paperwork, I was about to give up. I decided that the next time anyone asked me, I would just point "over there" like Hamilton had. Yet there was one more "clue" to be found—a clue that, amusingly, had been *published* back in 1983 in Stuart Jerome's reminisces about his own days in the Mail Room: *Those Crazy Wonderful Years When We Ran Warner Bros.* Reviewing Jerome's book one day, I discovered right there on page 98 that Jerome had stated unequivocally that Flynn occupied the downstairs right-hand corner apartment in the Star Dressing Room Building. On the next page, he says that "Bette Davis occupied the suite above Flynn's."[16] I'd read this book years earlier, probably before I worked on the lot and it had become my job to know such things. But seeing these sentences—in print yet—felt like both a triumph and a bit of a disappointment.

Today most "star" dressing rooms are actually elaborate trailers that are rented by the studio or the talent, towed onto the lot, and parked outside the soundstage where the actor is working. This practice actually echoes the usage of large furnished boxes as dressing rooms in the 1930s and on, which were on wheels, and often housed talent when parked inside or adjacent to the soundstages.

16. Writers Building

Jack Warner had a love-hate relationship with his writers. On a certain level, he admired their talent and their ability to be witty upon command. This was a skill that Warner, as a deeply closeted wit and raconteur, certainly both admired and resented. Yet the writers were more rebellious against Warner's authority than any other group in the studio, excluding actors.

Warner's writers were originally housed all over the studio. The reasoning was that any office with room for a typewriter was more than they deserved. Yet eventually it was decided that the wisest policy regarding the writers would be to place all the bad, disruptive eggs in one slightly less corruptive basket. To this end, he approved construction of a triangular, two-story "Writers Building" in 1933.

The building was surprisingly close to the main Administration Complex, where Warner kept his own office. Whether this was an attempt by the mogul to keep an eye on his writers, or a jab at his brother Harry, whose office was even closer to theirs, is hard to determine, but the building quickly became the social and political center of the studio, not surprisingly, because most of the greatest and most esteemed brains of the twentieth century ended up working in the building at one time or another.

The first great writer at Warner Bros. was future 20th Century Fox mogul Darryl F. Zanuck, who, using at least three pseudonyms, wrote most of the studio's product in its early years. In fact, many Warner writers like John Huston, Jerry Wald, Sam Fuller, Delmer Daves, Richard Brooks, Burt Kennedy, and John Milius went on to careers as directors or producers.

Others Warner writers were future literary lights on the way up, or faded geniuses taking Hollywood money on the way down. This group included Lillian Hellman, James Hilton, Raymond Chandler, Tennessee Williams, William Faulkner, Ernest T. Gann, Gavin Lambert, and Peter Viertel. Some occupants here were simply Hollywood's greatest screenwriters, among whom were Casey Robinson, Robert Buckner, Julius and Philip Epstein, Leigh Brackett, James R. Webb, Frank Nugent, Budd Schulberg, William Goldman, David Newman, Robert Benton, and Robert Towne.

Jack Warner didn't care *what* they were. He used to walk down the long hallways of the building listening for the sound of typewriters, the only way of convincing him that his writers were actually doing what they had been contracted to do. "Schmucks with Underwoods" is what he liked to call them, whether he heard typing noises or not. The studio's 1938 feature *Boy Meets Girl* had James Cagney and Pat O'Brien as Hollywood writers who sleep in their offices, but leave on a phonograph containing typing sound effects to fool their boss. Maybe that's where Warner got his suspicions.

Yet J.L. wasn't above, in his softer moments, expressing a grudging admiration for his scribes. "I never finished high school," he used to muse, "but I have the best writers in the world working for me." Among them were Jules and Philip Epstein, two brilliant identical twins who cowrote some of the studio's great pictures. The two of them fooled Warner for years by clocking in for each other. The one brother actually on the job would alternately assume the other's identity in order to fool the boss into thinking that both were always on the clock and diligently working at the same time. "It was like working at belts in a factory. The studio produced a picture a week," Jules, or maybe it was Philip, remembered later.[17]

Stuart Jerome, who worked in the Mail Room and lived to write a book about it, said that his favorite spot in the studio was the Writers Building; "situated in a cozy, quiet corner of the studio, far removed from the distracting turmoil of production, it was deliberately planned to give its occupants the solitude and serenity necessary for wooing the creative muse. In actual fact it was a boisterous madhouse, exemplified by two sections officially named the upper and lower wards."[18]

As the Hollywood contract system withered away, Warner, and his successors, increasingly used those wards as office space for studio tenants who weren't necessarily writers at all. In 1969, for example, an internal memo noted that rooms in the building were being leased by the following: Gordon Parks, the first African American to direct a Hollywood feature film (*The Learning Tree*); John Milius, who was drafting *Apocalypse Now* (which would not be released for ten years!); Jerry Lewis; Bill Cosby; Harold Hecht Productions; Ed Feldman, who was producing something called *Scuba Duba*; as well as producers William Mayes and William Miles, and writers William Roberts and William Marks.

From 1976 to 1980, producer Irwin Allen oversaw his pictures out of this building. Production illustrator Joe Musso recalls that Allen built a sauna and a wet bar in the annex on the northeastern side of the building.[19] He also adopted the stray cats that had infested the studio and built a home for them near the entrance. When Allen left the lot (he eventually returned to the studio through a deal with Columbia Pictures), nearby tenant Clint Eastwood agreed to take care of the cats for the departing producer. The cats are still cared for to this day. In the 1990s, the *Los Angeles Times* attempted to run a story on the studio cats, but the company requested that the article be suppressed out of a fear that people would throw their unwanted cats over the walls in order to give them a good home!

The next tenant in the building was the (Alan Jr.) Ladd Company (offices on the first floor), who here produced *Night Shift* (1982), *Blade Runner* (1982), and *The Right Stuff* (1983). *Once Upon a Time in America* (1984) and the successful *Police Academy* franchise were also mounted from this building during this era. In 1981, director Peter Hayms kept offices here for the production of the Sean Connery film *Outland*.

In 2010 the building was refinished, refurnished, and rededicated. A plaque was placed near the east entrance listing the construction date as 1935, which was off by two years. The Epstein brothers would have probably appreciated the subterfuge.

The plaque placed on the wall of the former Writers Building in 2009.

17. Casting Department

An invitation to this office was, for many years, the dream of every aspiring actor. Constructed as part of the original "Dressing Room 3," the casting office was managed by Solly Baiano, who scouted the talent, and Phil Friedman, who made the tough decisions about who would be offered the dream of stardom. The complex contained more than just a single office. In fact, there was a school of sorts inside the building, where unsigned and newly signed talent could partake in acting, voice, speech, and diction workshops. Sophie Rosenstein, coauthor of *Modern Acting: A Manual* (1936), was the teacher. A small stage used for rehearsals, schooling, and practice sessions was located inside the unit as well. Rosenstein, who managed these workshops, remembered that out of perhaps every five hopefuls who would be invited in for an interview, one, maybe, would be chosen to test. How many who made it on to stardom from there could only be speculated upon. She did admit that eliminations would most often be made on one of the following criteria: "lack of ability, lack of experience, photographic complications, and striking similarities to people already under contract."[20]

Today the former casting office, where stars were born and dreams were kindled or died, contains production offices and elements of the Warner Bros. Human Resource division.

18. Administration Complex

The entire area above 1st Street, running from the edge of the studio to the backlot, is almost entirely the corporate headquarters for Warner Bros. The original 1926 Administration Building, then as now, faced a circular driveway where executives and guests could park their cars. Almost immediately an East Administration Building was added, followed by a West Administration Building (original home of the Story Department) and its annex, which are now collectively called Building 1. The East Administration Building and the Main Administration Building were combined in 1934, and an annex was added that jutted out alongside and to

The Administration Building. 1930.

The front of the Administration Building after the first of its many facelifts. Note how the doors and windows have been widened and the Spanish influence was played down to reflect the deco-happy 1930s. 1938.

the east of the circular-shaped driveway, and south where it became the Costume Department. This labyrinthine structure is now known collectively as Buildings 2 and 3.

One corner of this complex contained the studio's on-lot barber shop and as such was one of the social centers of the lot, at least among the studio's executive class. Long before the gossip magazines ever got the news, patrons of the barber shop here were already well appraised of the fact that Humphrey Bogart and Lauren Bacall were a couple offscreen as well as on, and that Olivia de Havilland, according to a court ruling, would not have to serve out the time she had been suspended at the end of her contract. Barber Pat Reagan's interest in dressing up as Davy Crockett and competing in black powder rifle matches, off duty, presumably, was a frequent topic of conversation around the chair as well. Don Johnson (no relation to the actor) was the last barber at that chair, during the 1960s.

The president of the studio's office, then as now, was on the backside of the Circle Drive on the second floor, with a view of the Warner fiefdom offered by a large window. The general layout and the outer walls of the building are very similar to their look at the time of the original construction. But most of the building has been gutted and rebuilt several times.

In 1989, Building 2 was rededicated as the Daly-Semel Building, named after the popular longtime heads of the studio who occupied Warner's office suite from 1981 to 1999.

19. War Memorial

Most large industrial sites that existed in the 1940s probably at one time had some sort of commemorative plaque or monument dedicated to those employees who were engaged in the military during World War II. The studios in Hollywood were no exception. In 1944, the *Motion Picture Herald* reported that of the 19,600 workers employed in the film industry, fully one third, or 6,500, were by that time in one branch of the armed forces or another. The Warner Bros. monument was originally a free-standing metal plaque with each employee in the military listed alphabetically. In July 1944, a more permanent, stone monument (designed by Ralph Bates of the Maintenance Department) with the names of those serving on individual brass plaques was unveiled. In August 1945, after the battle of Iwo Jima, a sculpture representing the raising of the U.S. flag (created by Harry Platt of the Staff Shop and artist Pasquale Mannelli) was placed on top of the monument. A star was placed next to the name of any employee who lost his life defending his country. The names on these plaques were an inspiringly democratic jumble of the great and small in Hollywood: set painters and set designers and movie stars and movie moguls. Included on the plaques were a future president of the United States, Ronald Reagan, and the current vice president of the studio, Jack L. Warner, and his son Jack Warner Jr.

The Warner family had always been exceedingly patriotic. Jack had actually been born while the family had been trying to eke out a living in Ontario, Canada, but he and his brothers were eager to identify themselves as 100 percent American. In 1942, General Hap Arnold had approached Jack with the idea of creating a unit made up of experienced motion picture professionals for the purpose of creating military training and propaganda films. Initially the company was based at the old Vitagraph lot, but that studio, long unused and stripped bare, was insufficient to the task. Instead, the Hal Roach lot in Culver City (then not in use because Roach was himself in the military) was leased, reportedly for $1. Hal Roach ended up ahead of the game, though, because of the numerous and expensive improvements that the military implemented during its tenure there.

Jack Warner came out of the war an improved man as well. Commissioned a lieutenant colonel for his role in the FMPU, he had to get his staff to drill him from

Gary Cooper shows off his brand-new 1949 Ford Mercury 8 in front of the War Memorial. Cooper was on the lot shooting *The Fountainhead* at the time. 1949.

an army manual to learn the required officer lingo and mannerisms. His uniform, complete with a most impressive selection of medals and ribbons, came courtesy of his own Costume Department. But once he knew how to look, how to salute, and, more importantly, how to be saluted, J.L. discovered that he *liked* being a colonel. He would be addressed by that title for the rest of his life.

In the decades after the war ended, when real life for that war's veterans and for the rest of the planet could began again, most of the studios removed the memorials to their employees who had saved the world and made that world once again safe for Hollywood. Most, that is, except for Warner Bros. In the 1960s, the monument even cameoed in a movie, opposite no less than the studio's biggest female star, Natalie Wood, in the Hollywood-set *Inside Daisy Clover* (1965)—which added a John F. Kennedy–inspired "eternal flame" to the base.

Yet time, like soldiers, marches on. And in the 1970s and 1980s, the monument fell into neglect, the Iwo Jima statue started to decompose, and the Marines raising the flag started to look skeletal as the wire armatures under their uniforms became exposed to the sun and rain. An employee project to clean and polish the copper plaques designating those who had served was inadvertently botched in the 1990s when the newly polished placards were due to be reapplied to the monument and it was discovered that no one had taken note of which plaques had stars next to them. Yet salvation for the monument was on the way, and the statue was repaired and rededicated in 2006.

Today the studio has a second monument, dedicated to Warner Bros. veterans of other wars, on the Steven J. Ross Plaza, adjacent to the company store.

20. Costume Department

The studio's first dedicated costume building was constructed here in 1928. It was a long, two-story structure, with annexes, whose back wall butted against Dressing Room 1, and the side of which contained a payroll windows for extras. In the 1940s, it was staffed by 128 people.

Costumes continued to be stored here, and in those nearby and increasingly numerous annexes, until 1990, when the department was shuffled off to two buildings

A Costume Department interior. Note the racks of labels near the windows used for identification. Circa 1930s.

on the studio ranch property, where contemporary and television costumes were stored, and a third building on Thompson Street in Burbank, which housed period costumes. In 1994, the current 60,000-square-foot Costume Building was completed at the bottom of the Bridge Building Parking structure. Designed by Ronald Frink, the ground floor contains the department's administration, design, and wardrobe construction complex, as well as star dressing and fitting rooms.

In one corner of the building is a collection of dress mannequins, some of which are fifty years old or more. Interestingly, the names of the women whose measurements correspond to those of each body form have been written for decades in often now-faded black ink on each. So it is possible to note that a classic Warner star like Bette Davis has the same dimensions as a modern star such as Teri Hatcher.

Underground is stored eight miles of racked clothing, not including eight thousand purses or handbags, thirty thousand pairs of shoes, fifty thousand pieces of jewelry, and ten thousand hats stored on shelves. The new building is climate controlled, and the lights are all on motion sensors to protect the costumes from undue illumination, and also making a lone visitor feel quite isolated walking among the millions of pieces in a pool of light that turns on in front of him and clicks off after he has passed through during the journey.

21. Drug Store

This triangular shaped two-story building was constructed above Circle Drive in 1939. It straddled Olive Avenue and Rowland Avenue, which would later be renamed Warner Boulevard, and so was technically outside the lot.

Then, as now, the building contained small offices on both floors. Today this real estate is used by the Feature Production Department. On the ground floor facing the street was a small drug store ("Studio Cosmetics") and camera shop that lasted into the 1960s, servicing both headache-prone executives and curious tourists.

On New Year's Eve in 1958, it was at the gate in front of this building that Jack Warner Jr. tried to enter the studio, and, on orders from his father, was refused admittance by Security Department head Blayney Matthews. Warner Sr. had reportedly been unhappy with his son's performance during his convalescence from his auto accident in the south of France.

In 1954, while he was on the lot shooting *East of Eden*, a young actor named James Dean lived in one of the office apartments behind the drug store, apparently because his bohemian lifestyle didn't seem conductive to renting an apartment of his own. The studio was thus able to keep an eye on their young find, and at the same time Dean's Los Angeles–based friends were spared having to let him sleep on their couches.

Employees of the Mail Room at the time, many of whom were approximately the same age as Dean, used to be amused that the young star would stop by to shake

The former "Studio Drug Store" as it still looks on Olive Avenue. 2013.

envelopes containing the fan mail he was already receiving in order to ascertain if there was return postage money inside along with the usual request for an autographed photo. He would tear open these envelopes only and pocket the money. "What are you looking at?" he used to snarl. "They're addressed to me."[21]

22. Marion Davies Bungalow (Site)

Marion Davies was a major star in the 1920s and 1930s. She was also the mistress of newspaper magnate William Randolph Hearst, who promised free publicity in the Hearst press to any studio that would employ Marion. In 1924, while she was at MGM, Hearst constructed for her the most elaborate and opulent dressing room in Hollywood history. It was Spanish style, with fourteen bedrooms, a sitting room, a master kitchen, a study with a walk-in fireplace, a serving pantry, a dining room, and four baths.

In 1934, J.L. lured Marion and Hearst (who produced her films through his Cosmopolitan Pictures banner) north to Burbank, and Hearst determined that Marion's palatial bungalow would make the trip as well.

The structure had to be chopped into four pieces in order to be trucked to the studio. Even Jack Warner, no stranger to DeMille-style spectacle, marveled at the operation: "Streets were blocked, phone and electric wires were raised, and traffic was rerouted while this odd caravan rumbled toward Burbank. The cost was shocking, but Hearst was determined that his favorite star would not have an ordinary dressing room," he recalled.[22]

Ever Since Eve (1937) cast Marion Davies as a dowdy secretary and her bungalow, visible behind her, as a swanky estate. Robert Montgomery, right, seems suitably impressed with both of them.

This "dressing room" remained in Burbank until 1937, when Marion, Hearst, and the bungalow all moved on. Interestingly, they left behind an annex building, built in the same style, which would later be James Cagney's dressing room and play James Mason's dressing room in *A Star Is Born* (1954). The structure continued to be used as an office, including, for a time, by Hal Wallis, Milton Sperling, and most recently producer Joel Silver. No better contrast between the Hollywood of old and of today can be found than in the realization that Silver, in particular, one of the most powerful people in today's film industry, long ran his empire out of what was once an actress' guest cottage.

23. Frank Sinatra Office

Across the sidewalk from the remains of the Davies bungalow, and down a leafy walkway built after Marion's bungalow had departed, can be found an elaborate office complex built in 1964 by Jack Warner for his friend, Frank Sinatra. With the possible exception of Al Jolson, whom Warner liked immensely, there was never another actor whom Jack Warner would have unhesitatingly used the word "friend" to describe.

Sinatra was everything that Warner wanted to be. But in his heart, J.L. knew that, even with all his power and fame, he could never be as confidant, witty, tough, or attractive to the ladies as Sinatra was. Because Warner saw so much of himself, or at least so much that he wished himself to be, in Sinatra, he tolerated more of the singer's shenanigans with less complaint than he would have with any other star.

Sinatra had made *Young at Heart* at the studio back in 1954, and his indifference to the project had not made the experience a particularly happy one. But J.L. had courted Sinatra relentlessly afterward to come back to the studio. The six films they made together in the 1960s were not particularly distinguished—all of them look like they were more fun to make than they are to watch—but Warner was so flattered to have Sinatra and his rat-pack buddies on the lot that he happily looked the other way when the films they made went over budget and the results were lackluster.

Sinatra's first office on the lot was, naturally, in the Star Dressing Room (second floor). But J.L. promised to build him better quarters. The resultant bungalow, complete with library, wood-paneled office suites, and, naturally enough, a well-stocked wet bar, certainly rewarded Sinatra for his comparative patience.

Yet as Frank Sinatra's brand of cool cooled off itself in the late 1960s and the Hollywood that he and Warner had ridden roughshod over for so many years was swept away, younger, more relevant actors, and even actor-singers came onto the lot, and eventually ended up occupying Sinatra's own office suites.

First Artists was a production company that, in the style of United Artists in the 1920s, attempted to bring together the predominant talent of its era as creative producers of their own product. To that end, in 1969, Steve McQueen, Barbra Streisand, Sidney Poitier, and Paul Newman leased Sinatra's old offices as their headquarters. The experiment was not a success, and in recent decades, producer Quinn Martin, director Richard Donner, and producer Joel Silver have occupied the building.

24. Postproduction Complex

First National constructed the studio with no provisions for the coming of sound. None of the four original stages were soundproofed, and there were no sound recording or editing facilities in any of the long-range plans for the complex. Significantly, the first building the Warners construed on the property was the Music Building. At the building's dedication in 1929, Jack Warner allegedly called the building "our first Burbank erection." That structure was also called, less descriptively, the Warner Building and the Warner Administration Building at different times in the 1930s.

In 1929, the "New Dupe Building" was constructed just behind it, and behind that quickly rose the "Recording Building." The last two buildings are still used for

The first building that the Warners constructed on their lot (in 1929) was the structure on the right; significantly, it was designated for use in postproduction. 1968.

editing and sound recording, although the latter has been largely replaced with a bigger structure.

Built in 1928, the Recording Building was the equivalent of the airless bunker that Sam Warner used on the Sunset Boulevard Studio lot. Sound originating on the set went from a microphone into an on-set mixing board, where, in the 1930s, audio from up to three microphones could be recorded. From there, using feeds running underground through caverns that circumvented the studio, the audio went into an amplifier in the recording rooms located on the ground floor of this building. Through the use of a patch panel, any room could receive sound from any wired location on the lot. This system, designed by department head William Mueller, was, as cumbersome as it sounds, technology that was cutting edge for its era.

The sound was recorded on disc during the Vitaphone days, and optically on film until the early 1950s, when a more versatile magnetic tape format became the industry standard. In the 1990s digital audio changed the business, and operations inside this building, once again.

Two screening rooms (numbers 4 and 5), with a combined capacity of 161 seats, can be found on the second floor of the "Recording Building." Screening Room 4 was featured in the film *A Star Is Born* (1954) in a scene in which Judy Garland stumbles into the room during the screening of the world's noisiest western.

Across the street from this complex is a large building that was built in 1928 and contains what was originally referred to as "Sound Stages 1 and 2." As the

The Scoring Stage, where musical selections are recorded to accompany the action onscreen, is one of the most evocative places in the whole studio. Here, Robert Alda (on screen), as George Gershwin, gets his music sweetened by a full orchestra, for *Rhapsody in Blue* (1945). The 1929 Steinway piano, right, is still on the stage and was once a favorite of singer Frank Sinatra.

other stages were gradually soundproofed, this building was assigned the designation of "Sound Stages 9 and 10" (with yet another Costume Department annex on its southern end). From 1929 on, the structure was used for recording music, and it quickly evolved into the Scoring Stage, still used today.

The Warner Bros. Scoring Stage is legendary for the peerless sound quality that it produces. It is 65 feet wide by 80 feet long, with concert hall–style floors and walls, which are original despite numerous upgrades to accommodate the digital era. The room can accommodate up to a ninety-piece orchestra and has witnessed the creation of the music for hundreds of great movies as conducted by all of the great Hollywood composers.

It's impossible to step into the room and not hear some of these pieces in one's head even on days when the stage is not working. The very walls seem saturated with music. A 1929 Steinway piano in the corner was a personal favorite of Frank Sinatra and is still used daily. If the room seems visually familiar as well, it is because it has been used as a set, at least twice, playing a Hollywood studio scoring stage both times. In *It's a Great Feeling* (1949), Doris Day visited the Stage. Five years later, James Mason proposed to Judy Garland there in *A Star Is Born*.

One thing that has changed is the name on the door. For decades, the stage was referred to as the Leo Forbstein Scoring Stage, after the longtime (1931–1948) head of the Music Department. In 1999, when it was rumored that the stage was going to be shut down, actor Clint Eastwood, who had been using the stage to score his films for decades, interceded. Not only was the stage not closed down, but it also was refurbished and rededicated as the Clint Eastwood Scoring Stage.

Dick Mason, who we met earlier, remembered that in 1958, when he was hired out of high school to work in the Mail Room (at $1.44 an hour), he was sent to deliver something to the Scoring Stage on his first day. When he entered the room, a big orchestra was conducting a score for a western that was being projected on the big screen. When the light came up, he recognized that the composer on the podium was Dimitri Tiompkin, who was recording the score for *Rio Bravo*. "I remember thinking right then that this was the best place in the whole world," he remembers. "I couldn't understand why anyone would ever want to leave."[23] Warner Bros. would turn out to be the only employer Mason would ever have.

The warren of offices and bungalows surrounding this building, and stretching out nearly to the backlot, still houses numerous editing- and post production-related departments. Foley, where sound effects are created; ADR (automated dialogue replacement), where voices and effects are dubbed; and numerous transfer, restoration, and mastering facilities—all the finest in the world—are all housed here, servicing both Warner Bros. and other studios' product.

All of this was overseen, in the 1960s, by Rudi Fehr. Fehr had been an influential film editor, and then had been the head of the entire Warner Bros. Post Production Department for decades by this point. But when the studio forced him to "retire" in 1976, Fehr managed to get the last laugh at the age of seventy-four by scoring an Oscar nomination, shared with his daughter Kaja, for *Prizzi's Honor* (1985). This late-career "comeback" film was directed by another Warner Bros. expatriate, seventy-nine-year-old John Huston.

25. Commissary

The Commissary, "where the stars eat," opened in 1925 even before the studio proper, presumably to service both the production and construction crews on the property. Originally it was privately operated. After four months it burned to the ground, was rebuilt, and reopened, this time with First National as the sole owner-operator. At the time the staff included ten waitresses, two cooks, a dishwasher, and a busboy. Six more waitresses were eventually hired. One of them was Kathryn Higgins, who in 1929 would end up managing the place.

In 1930, the building was enlarged again. The capacity inside was increased from 240 to 350 people. In 1936, that number was ratcheted up to 550. Today, the building and its outside dining plaza can service about eleven hundred.

The Commissary's function was, and is, not only to service in-house diners, but also to cater meals on any of the soundstages or on location, or to provide brown-bag

The Green Room was a fancy name for what today is the fine-dining area on the eastern side of the Commissary Building. Circa 1950s.

lunches or dinners for staff. They also were, and are, responsible for managing the executive dining room in the Administration Complex and the Fine Dining Room, located on the eastern side of the Commissary Building.

For many years the Studio Store, where employees and their starstruck guests could buy Warner Bros. crew shirts or a Bugs Bunny ash tray, was located next the Commissary as well. Eventually it moved to the future Tour Department office at Gate 4, and finally to the former Costume Building, where in 2004 it was renamed "Central Perk," after the coffee shop in the series *Friends*. For ten years (1991–2001), Warner Bros. Studio Stores could also be found in shopping malls and tourist destinations around the world.

In the 1940s, the Commissary was officially renamed the Green Room (later still, it would be called the Blue Room). Publicity at the time stated that Errol Flynn was "a light eater," that Bette Davis "between laughs eats hot dogs," and that "Joan Crawford invariably orders cold turkey and fruit salad topped with a mayonnaise dressing which she makes herself and brings to the studio."[24]

In 1991, as part of that studio's ongoing rededication of their lot, and in order to follow studio President Gary Credle's dictate to make every part of the property a filmable location, the front of the Commissary was resurfaced with backlot brick and an artificial second floor was added. Thereafter the Commissary could be used

An interior view of the Warner Bros. Commissary. Circa early 1940s.

as an extension to the adjacent backlot Brownstone Street set, and could appear on camera whenever the set was photographed, thereafter allowing the Commissary "where the stars eat" to become something of a star itself.

26. Schoolhouse

From the 1930s into the 1960s, children were employed on the lot in sufficient numbers to warrant the construction (in 1931) of an accredited schoolhouse, staffed with a real teacher, Mrs. Lois Horne. Debbie Reynolds remembers Horne as a "tall, thin, formidable woman with grey hair pulled back in a bun."[25] Students who were needed on the set were tutored individually in order to meet state requirements as well.

Warner Bros.' primary child star during the 1930s, a rare golden era of stardom for both women and children, was the cherubic Sybil Jason, whom Warner signed in 1935 as competition to Fox's pint-sized dynamo, Shirley Temple. The following year, Jason managed to steal scenes from no less than Al Jolson in *The Singing Kid*. Long-term screen immortality was not to be hers, however, and Jason ended her career at Fox supporting Shirley Temple herself. In her later years, Ms. Jason was a beloved "honorary member" of the International Al Jolson Society, the members of

Bette Davis seems slightly disinterested in her young costar, Glenn Ford, during a break in the production of *A Stolen Life*, in which they were appearing together. 1946.

whom reveled in the company of one of their heroes' actual costars, and she had her own fan club as well, which lasted until 2010. Sybil herself lasted until 2011.

The school building itself didn't survive quite so long. When there were no longer enough child stars to keep Mrs. Horne busy, the school was closed and the building was later used by the Mail Room. In the late 1970s, superstar Burt Reynolds kept offices here. In 1993 Clint Eastwood pointed out that there was a gymnasium where he and other employees could work out on site at Paramount, but not at Warners, and inquired as to why that was.

Actually, the studio once did have a gymnasium, in a redesigned set storage building managed by a former champion welterweight boxer with the colorful moniker of Mushy Callahan, whom Jack Warner had first admired in the ring and then employed. But both the building and Mushy were both long gone by the time Eastwood made his fateful suggestion. So the former schoolhouse was demolished, and a larger, two-story structure was erected on the site as the studio fitness center.

An open alcove to the right of the front door to the new building was big enough for a basketball hoop and an abbreviated court as well. But when the cast of TV's *ER* (1994–2009) started using it on a regular basis, and many a female personal assistant started finding reasons to walk by or to eat lunch across the street and ogle that series' basketball-crazy star, George Clooney, management decided something needed to be done to enlarge the court to regulation size.

In 1996 Studio Operations had built an enclosed, but temporary, basketball court in Parking Lot H for superstar Michael Jordan to practice on while he was shooting *Space Jam*, so they already knew what was involved. After some contemplation they instructed their engineers to scoop out the backside of the Brownstone Street façades, which were on the other side of the Fitness Center—the inside of which were currently being used to store lighting equipment—and use this real estate to enlarge the court to regulation size. This was done, and the result was much appreciated by the fitness center members, the *ER* cast, and a great many personal assistants.

27. Warner Records

Warner Records was founded in March 1958, when Rudi Fehr pointed out to Jack Warner that it would cost less to start a record company than the budget of a single picture at the time. The department opened here on the site of the old Camera Machine Shop. Early Warner Records hits were novelty items by the likes of comedian Bob Newhart and *77 Sunset Strip* star Edd "Kookie" Byrnes. But in 1963 Warner Records merged with Frank Sinatra's Reprise Records, which was heavily in debt. Sinatra's legitimacy in the recording industry and his star power ultimately made the merger a successful one, and the company had a long and largely profitable run. By 2004, however, the music industry overall was in dire financial straits, and the entire division, which was now housed at the nearby corner of Riverside Drive and Warner Boulevard, was sold to an outside private equity group. One of the tenets of the sale was that Warner Records, although an outside company, could continue to use the Warner trademarks and logo, which it still does.

The original Warner Records Building is still used as office space. In the 1970s, Lorimar Telepictures was headquartered there. At different times, producers Paula Weinstein and Reinhold Weege, and actors James Garner (in 1978 while shooting *The New Maverick*) and John Travolta, have also rented offices in this building.

28. Film Vaults

The sum total of everything the studio has done is contained in its film vaults. Originally, the highly flammable nitrate film elements were stored in several two-story, multiple-room bunkers, and two smaller buildings south of the Administration Complex. The oldest surviving vault, built in 1936, was constructed behind, but predated, the film laboratory alongside Hollywood Way.

Its sister, which was slightly smaller, was situated next to a truck shed on the backside of Brownstone Street. A third building of the same design stood slightly to the south of the water tower. Film was also stored in the basement of the Mill and all over the lot, especially after nitrate film stock was phased out in the early 1950s and less combustible film elements were made available.

The last surviving nitrate-safe Film Vault on the Warner lot is this imposing, bunker-like structure, located behind the Film Lab and built in 1936. 2013.

The film vault behind Brownstone Street was removed in 1995. The Warner Bros. Museum and the 516-seat Steven J. Ross Theater were constructed on the site. Today the studio's primary on-lot film vault is the former Soundstage 20, which had been constructed in 1939, and until 1992 had been used most often for wardrobe storage. The new vault preserves color film at 35 degrees Fahrenheit and the more resilient black-and-white prints at 45 degrees, with backup elements housed both digitally and in key locations around the world, including a salt mine 650 feet below the surface in Kansas.

The on-lot vault is estimated to be the home of more than six thousand features, sixty-five thousand television episodes, and twenty thousand shorts.

29. Film Lab

The laboratory building was original constructed in 1938 just outside of the studio gate at the corner of Rowland Avene and Hollywood Way. Although laboratory operations were usually contracted out (at one time, in the 1950s, Technicolor managed the operation), most of the eighty employees were paid by Warner Bros. and

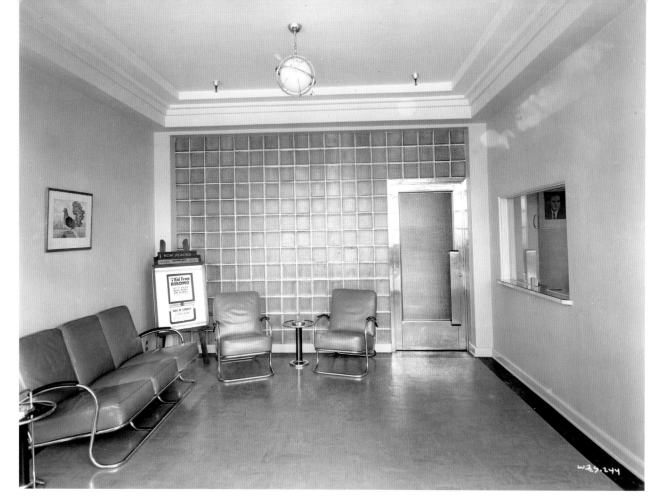

The Film Lab lobby, designed in the exquisite Art Moderne style. 1938.

some of their jobs with the studio went back to the original Sam Warner lab constructed in 1924 on Sunset Boulevard.

The 19,000-square-foot building was designed (by Bert Titlebaum) to be the best in the industry. It was constructed at a cost of $500,000, with air conditioning throughout and an appealing Streamline Moderne look that made the building, from the outside at least, look a little bit like an ocean liner beached incongruously in a parking lot.

In the 1940s it was estimated that more than 75,000 feet of negative film was exposed on the stages of Warner Bros. each week—some 4 million feet a year. This film was all sent to this building for processing. The resultant positive print was then assembled according to instructions and synchronized with the soundtrack, which had been converted to 35 mm film, on an upright editing machine called a Moviola. The camera negative would be filed and stored in a fireproof vault and would ultimately be sent to a printing room where it would be timed, corrected and assembled, married to the soundtrack, and duplicated to match the edited positive work print. These prints would be the ones ultimately shipped out the gates and to theaters.

Like every building on the lot, the film lab was often used as a filming location. In *Romance on the High Seas* (1948), for example, it played the "Miracle Drug

Company," and in *My Dream Is Yours* (1949), it was a radio station. Both films headlined Doris Day.

Today the building, still whimsically nautical in appearance, is managed by the Postproduction Department.

30. Tiger's Den Club

As with many things in Hollywood, taking a tour of Warner Bros. was long an experience one could have only if blessed with connections at the studio. Jack Warner enjoyed showing off his factory, and in particular his trophy room, to guests, which included American presidents, royalty, ambassadors, contest winners, dignitaries from around the world, scientists, and sports figures, as well as exhibitors, independent theater owners, new talent, popcorn growers, and others associated, however tangentially, one way or another, with the entertainment industry. Even though the studio produced short subjects, such as *Musical Movieland* (1944), which implied that regular tours for regular people were also the norm, this was most definitely not the case during this period.

Usually, the Mail Room boys were entrusted with studio tours, as many of the executives whose guests they were escorting would not have known what was shooting in which stage and would not have been able to find that stage with a compass and a map. The Mail Roomers, however, knew the studio better than any of its executives did, and relished being able to put down their mailbags for an afternoon and show off.

The site of the old Tiger's Den Club, with the Film Lab sprawling behind it. 2012.

A memo dated March 21, 1946, however, addressed the studio tour situation in an entirely different light:

IMPORTANT

    Now that vacation time is in the offing and with travel restrictions lifted, we are being deluged with requests for tours through the studio. You can, of course, appreciate that we must take care of a normal amount of visitors for business purposes and for good public relations with certain of our exhibiters.

    However there is a definite limit to the number we can take care of and we, therefore, ask everybody's cooperation in politely but firmly rejecting any requests from friends, relatives, and "visiting firemen," who want to visit the studio. It only causes a slow-up of our operation and certainly is not helpful to our artists to be placed under the strain of having a constant group of onlookers.

    I would appreciate your attention to this request as we do not want to be placed in the embarrassing position of having to refuse you passes.

    Jack Warner

Embarrassing positions were no longer such a concern when, in 1973, Warner Bros., or rather The Burbank Studios, or "TBS" as the lot was known at the time, opened a tour department that was, for the first time, available to the general public. In 1964 Universal Studios, Warner Bros.' neighbor, had instigated a tour of their backlot via "glamour trams" (pink and white carriages pulled by diesel-powered tractors). The Universal "tour" was always designed to include staged material orchestrated for the amusement of guests—although in the early days, more of the working studio was also included than would be common in later years. At Warner Bros. it would have been be financially impossible to re-create or alter anything on the lot for visitors, as the tours would be kept very small, and would be limited in frequency in order to not interfere with production.

As had been done in the past, Dick Mason, a former Mail Room employee, was chosen to head the department, which initially operated out of a corner of producer Quinn Martin's office building and later moved to a shed in a parking lot between Hollywood Way and Cordova Street. Mason's initial involvement was almost inadvertent. "I was brought in by management at TBS as a consultant, because I'd been giving tours unofficially for years. We never thought of making money at it. I think we charged $3.00 when we first opened to the public,"[26] he remembers with a chuckle. There was no money for advertising, so the tour stayed alive through word of mouth, and therefore many of the guests continued to be associated, somehow, with the industry.

    Anyone wishing to book a tour would need a reservation and a drive-on pass to enter the studio for their appointment. Sometimes the prospective guest, upon being issued a pass, would not be able to find the tour office, and so would spend the day wandering around the lot looking for it, and therefore get his "tour" anyway, unaccompanied and for free.

Mason's unvarnished working Hollywood tour was an immediate success, almost in spite of itself. Fans and the press called it the "anti-Universal," and many guests came back multiple times because it was always different, and because no other studio in Hollywood offered anything quite like it.

In the 1990s the department was moved to a better location at the mouth of Gate 4 and Hollywood Way. The building Mason inherited had been a dance rehearsal hall constructed in the late 1930s. In the swinging 1960s, the thing had been transformed into a rather unsavory go-go club called the Tiger's Den, and at the time the Tour Department moved in, it was the Studio Store. With the new building, the public could now enter from the street to enquire about a tour without getting a pass to enter the lot first, although reservations were still strongly suggested. At the

A local travel magazine's proposition (for lack of a better word) to the tourist trade. 1974.

same time, the studio purchased (initially) two- to twelve-seat golf carts, allowing guests to be driven across the lot for the first time. Until this point most of the tours had been on foot and very dusty and strenuous—although an ancient, rebuilt golf cart Mason had inherited from another department had been used for smaller tours up to this point, and had been much fought over by his foot-weary staff.

With Dick Mason's retirement in 2000, Danny Kahn of the Operations Department was brought in to make the tour smoother, more commercial, and more corporate. He lobbied to increase the number of tours, to advertise, and to move the department across the street from Gate 5, to the lobby of an office building previously used by Columbia Studios (built in 1988, it is now called Studio Plaza). Wisely, he kept the intimate, private aspects of the tour that always appealed to guests by increasing the number of tours without increasing the number of people *on* the tours. His jiggering paid off handsomely. The VIP Tour Department is consistently one of the studio's most lucrative departments. Even Jack Warner might have approved.

31. Water Tower

The studio water tower rose in 1926 as part of the initial studio construction push. Oddly it did that rising hundreds of yards away from where it is now.

Initially, the 133-foot tower, with its hundred-thousand-gallon tank, was assembled next to the site of the Fire Department and dead center in the original lot's layout. The water tower, like similar structures in other industrial sites, was intended as a firefighting and factory tool and was never used to supply the plant with drinking water. By the 1930s, however, it had become apparent that the most flammable part of the studio was not the administration and soundstage complex, which the tower was then casting its shadow across, but the craft and technical departments, and the backlot, all of which were far to the south or the east. The Long Beach earthquake that rocked the studio in 1933 and the devastating lot fire of 1934 bore this out.

In 1937 it was finally decided to do something. The tank was dissembled, the scaffolding that supported it was taken down, and the entire monolith was laboriously trucked across the lot, where the process was repeated in reverse at the end of Hollywood Way—it stands there today.

The water tower, somewhat inexplicably, has always been a most potent symbol of the studio and of movie studios in general. "There is no bigger totem of Hollywood than the Warner Bros. water tower,"[27] actor Ben Affleck recently observed. This is true, yet odd, since the logo painted on its tank was originally, and through the 1930s, not that of Warner Bros. at all, but of First National Pictures, and in the 1970s and 1980s of The Burbank Studios. It should also be noted that such an object as a water tower is still a familiar site at any large industrial site and by no means unique to the motion picture industry.

The water tower in its original location with its original decoration. Note that the logos for Vitaphone and First National are included— but not that of Warner Bros. This paint job was used from 1926 to 1939.

The Warner Bros. Water Tower with its traditional (1939–1967) shield logo.

The Warner Bros. Water Tower
after the sale to Seven Arts.
1967–1969.

The Warner Bros. Water Tower
during the Burbank Studios era.
1972–1990.

The Warner Bros. Water Tower as it (usually) looks today.

The Warner Bros. Water Tower's appearances on screen are also surprisingly few. It's most inadvertently amusing cameo is in the Karl Malden vehicle *Phantom of the Rue Morgue* (1954). In that film, the camera observes a Parisian Street fair on the backlot French Street set. A girl on a trampoline is followed by the tilting camera as she, and the camera, pivots progressively higher with each trampoline leap. The very last time she jumps a little bit too high, however, and the WB water tower is briefly rendered visible, even though the setting is faraway Paris! More recently, the same tank was used as a prop in *Looney Tunes: Back in Action* (2003), in which it is upended by a runaway Batmobile. The water tower was best utilized, however, by the animated Saturday morning TV series *Animaniacs* (1993–1998), in which it was the home of the title characters: the "Warner Brothers," Yakko and Wakko, and their sister Dot.

Also painted, but not so animated, is a rendering of the water tower on a backlot wall perpendicular to the actual tower at the studio. The painting, courtesy of the Scenic Arts Department, is supposed to depict part of New York City in order to extend the New York Street set that is nearby. But, inexplicably, the clever artists also included the silhouette of an adjacent and very familiar Burbank water tower as reflected in a "window."

Jack Warner allegedly liked to end arguments with his staff by pointing out the window and snarling, "Whose name's on the water tower?" In 1967, however, J.L. tried this line on Warren Beatty during the production of *Bonnie and Clyde*. Without missing a beat, Beatty shot back, "Actually those are my initials, J.L."

Incidentally, the water tower, ever since 1971, no longer actually holds water. In fact a recent internal engineer's survey strongly suggested that it never be filled with water again. So like a lot of people in Hollywood, the Warner Bros. water tower now looks good, but doesn't really do anything.

32. Television Building

In the mid-1950s, Jack Warner hated television. He so disliked the upstart medium that, allegedly, he would not allow televisions onto the lot even to be photographed as props. An oft-told story goes that until the late 1950s, if a script called for a scene set in a suburban living room, it would be a living room that, bizarrely, did not yet have a television. If this tale is true, it ignores such well-remembered pictures from this period as *A Star Is Born* (1954) and *Rebel without a Cause* (1955), both of which featured televisions—although, admittedly, the feared black box was not depicted in a particularly flatteringly light in either.

What is true is that Warner, like Hollywood's other aging moguls, was frightened by television's undeniable potential to keep audiences at home rather than buying tickets to see movies in the local cinema. Nevertheless, he reluctantly realized that, like sound and color, television was an innovation as well as an invasion. And a source of income as well as of competition.

In March 1955, Warner Bros. Television was born. William T. Orr, a capable studio executive and Jack Warner's son-in-law, was the first president of the unit (*Dragnet*'s Jack Webb would be the second). Warner ordered this two-story office complex next to the backlot constructed in 1958 to service his initial television offerings. The building was the first such structure ever erected inside a Hollywood movie studio for the purpose of television production.

At the ground breaking for the new $600,000 building, J.L was photographed holding tight to a shovel and to starlet Natalie Wood. His trademark shark's grin to the camera seems a little forced this time, although he may have been comforted by the fact that Wood, at least, was a budding *movie* star.

Jack Warner in 1961, surrounded by his television stars, and a few feature film performers and executives for good measure. From left: Donald May, Gary Vinson, Efrem Zimbalist Jr., Will Hutchins, Poncie Ponce, Clint Walker, Connie Stevens, Peter Brown, unknown, Margarita Sierra, Mike Road, Rex Reason, Dorothy Provine, John Russell, Peggie Castle, Chad Everett, William T. Orr, Anthony Eisley, Angie Dickinson, Jack Kelly, Jack Warner, Andrew Duggan, Natalie Wood, Richard Long, Hugh Benson, Ty Hardin, Diane McBain, Van Williams, Edd Byrnes, Roger Moore, Sharon Hugueny, Robert Conrad, unknown, Jaqueline Beer, Roger Smith, Louis Quinn, Ahna Capri, Ronnie Dapo, Peggy McKay, Carol Nicholson, Tim Rooney, Grant Williams, and Shirley Knight.

Just to the north of this building is a nondescript office complex (built in 1959), which today is used for editorial work, but in the 1960s housed Batjac Productions, John Wayne's production company.

33. Cartoon Department

The single most recognized figure in the history of Warner Bros. isn't any of the Warner Brothers themselves, any of the stars who worked for them, the studio, its water tower, or its shield logo. The studio's single most recognizable figure, perhaps one of the few nearly universally recognizable figures in recent history, is actually a cartoon rabbit.

When I was a clerk in the Tour Department in the 1990s, I'll never forget talking to a woman who was upset that her eight-year-old son couldn't go on the studio tour (for the record, the age limit was ten at the time, and it has since been lowered to eight). "But why wouldn't you want children to see where their favorite cartoons are made?" she pleaded. I tried to explain to her, as nicely as I could, that the cartoons she was referring to were decades old, and furthermore that many of them had not been made on the lot, and that even if they had been, and even if they were being made there today, watching an artist hunched over a drawing board sketching funny pictures of a rabbit would not be much fun for either the eight-year-old or the artist.

She tried again. "If you aren't making Bugs Bunny," she said, "then whatever do you do here?"

I dropped the bombshell. "This is a movie studio, Madam; we're the biggest producer of film and television product in the world."

The lady was astonished. "You mean that Warner Bros. makes *real* movies too?" she sputtered.

Her opinion of the studio's product is not unique. To many people, in spite of seeing the WB logo on TV shows and feature films countless times for their entire lives, Warner Bros. will always be only the place where Bugs Bunny works.

This was not always the case. In fact, animation genius Chuck Jones used to love to tell the story of how when one of their cartoons won an Academy Award, Jack Warner, who seemed to think that the "cartoon guys" were more than a little bit eccentric, was required to show up at a banquet to congratulate his animators, where he thanked them for making "those funny Mickey Mouse cartoons."

Warner probably really did use that line. It would have been just like him to make a joke like that. But make no mistake, it was a joke. J.L.'s daughter Barbara has said that her father dutifully screened every cartoon the studio made at home with his family and that both she and her father were as amused by Bugs Bunny and his pals as the rest of the world was, and is today.

And yet, for many years, the cartoon division was neglected and underfunded and ignored.

Left to their own devices, the animators then did pretty much what they wanted. So it's odd that the sensibility of these cartoons reflected that of the live action films as much as it did. Warner Bros. cartoons, and Warner Bros. cartoon characters, were just as hard-boiled, combative, and anti-establishment as their live-action counterparts. Bugs Bunny is a little bit Humphrey Bogart, crossed with a little bit of Al Jolson at his most aggressive and grandstanding. And today, with the audience for classic movies in black and white growing depressingly smaller with each passing year, it is the cartoon archetypes and not the flesh-and-blood performers that general audiences are most likely to still recognize.

The Warner Bros. cartoon division started in 1930. The studio had found itself in need of animated shorts to fill out the program of feature films and shorts they were booking into their theaters. Producer Leon Schlesinger's product, then being produced by the Harman-Ising Animation Studio and later by Leon Schlesinger Productions, fit the bill perfectly, because they were cheap. Schlesinger, who spoke with a lisp right out of one of his own cartoons, produced his product out of several offices at the Sunset Boulevard Studio as an independent producer, until 1944, when he sold the company to Warner Bros. but stayed on as consultant.

One of the buildings on the Sunset lot—no one agrees exactly which one—acquired the nickname "Termite Terrace" (animator Tex Avery is usually given the credit), and everyone found the name so amusing that the animators took it with them when they moved to slightly better quarters facing the street, and even after they left that lot to go to Burbank.

I Haven't Got a Hat (1935) was a breakthrough for the division. Until this point, most of their animated characters had been "inspired by," to put it nicely, other studios' more popular animated performers. But this film, which introduced Porky Pig, showed that original character animation, and even a most welcome touch of pathos, were no longer beyond the grasp of Schlesinger's crew.

Daffy Duck made his debut in 1937, and Elmer Fudd and Bugs Bunny in 1940. Interestingly, as audiences grew up watching these performers, and their children and grandchildren followed their example, these characters, like their audience, and like the studio's most enduring live actors, actually seemed to evolve to reflect the passing of years. Today, these cartoons are syndicated and run out of sequence, so the evolution of their characterizations is harder to track. But it's interesting to note that Elmer Fudd, for example, in his earliest cartoons, very much physically resembled, but for a slightly elongated physique, the character that modern audiences recognize today. In 1941, however, after Pearl Harbor, he inexplicably became uncharacteristically obese. Trying to get out of military service perhaps? He eventually lost the weight, only to evolve beyond his earlier, ineffectual hunter characterization, into variously, a suburbanite, an office worker, an unlikely opera star, and even a wealthy capitalist during the prosperous 1950s. Through it all, he retained his essential milquetoast persona, and yet it was hard to escape the feeling that he, and we, were on life's twisting journey together. And because Elmer Fudd was always Elmer Fudd, unlike Errol Flynn, for example, who could be a pirate in one film and a prizefighter in the next, we were always invested in his continuing story arc and his (many, many) failures. Think about how different Elmer's life may have turned out if, just once, he had captured that "wascally wabbit."

In 1952, with the Sunset Studio's sale, the unit was moved to the big plant in Burbank, where, in the most remote, most distant corner of the backlot, this peculiar E-shaped structure was created. The unusual physique of the building was an attempt to give each of the artists both a window and natural light at some point in the day. The unusual location was an attempt to keep the animators and their unconventional antics as far away from the "normal" people on the lot (whomever they may have been) as possible. Yet, in retrospect, perhaps the care with which the building was designed may have been an indication of Jack Warner's begrudging affection for the division.

Tom Ray, a longtime animator at the studio, remembered that the new building was sandwiched between the Los Angeles River and the backlot western set, "Laramie Street." "I used to walk through the western street every day to get to my car," he said. "One day they were just throwing away a bunch of barrels and saloon doors and such. I asked if I could have them, they said, 'Sure.' So I started taking stuff home every time a western wrapped out there and putting it together again in the back yard of my place in Culver City for the kids. After a few years I had a miniature Laramie Street right there in back of my house."[28]

In 1962, due to the decline of theatrical shorts and the immense backlog of releasable cartoons made to that point, the division was closed. The following year, the building itself was leased by DePatie-Freleng, an independent animation company founded, after the closing of Termite Terrace, by Warner Bros. alumni David H. DePatie and Friz Freleng. Warner Bros. did eventually contract with DePatie-Freleng to produce a limited amount of product using their classic characters, and many Warner Bros. alumni, both animators and animated characters, found employment at their old studio.

In the early 1960s, animation history was again made at (if not by) the studio, when DePatie-Freleng was contracted by United Artists to produce the animated credits for a feature film, *The Pink Panther* (1963). The success of this sequence led to a stylish (and successful) cartoon series, the first of which, *The Pink Phink* (1964), would win them an Academy Award.

In 1967 Warner Bros. decided to produce their cartoons in-house again, and so they reclaimed the Animation Building for this purpose. For the most part, these latter-day cartoons were unsuccessful, and after two years the department was shuttered once again.

In 1994 Chuck Jones, who was then eighty-four years old, returned not only to the lot but also to the Termite Terrace building on the lot once again to produce some animated shorts for the studio. Memorably, he arranged to have his mail delivered to the building via a mail box positioned on a post next to a rabbit hole. The name on the mail box: "B. Bunny," of course.

He and his animators, a combination of veterans (a few who had been at the studio nearly as long as Jones had) and beginners thrilled to have the opportunity to work for the man whom Robin Williams called "the Orson Welles of cartoons,"[29] even drew caricatures all over one of the walls. When Jones left the office for the last time in 1996 (he would die in 2002), John Schulman, the studio's Council General and a personal friend of Jones, had the drywall removed so that it could be preserved.

Today, the rabbit hole mail box, like the wall, is long gone. But the building is still there, still tucked away in a hard-to-find corner at the very edge of the studio. The Music Department has offices there, and television shows, including the long-running (1996–2005) TV series *Everybody Loves Raymond*, rent out the other storied and still very well-lit offices.

FOUR

·····························

The World on a Soundstage

FOR SOMETHING as iconic as the Warner Bros. stages, they are also somewhat mysterious. The numbers on the stages have been changed numerous times. The original soundstages on the lot, numbers 1–4 (built in in 1926) and 5 and 6 (built in 1927), were not soundstages at all, as they were designed for the shooting of silent pictures and had to be expensively retrofit. In fact, the phrase "soundstage" was first used on the Scoring Stage complex (as in "Soundstages 1 and 2"), apparently with the intention that the stages where sound was recorded in was to originally encompass an entirely different, and parallel, numbering system. When it was decided that silent pictures were no longer viable, these original "soundstages" were renumbered as Stages 9 and 10 and folded into the general stage sequencing. This means that at Warner Bros., there were no Stages 9 and 10 (even though two rooms inside the Scoring Stage building were designated as such), until the entire complex was renumbered in March 1972. At the time, many of the large stages were also being divided into smaller shooting spaces to accommodate television. The original number sequencing, which had stopped at twenty-four before, represented only twenty actual stages (there were no Stages 9 and 10 remember, Stage 21 had burned down long before, and Stage 20 was, in 1972, being used for storage). So with the new numbers, the same quantity of stages on the lot suddenly jumped to twenty-eight. To add to the confusion, "unlucky" Stage 13, which had been coyly referred to up to this point as Stage 12A, would now be skipped entirely—Stage 12 would be next to Stage 14 under the new system. Also, Stages 27 and 28 would be divided after the renumbering, and so had to be designated as Stages 27 and 28, A and B. Very confusing.

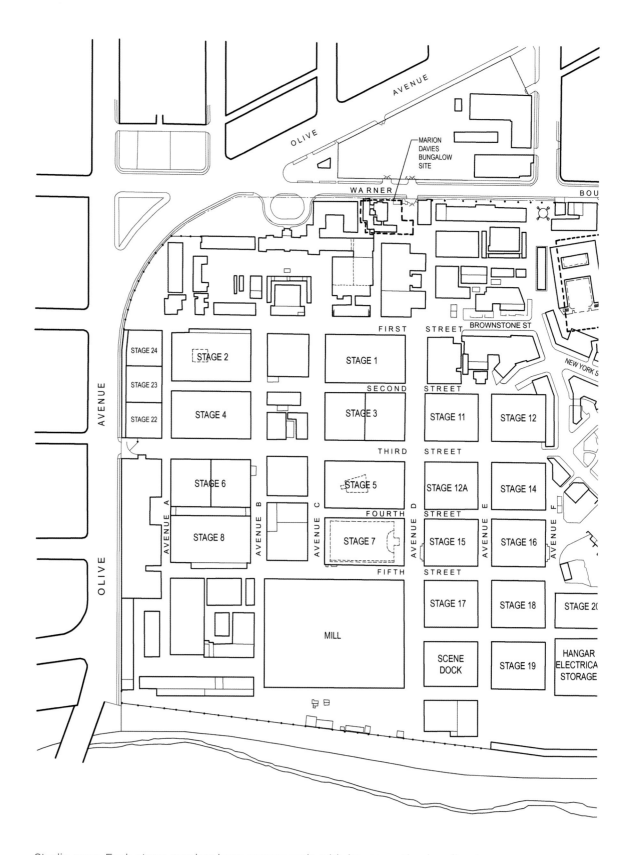

Studio map. Each stage number here corresponds with its respective heading in this chapter. Courtesy of Robert Lane.

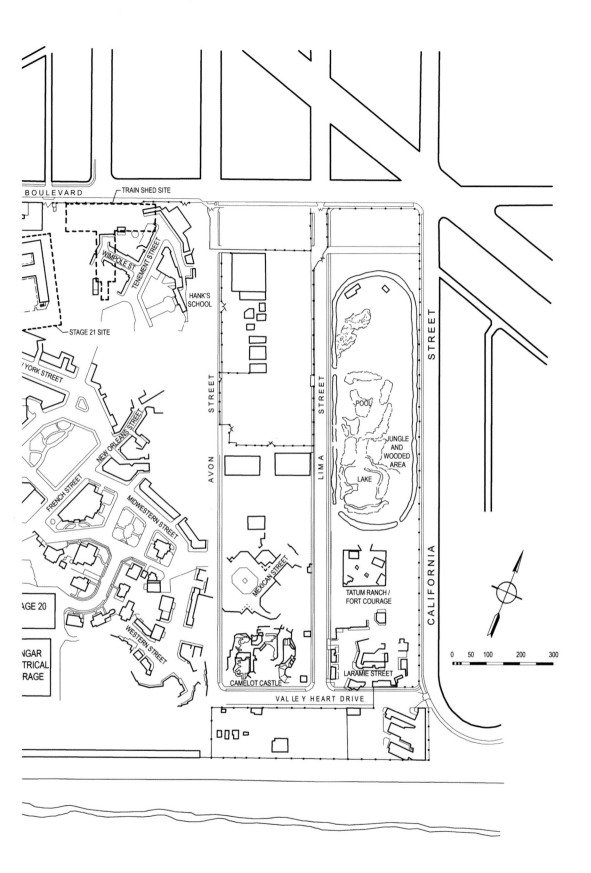

BOULEVARD — TRAIN SHED SITE

WIMPOLE ST

TENEMENT STREET

HANK'S SCHOOL

STAGE 21 SITE

NEW YORK STREET

NEW ORLEANS STREET

FRENCH STREET

MIDWESTERN STREET

AGE 20

ANGAR
TRICAL
RAGE

WESTERN STREET

AVON STREET

LIMA STREET

MEXICAN STREET

CAMELOT CASTLE

VAL LE Y HEART DRIVE

POOL

JUNGLE AND WOODED AREA

LAKE

CALIFORNIA STREET

TATUM RANCH / FORT COURAGE

LARAMIE STREET

0 50 100   200   300

Dean Ricca, one of the senior studio guides, once told me that he had a woman as his guest on the tour who told him that *Casablanca* (1942) was the all-time favorite movie of both herself and of her mother, who had recently passed away. Knowing very well that the closest that film had ever gotten to the real French Morocco had been the studio's eastern gate, the woman had told Dean that she had gone to California because her mother had requested, from her deathbed, that she go to where "*Casablanca* was shot" to say goodbye to her.

Knowing this, Dean looked up the stage number for *Casablanca* and discovered only that Rick's Café had been created on "Stage 8." But, also knowing about the renumbering, he had been a little unsure if Stage 8 in 1943 had been the Stage 8 of the twenty-first century. Yet, when the day of their tour arrived, hoping for the best, he had dutifully driven them out to the current Stage 8 and told her that, yes, he thought this had been the spot. With the rest of the tour group, Dean had watched the woman walk hesitantly up to that stage. "She leaned on the stage with one hand. The other hand she put on her heart and she spoke to her mom," he remembered. "She was so happy. But everyone else on the tram was crying. Including me."[1]

Actually, Dean needn't have worried. It turned out that among all the stages on the lot, Stage 8 is unique in that it is the only classic-era stage on the lot, save one other, that *hasn't* been renumbered. It was designated as Stage 8 when it was constructed in 1927. It was Stage 8 when it was Rick's Café, and it is still Stage 8 (at least on its eastern side) even today.

In referring to any of these stages, for the sake of clarity, we will use the old numbering sequence, which was in place in the 1960s, with, for reference, the current stage number listed in parentheses alongside it for the introduction to that stage only.

Still, the stages at Warner Bros. don't give up their secrets easily. Walk into any one of them, and pull the massive "elephant door" (named, presumably, because it is big enough to walk an elephant through) behind you closed. Suddenly it's like walking into a different world. The almost two-foot-thick walls, padded and soundproofed to keep out as much as 80 percent of the outside world, make the air inside feel different from that of the real world. And when the door latches, there is sometimes a slight sucking noise as that air equalizes.

Human voices sound slightly different inside a soundstage. Depth and perspective and perception seem to change slightly inside a stage as well. These stages are *big* places. And when one of them is empty, they feel very large indeed, yet oddly, paradoxically, they actually, counter-perceptibly, feel even larger when they have sets standing inside. It's possible to wander through the sets on a soundstage for what can feel like hours without ever getting to that stage's outer wall. Halls and doorways and rooms and streets inside a stage can feel like they go on forever. Part of this is done through tricks and false perspectives, and part of it can be chalked up to being initially unfamiliar with how these sets are laid out. But it still feels . . . strange, how the stages seem to expand and stretch out when they are being used. Ask anyone who has visited or worked on a soundstage; it's unexplainable. And it's undeniable.

On these stages have worked, arguably, the most popular and creative individuals of the twentieth century and beyond. Today Warner Bros. shoots its pictures in soundstages all over Los Angeles and all over the world. (Despite what people might think, few sustained sequences are, even today, shot in *actual* offices or apartments or casinos or kitchens.) Yet one hopes that today's stars, when working for the studio and *at* the studio, can appreciate that when they recite their dialogue inside one of these huge, barnlike, structures, their words and faces are being recorded in the exact *same* place where Humphrey Bogart or Bette Davis or James Dean or Marlon Brando or Paul Newman stood and inspired or amused generations.

Recently, the studio put plaques on each of their stages designating which films had been shot inside. This was a wonderful idea. Disney had done something similar a few years earlier, and Paramount and Fox would follow with their own signage a few years later. It's amusing, however, to hear people look at these plaques and remark about how amazing it is that after all these years only twenty pictures had been shot inside the stage in front of them. Even Warner Bros. Chairman and CEO Barry Meyer once made that mistake in a *Los Angeles* magazine piece.

Actually, for every film listed, dozens, hundreds, thousands of pictures have actually been born inside—the truth is that inside these stages, more films had been made than anywhere else on the planet.

People visit movie locations around Los Angeles and in other cities almost as a holy pilgrimage. They drive for hours and take photos and put up monuments to the fact that a favorite film or TV show had been shot on a particular spot. Yet they seldom seem to realize that while this is probably true, it is back at this studio and inside these stages where their favorite scenes had probably been created, often using symbolic architecture only suggesting a city park, or the Statue of Liberty, or a railroad depot. Soundstages are where most movies are in fact "made," and yet, because they seldom carry a lasting physical record of any one film, and because these stages are not generally accessible to a film's fans, soundstages are seldom thought of as being a movie's "location," even though most films and TV shows are shot inside them.

Because so very many of our shared movie memories have been created on these stages, it is, then, impossible to provide more than a cursory tour of Warner Bros. soundstages. That said, I'm going to try to do just that. So here, then, stage by stage, as numbered in the 1960s, and for the first time anywhere, is a tour of the stages of Warner Bros.

Where movies are made.

Stage 1 (Stages 12 and 18)

Built in 1926 for $63,582.

This 30,856-square-foot stage's northern wall is covered from rim to rafters with a beautiful growth of ivy that is not duplicated anywhere else in the studio. We do know that the ivy was attached to the wall in 1952. But an oral tradition has always

Stage 1, or rather a corner of it. Evidently, a western is shooting inside. Note the sealed-over doors from the pre-sound era. Circa 1930s.

held that the ivy was planted at the personal behest of Mr. Jack L. Warner himself, whose office did, and does, overlook this wall—a wall that presumably blocked the mogul's personal view of his fiefdom. According to this same story, J.L requested not only that the ivy be strung to the wall, but also that it needed to be strung to the wall overnight and be in place for whenever J.L happened to glance out the window the following morning. So, according to the story, the beleaguered Greens Department was forced to supplement any real ivy they could find or steal with cloth "stand-ins" painted green, until the real thing could fill out the gaps. Which it quickly did.

The interior of Nottingham Castle and the famous Errol Flynn–Basil Rathbone duel for *The Adventures of Robin Hood* (1938) were created inside this stage. In 1942 it was the home of the fogbound Casablanca airport in *Casablanca* (1943). Incidentally, the oft-repeated story about how a miniature plane was made to look full-sized using midget mechanics is, according to assistant director Lee Katz, apparently true.

In 1972, John Wayne's surprising death scene from *The Cowboys* (1972) was staged here. The blockbuster miniseries *Roots* (1977) and its sequel, *Roots: The Next*

A musical number for *Colleen* (1936) featuring Stage 1 and several of the extras pictured in our photo of the Studio Fire Department in chapter 3.

Generation (1979), also worked here. The legendary band the Eagles played their first concert in fourteen years inside this stage in 1984. I used my passkey to slip inside a stage door to watch them perform and was immediately tossed back outside by the biggest security guard I've ever had the misfortune to be caught sneaking around by. For the television series *Gilmore Girls* (2000–2007), Yale University was created, inside and out, here on stage as well. I once took a group of real Yale students inside. They were impressed, if not convinced. . . .

Ronald Reagan's finest moment on film as an actor was recorded here. In the early 1940s Reagan was an adequate, if unexciting, leading man. But the role of the needlessly maimed Drake McHugh in *Kings Row* (1942) inspired and obsessed the young actor. "Where's the rest of me?" Drake memorably shrieked into the rafters of this stage upon learning that his legs had been amputated. "No line of my career has been so effective in explaining to me what an actor's life must be,"[2] he said in an autobiography that used the line as its title. Decades later, as a former president of the United States, Reagan would return to the stage for the studio's rededication. Perhaps, even then, Reagan was seeking an answer to his question.

Stage 2 (Stages 4 and 11)

Built in 1926 for $61,785.

This 30,856-square-foot stage contained the studio's original underwater tank. The floor could be opened to reveal a concrete-and-metal, triangularly shaped swimming pool inside. The pool was kept empty until a script set during a storm at sea, or on the canals of Venice, or in a back yard swimming pool needed it. Then the floor on top was pulled away and the tank would be filled. An interesting feature of the tank was the glass portholes cut into the walls of the tank. By positing a camera on the dry side of these windows and looking in, underwater sequences could be filmed without having to submerge the camera. This stage and the tank inside were particularly popular with director Busby Berkeley for his absurd and astonishing spectacles whenever they needed to be set on, or in, water.

The tank has not been used in decades. Very few people at the studio remember or even know that it is still there. But, still, there it is. Even today it is possible to enter the cavernous stage, used famously as the *Washington Post* city room in *All the President's Men* (1976) and most recently for television series like *Murphy Brown* (1988–1998), *ER* (1994–2009), and *Chuck* (2007–2012), and open a well-hidden trapdoor leading under the floor. After crawling through a passage infested with decades of dust and cobwebs, a brave visitor can still look through these portholes, now bleeding rust and thick with grime, and into the long-dry pool where once swim-suited chorus girls kicked their long legs and hoped for stardom.

In the 1930s, dressing rooms were constructed against the northern wall of the stage; these are still used today as offices.

Stage 3 (Stages 14 and 17)

Built in 1926 for $61,940.

This is fairly typical of the Warner soundstages. It was 33,000 square feet before it was divided, in the 1960s, into Stages 3 and 3-A, and 35 feet high to the catwalks. Walking inside, the place feels, when empty, much like any other stage on the lot. Likewise, the talent that has worked here is, if anything, typical.

But let's do something different and look, for just a minute, at that talent. In this representative stage, then, has toiled, at various times throughout the decades, among many, many others, the following: Humphrey Bogart, Paul Muni, James Cagney, Bette Davis, Gary Cooper, Ingrid Bergman, Peter Lorre, Ginger Rogers, Jack Benny, Joan Crawford, Errol Flynn, Barbara Stanwyck, Alfred Hitchcock, Elizabeth Taylor, Marlon Brando, Vivien Leigh, Judy Garland, James Dean, Jack Webb, Boris Karloff, James Stewart, Rock Hudson, James Mason, Montgomery Clift, Andy Griffith, Tony Curtis, Natalie Wood, John Wayne, James Garner, Efrem Zimbalist Jr., Rosalind Russell, Jack Lemmon, Sandra Dee, Raquel Welch, Lynda Carter, Meryl Streep, Sylvester Stallone, James Earl Jones, Sally Field, Dennis Quaid, Teri Hatcher, George Carlin, George Clooney, Steve Carell, Anne Hathaway, Drew Carey. . . .

Stage 4 (Stages 5 and 10)

Built in 1926 for $61,518.

The Life of Emile Zola (1937), the studio's first Best Picture Oscar winner, was shot inside this 30,856-square-foot stage, as was some of *Yankee Doodle Dandy* (1942), which bagged Cagney his only Oscar. Many fans prefer 1949's *White Heat*, which afforded Cagney his most psychotic gangster characterization—this was also created inside this stage.

Most of *Rio Bravo* (1959) was shot on location in Tucson, Arizona, although it would surprise that film's many fans (including director and fan Quentin Tarantino) how much was also shot inside this stage. The first season of the beloved sitcom *Friends* (1994–2004) was shot here, as was, for most of their long runs, *Full House* (1989–1998) and *Everybody Loves Raymond* (1996–2005). For *Full House*, a neon sign recreating that series' onscreen logo was attached to the stage's southern wall. I've often wondered what happened to that sign when the show ended.

Stage 4 in the 1940s.

Stage 5 (Stage 15)

Built in 1927 for $76,744.

For the remarkable story of this 25,960-square-foot stage, see the "Stage 5 Departments" section in chapter 3.

Stage 6 (Stages 6 and 9)

Built in 1927 for $63, 455.

Kismet (1930) shot an elaborate "harem swimming scene" inside a specially constructed pool inside a raised floor on this 30,856-square-foot stage. The scene increased the film's budget by $50,000, but its ultimate effectiveness is unknown because the resultant film is one of comparatively few Warner Bros. (actually First National, in this case) pictures that are now considered lost. The negative was probably destroyed in the 1934 fire.

"Hooray for Hollywood," which became an anthem for the entire motion picture industry, was first performed on this stage in 1937's *Hollywood Hotel*.

On February 6, 1963, another fire burned the roof off of this stage and destroyed the sets for *Mary, Mary* (1963), which was shooting inside. The original, rounded

Stage 6, second building on the left, and a lonely-looking security guard. Circa 1940s.

barnlike rooftop, with a horizontal ventilation shaft running across the top, was replaced, on the cheap, with a squared-off roof, noticeably different from that of any other stage on the lot, a distinction that it retains to this day.

In the 1960s, this stage was divided into Stages 6 and 6-A.

Stage 7 (Stage 16)

Built in 1935–1936 for $127,544.

This most storied of locations was less than a year old when the Production Department assigned *Cain and Mabel* (1936) to this stage, changing its destiny forever.

Cain and Mabel was a Cosmopolitan Production. Cosmopolitan was the name of William Randolph Hearst's company, and so the star of the picture was Marion Davies. For Marion's costar, Hearst had borrowed Clark Gable from MGM. Gable disliked the script. And he disliked being loaned out, although his last loan out,

Cary Grant and Priscilla Lane on the way to Stage 6, where *Arsenic and Old Lace* was in production. 1941.

to Columbia for *It Happened One Night* (1934), had netted the actor an Academy Award. Most of all, Gable disliked having to shave off his trademark mustache, which was considered inappropriate for his *Cain and Mabel* character, a prizefighter.

For the "I Sing You a Thousand Love Songs" number, it was determined that the brand-new, 31,388-square-foot stage was not tall enough for some of the gargantuan choreography referenced in the script. Now, to a non-engineer it would seem that if one had a building that was already a formidable 67 feet high and wanted it to be 30 feet taller, the thing to do would be to just knock off the roof and build up to the required size. That might well have been good enough for Warner Bros. But it wasn't good enough for Cosmopolitan, for Marion Davies, or, most importantly, for Hearst, whose dollars were financing the production and the production number. So instead it was somehow decided to dig under the base of the stage, insert hundreds of hand jacks, and then, apparently using unemployed actors as modern-day galley slaves, to laboriously crank the building up, inch by inch, by hand, while building a new bottom half underneath! "A guy would blow a whistle and everybody would

Stage 7 during its pyramid-like
rise into the heavens. 1935.

take a turn, pull one turn on the jack," Grip Department employee Champ Mila-man, who was there, remembered.[3]

The story seems almost impossible to believe. And its latter-day reputation as Hollywood's equivalent to the building of the pyramids (or perhaps the Tower of Babel is a better analogy) notwithstanding, it would be easy to dismiss the tale out of hand were there not photographs and even moving images of the building rising into the sun still in existence.

The stage itself also stands as irrefutable proof of the event itself, of course. An inspection of the rather awe-inspiring building, which still towers over everything else on the Warner lot, reveals that halfway up, at the bottom of the buttresses that support the walls, there is still a visible "seam" connecting the two sections. And the stage as it stands today, at 98 feet high, is still the tallest purpose-built sound-stage in the world. So tall is it that, not coincidentally, it is also the only soundstage anywhere in the world with a restroom in the rafters on the top (men's room only).

Clark Gable, Marion Davies, and director Lloyd Bacon look on as Stage 7 is vertically enlarged for *Cain and Mable* (1935).

Apparently, this amenity was added because it would have taken too long or caused too much of a work delay to let the technicians in the rafters climb all the way down onto the floor every time that nature called. I used to climb into those rafters far above the stage floor on occasion myself, and I can testify that in addition to a men's room, those rafters are also equipped with very colorful, and very obscene, graffiti from the 1930s.

Less irrefutable proof exists for the most delicious, if unverifiable, detail of the story. According to studio legend, as the building rose into the sky, someone started to worry that when the day came to lower the original stage into the recently erected base section, the whole thing would collapse like an oversized house of cards. The ingenious solution? That blocks of ice be positioned in the gap between the sections. It was pointed out, not unreasonably, that as the ice melted, it would allow the top half of the stage to settle slowly and safely into the bottom half, and into Hollywood history.

The epilogue to the story, if the stages continued usage isn't one itself, this that when *Cain and Mabel* was released to a less-than-eager public, it belly-flopped. Davies only made one more movie, the equally unloved *Ever since Eve* (1937), after which she retired. Gable went back to MGM, where his memories of the film presumably lasted no longer than it took him to regrow his famous mustache. He would return to Warner Bros. only once, more than twenty years later, for 1957's *Band of Angels*. One wonders what the older Gable must have thought, driving back onto the lot after all that time and seeing Stage 7 still casting its mighty shadow across all it surveyed.

The reengineering of the stage did not end in 1935. In 1941, for *Sergeant York*, the publicity department got a lot of press describing the construction of a full-sized mountain that could be revolved on a merry-go-round-type base in order to shoot multiple "locations" representing different facets of Gary Cooper's character's Tennessee homeland. The set, which also included 200 feet of gurgling mountain stream, a forest of actual and simulated trees, and a farmyard, garden, and cabin, all came in particularly handy when rain made filming many scheduled actual exteriors impossible. Donaho Hall, the film's colorfully named "Tennessee technical advisor," proclaimed the set "realistic enough to make a hound dog go smellin' around for coon tracks." A compliment, presumably.[4]

When Stage 21, the aquatic stage, burned down in 1952, the Production Department eventually realized that they would need another large space in which to shoot water-based sequences. Stage 2 was no longer suitable, and a triangular-shaped pool next door on Stage 5 was too small as well. The solution, implemented in 1953 for *South Sea Woman* (1953), was to dig a large swimming pool (192 by 113 feet by 5 feet, 9 inches deep) into the floor of Stage 7, which, when combined with the additional overhead space, would make it the most versatile shooting location in the world. Ingeniously, the pool was designed so that when the floor was opened up and the tank inside left dry, sets could be constructed on the floor of the pool, thus allowing even more height to build up into. A second pool, measuring 90 by 100 feet, and 20 feet deep, was later added inside the first, increasing the total water capacity to some 200,050,000 gallons. When the tanks are not being used, or the height they afforded is not desired, the floor can be replaced, although that process is an expensive one.

Sometimes, dirt was used to fill the pool instead of water. For *Darby's Rangers* (1958), when the soil that had been used to fill the tank was removed, it was ultimately trucked out to the backlot, where it was discovered there was enough there to significantly enlarge the studio's Jungle set.

Wet or dry, there is no doubt that Stage 7 has hosted some of history's great films and/or great sets. For example in *Rebel without a Cause* (1955) much of the legendary chickie run sequence was shot on the floor of the stage. In *Giant* (1955), *My Fair Lady* (1964), *Camelot* (1967), and *Murder by Death* (1976), the great halls from great family homes were built on the stage floor. For *Disclosure* (1994) a nine-story Seattle office complex was created nearly full-scale on the stage. In *Maverick* (1994), a Mississippi riverboat gambling salon was built in the space with special motors installed to rock the overhead lighting fixtures to mimic the movement of a boat on a river. In *Executive Decision* (1996), a jet airplane fuselage was itself hung from gimbals in the stage rafters to simulate flight.

In 1963, a seventeen-year-old Steven Spielberg reportedly snuck onto this stage during the production of *PT 109* and got to watch part of a spectacular scene in the tank in which future president John F. Kennedy (played by Cliff Robertson) has his boat scuttled by a Japanese destroyer. Before the scene was completed, however, the would-be director was noticed by a security guard, who escorted him off of both the stage and the lot. Years later, when Spielberg returned to the stage to shoot *Jurassic Park* (1993), someone who remembered the *PT 109* incident reportedly put up a "Welcome Back Steven" banner above the door. Spielberg subsequently shot part of *Indiana Jones and the Kingdom of the Crystal Skull* (2008) inside the stage as well.

Other pictures that utilized the tank filled with water include *The Old Man and the Sea* (1958), for which Spencer Tracy spent most of the movie sitting in a small boat talking to a big rubber fish; *The Great Race* (1965), which floated a car on an manufactured ice floe; *The Goonies* (1985), which utilized a full-sized copy of *The Sea Hawk's* "Falcon" as a pirate vessel trapped in an underground cavern; *The Perfect Storm* (2000), for which an actual New England fishing vessel was floated inside the tank; *Poseidon* (2006), which re-created an ocean liner, upside down; and *Inception* (2010), which flooded an Asian temple on the stage.

The building has been utilized in interesting ways from the outside as well. *The Roaring Twenties* (1939) used it as a bootlegger's warehouse. *Desperate Journey* (1942) cast the exterior as a munitions plant. *I Was a Communist for the FBI* (1951) ingeniously used the support columns along the north wall as part of a railroad tunnel, and it brought in a real train on a real spur track to supplement the realism of the sequence.

This stage, unique in so many ways, earned a distinction no other soundstage has ever attained in the 1990s when, using the new numbering system, Stage 16, as it was then called, became the name of a themed restaurant based on famous Warner Bros. films at the Venetian Hotel in Las Vegas, Nevada. The venture was not a success. Apparently, there can only be one Stage 16.

Stage 8 (Stage 7 and 8)

Built in 1927 for $63,353.

This 30,856-square-foot stage was Rick's Café. But it has been much more. It was Philip Marlowe's shabby office in *The Big Sleep* (1946), it was the fateful rail car in *Strangers on a Train* (1951), it was Judy Garland and James Mason's Malibu getaway in *A Star Is Born* (1954), and it was the site of much domestic distress in *Who's Afraid of Virginia Woolf?* (1966). In the television era, it has been the home of *Kung Fu* (1972–1975), *Step by Step* (1991–1998), and *Without a Trace* (2002–2009).

Stage 11 (Stage 19)

Built in 1935–1936 for $50,597.

This 10,507-square-foot stage rose at the same time as *seven* other stages. The 1934 fire was partially responsible for the construction spurt that pushed the front lot west over some of the destroyed backlot parcels and caused the backlot itself to spill across Avon Street onto previously undeveloped real estate.

It's probably inadvertent, but some stages seem to lend themselves to certain genres. Stage 11 is an excellent example. A pretty band singer named Doris Day made her debut on this stage in 1949's *Romance on the High Seas*. She immediately became one of the studio's favorite stars, despite the fact that, Jolson and Busby Berkeley notwithstanding, the studio had no particular affinity for musicals. Yet Day would go on to make at least four more of them on this stage alone: *Young Man with a Horn* (1950), *Calamity Jane* (1953), *Young at Heart* (1955), and *The Pajama Game* (1957).

Other films with musical numbers shot on this stage include *Yankee Doodle Dandy* (1942), *This Is the Army* (1943), *Damn Yankees* (1958), and *Inside Daisy Clover* (1965). Lifetimes later, a short-lived and decidedly offbeat television series, *Pushing Daisies* (2007–2008), on this same stage inexplicably and against all logic started incorporating occasional old Hollywood-style musical numbers into its storylines as well.

If they only knew . . .

Stage 12 (Stage 24)

Built in 1935–1936 for $47,130.

In the late 1920s, before this stage stood here, the studio constructed an interior theater set near this site containing a complete proscenium, an auditorium, and even a raised ceiling behind the stage set for lifting scenery up into. This set was burned in the 1934 fire, and the 21,014-square-foot Stage 12 rose from its ashes.

Doris Day smiles slyly at the crew and equipment surrounding her on (presumably) Stage 11, for *Calamity Jane*. 1953.

One of the most interesting experiments in cinema history was conducted in 1948 when Alfred Hitchcock chose for his first color film an adaptation of a rather long-winded play, *Rope*, by Patrick Hamilton, which in turn had been based on the real-life Leopold-Loeb killings. What made the picture Hitchcock created from this material truly unique, however, was his decision to shoot the entire movie in a single take—actually, ten takes with the "cuts" disguised to appear invisible.

To quote a publicity release at the time, "Hollywood Skeptics said it couldn't be done. Too many airplanes flying overhead to spoil the soundtrack. One of the actors was a cinch to forget his lines. How could a crew member hold back a sneeze that long? The floor might squeak. The cameraman might miss his focus on one of the shots. . . ."[5]

The upside was that with every shot, a full reel, 950 feet of film, was exposed, equaling a remarkable 11 percent of the finished film, which must have made the studio accountants happy, until they realized how many days of planning and rehearsal went into that single unbroken take.

Stage 12, renumbered Stage 24, in the left foreground, as seen from the roof of the Fitness Center. 1998.

Because of the demands of the project, nearly the entire movie was shot within the walls of this stage (the trailer, which included scenes on a park bench not seen in the film, was shot on Stage 7, and the credit sequence on Brownstone Street). The story had to be told in real time, like a Greek play, so a realistic sunset had to be created to reflect what needed to be seen from the windows of the film's set. Fiberglass "clouds" were constructed and manipulated in order to simulate, in real time, a sun setting over the thirty-five square miles of New York that would have been visible from the film's 54th Street apartment setting.

That same apartment set was reused later that same year for the early Doris Day vehicle, *My Dream Is Yours*, for a Bugs Bunny–starring animated sequence. This time, the film was shot and cut like a conventional picture.

The TV series *Friends* (1994–2004) occupied both this stage, and the love and attention of much of the world, in the 1990s. So popular was the series that when its final episode aired, the studio took the unprecedented step of rededicating Stage 12, which was then known as Stage 24, as "The Friends Stage." Jay Leno even broadcast his *Tonight Show* series live from the stage on May 6, 2004, for the *Friends* series finale.

Several years after that finale, Matt LeBlanc, one of the stars of *Friends*, gave an interview to *Vanity Fair* magazine in which he mused about his own experiences, those of his costars on that series, and, without realizing it, those of many others who had worked and loved and innovated in that building before him. "We could never leave the stage," he said. "Metaphorically speaking. Still can't. Still on that stage. That will follow us around forever."[6]

Stage 12a (Stage 20)

Built in 1935–1936 for $44,265.

This 21,014-square-foot stage should have been Stage 13. But no one was about to let that happen. It was often used for casting, wardrobe, and makeup tests. In 1973, when the stages were renumbered, it was divided into two smaller stages, 20 and 23. Yet, in 1995, the divider was removed so the stage could accommodate big-budget features like *Batman Forever* (1995), *Soldier* (1998), *Wild Wild West* (1999), *Disney's The Kid* (2000), *Solaris* (2002), and *Poseidon* (2005).

Peter Lorre, Humphrey Bogart, Sydney Greenstreet, Helmut Dantine, Claude Rains, John Loder, Philip Dorn, George Tobias, and Victor Francen walk right past Stage 12A, right, on their way to the *Passage to Marseille* set. 1944.

Stage 14 (Stage 25)

Built in 1935–1936 for $45,786.

This space was utilized for Errol Flynn swashbucklers, gangster films, westerns, melodramas, and, from the late 1950s onward, television westerns. *Cheyenne* (1955–1963), the studios' first hit series, was a frequent tenant. *Colt .45* (1957–1960), *Sugarfoot* (1957–1961), *Maverick* (1957–1962), and *Bronco* (1958–1962) all appear to have ridden through the stage as well.

The last great western to regularly utilize this 21,280-square-foot stage was *Bonanza*. During most of its very long run (1959–1976), *Bonanza* was shot at Paramount. But in May 1970, the series moved to Warners, where it was based until its cancelation. The Ponderosa Ranch from that series was a long-standing set on this stage. Several employees on the lot, when the series was canceled, recalled going to the wrap party on a Friday and then coming back to the stage on Monday only to find that the Ponderosa set, which had always seemed as stable as a redwood, had already been struck, and the stage was now eerily empty.

Stage 15 (Stage 21)

Built in 1935–1936 for $46,664.

The Wrong Man (1956) was the last film that Alfred Hitchcock made at Warner Bros. Hitchcock insisted on his Art Department's building a miniature elevated train outside the window of one of the sets on this stage, even though it had nothing in particular to do with the scene going on inside. The train, when outfitted with miniature passengers and miniature lights, and rigged to run on a miniature track, was barely visible on screen, but seemingly fascinated Hitchcock more than the script he was filming did.

Years later, in *Pee Wee's Big Adventure* (1985), Pee-Wee Herman's fascinating rampage across the studio lot began here as well.

I brought director Stanley Kubrick's daughter Vivian to this 21,014-square-foot stage in 2003 when she was entrusted to me on her visit to the studio. As the only feature shooting on the lot at the time was an irreverent film version of the TV series *Starsky and Hutch*, I was a little worried that the great filmmaker's daughter would not be received on the stage with the proper reverence. I needn't have been. Director Todd Phillips was so thrilled to have her on his set that he virtually shut down production, probably costing the studio thousands of dollars, so he could graciously entertain her and her family.

Stage 16 (Stage 26)

Built in 1935–1936 for $49,787.

This 21,280-square-foot stage is currently the home of the successful sitcom *Two and a Half Men* (2003–). Sequences from both *My Fair Lady* (1964) and *Wait until*

Dark (1967), two of Audrey Hepburn's most successful movies, were also filmed inside. But most often, this stage has hosted lesser stars, or rather major stars in lesser projects.

For example, Gene Wilder, who started his career as a comic supporting actor here on the lot with *Bonnie and Clyde* (1967), was unfortunately unable to translate his popularity into a successful sitcom with *Something Wilder* (1994). Longer lasting, but still falling short of earlier glories, were Stage 16 tenants William Shatner with *T.J. Hooker* (1982–1986) and Brooke Shields with *Suddenly Susan* (1996–2000). David Carradine, whose *Kung Fu* (1972–1975) had been a major, if cultish, success, teamed up here with Brandon Lee, the son of another star who had found fame at Warner Bros. (Bruce Lee), for *Kung Fu: The Movie* (1986). But martial arts lightning did not strike again, and both Carradine and Lee would ultimately die in mysterious, if unrelated, accidents while shooting other projects.

In 1993, painted French-styled façades were added to the eastern wall of this stage, which is at the very end of the backlot French Street set, successfully supplementing the street's usefulness as assorted Gallic-influenced locations.

Stage 17 (Stage 22)

Built in 1935–1936 for $45,107.

This 21,600-square-foot stage, which sits opposite the Mill, was Mildred's restaurant in *Mildred Pierce* (1945), the top floor of the storm-swept Hotel Largo in *Key Largo* (1948), and, perhaps most movingly, the smoky "Downbeat Club" where Judy Garland sang the torchy ballad "The Man That Got Away" in *A Star Is Born* (1954). The number is so heartbreaking that Bosley Crowther, in his famous review of the movie, must have been referring to this song when he remarked how it "Makes the heart flutter and bleed."[7]

Stage 18 (Stages 27 and 27B)

Built 1935–1936 for $44,179.

Barbra Streisand's remake of *A Star Is Born* (1976) was partially shot in this location across the street from where the Garland version was shot. Also shot inside this 21,014-square-foot stage was *Black Legion* (1937), *Dark Victory* (1939), *The Roaring Twenties* (1939), *Strangers on a Train* (1951), *The Left-Handed Gun* (1957), *Camelot* (1967), *Time after Time* (1979), *The Long Riders* (1980), *Outbreak* (1995), and the TV series *China Beach* (1988–1991), *Cold Case* (2003–2010), and currently *Heart of Dixie* (2011–).

Stage 19 (Stages 28 and 28A)

Built 1936–1937 for $51,798.

Sometimes, it isn't just sets on the backlot that are reused. During production of the TV series *Sisters* (1991–1996), a standing set on this 21,014-square-foot

Pee-Wee Herman races past a backdrop depicting renumbered Stages 17 and 18 in *Pee-Wee's Big Adventure*—which the real Stages 17 and 18 are then revealed as being behind. 1985.

stage that was playing Swoosie Kurtz's upscale home in that series was repurposed by the TV movie *A Walton Thanksgiving Reunion* (1993) to play John-Boy's fiancée's upscale home.

In this case, no one noticed. But sometimes this cannibalization can cause some confusion. Another TV movie, *Moviola: The Scarlett O'Hara War* (1980), staged a sequence here in which producer David O. Selznick (played by Tony Curtis) holds a press conference to announce his production of *Gone With the Wind* (1939). Scenic Arts was commissioned to paint a backdrop depicting that film's "Tara" plantation to use as set dressing in the scene. When production wrapped, this backdrop, as was the custom, was rolled and put into storage for potential reuse. Some years later, this piece was "discovered" in Scenic Arts, and the plantation it depicted was recognized as Tara. So it was, at least for a time, reasonably assumed that this backdrop really was used in *Gone With the Wind*.

Stage 20 (Now Building 48)

Built in 1939 for $21,352.

Although this structure was intended for use as a soundstage and was designated as Stage 20, little actual production seemed to happen here, perhaps because, for unknown reasons, it was immediately divided into thirds. The largest section, the western half, was designated as the "scene stage." The eastern parts were referred to as the "paint stage" and the "hardware stage." Circa 1967, it was reclassified as an "equipment storage" building. During The Burbank Studios era, it was used for wardrobe storage. It was converted into a refrigerated film vault in 1992, which remains its purpose today.

Stage 21 (Site)

Built in 1939 for $125,000 (estimated cost).

Purpose built for *The Sea Hawk* (1940), Stage 21 was the largest soundstage on earth and the most unique. "Built of stock trusses, it's 142 feet long, 138 feet wide, and 66 feet high from the stage floor to the underside of the giant steel beams. In it are parked two full sized ships that can do everything but turn somersaults," a

Stage 21, just above the water tower, was the largest sound stage in the world. The backlot Train Shed is visible in the foreground. 1951.

Stage 21 under construction. 1939.

breathless article in the *Los Angeles Times Sunday Magazine* told its readers in 1940.[8] Actually, for once, the press deflated the stage's dimensions considerably; the length of the stage was actually an even more head-shaking 240 feet.

Both the two eighteenth-century ships inside, a British man-of-war and a Spanish galleon—named, respectively, the *Falcon* and the *Albatross* (the later sometimes referred to as the "Galleass" or the "Alverez")—were approximately 136 feet long and 56 feet high each to the top of the masts. Each ship was constructed to sit on a steel platform submerged in an indoor lake, which averaged from 3 to 12 feet deep, and move through the water via a series of submerged tracks. Enormous rockers, designed by Elmer Smith of the Mechanical Department, could simulate the pitch of the ocean on either ship. It is said that actual sea sickness among the cast and crew was not uncommon. The equipment was designed so that when the water was drained, scenes involving earthquakes for future films could utilize the same technology.

Along the walls was hung a 600-foot-long backdrop depicting more water, of the painted variety, and a realistic blue sky designed by *Sea Hawk*'s art director, Anton Grot. On one of the walls, a 48-foot-wide section could be removed, opening up the stage to another outdoor lake that fronted the existing backlot Bonnyfeather Street, as well as a quaint fishing village, an ocean liner, and other water-based

Errol Flynn and his mates, at sea on Stage 21, for *The Sea Hawk*. 1940.

settings. With the wall open, the outdoor and indoor sections could be turned into a single enormous set. The opening was also used to float the ships, which had been constructed in the Mill, into the stage via the lake.

The studio apparently had plans to follow up *The Sea Hawk* with a series of expensive aquatic pictures, but ultimately, although that film was a success, World War II and the crippling loss of foreign markets that came with it curtailed these expensive ambitions. In fact, the publicity department claimed that *Operation Pacific* (1951) marked the first time the tank had been flooded since *Captain Blood*! This publicist had meant to say *The Sea Hawk*, but his statement about the infrequent usage of the Stage 21 lake wasn't true either. *Out of the Fog* (1941) and *Across the Pacific* (1942), for example, had shot aquatic sequences utilizing the tank. *The Big Sleep* (1946) also had partially flooded the stage for the "Lido Pier" sequence, where the body of a chauffeur, killed by an unknown individual, is discovered in a submerged car. But it is true, sadly, that the opportunity for more period seafaring adventures, with Errol Flynn, hopefully, had in the years since

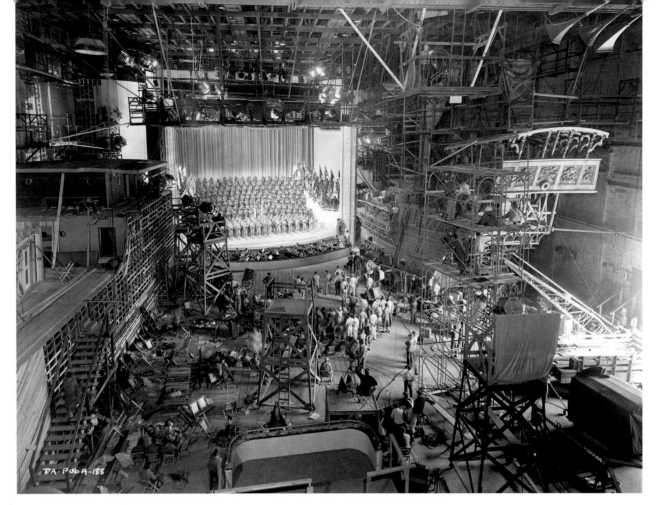

This Is the Army (1943) shooting the lavish "This Is the Last Time" musical number on Stage 21. The water is gone, but the ship *Falcon* is still there, right.

1939 been largely squandered. Squandered in this instance not due not to a lack of resources, interest, or audiences, or to internal studio politics, but to the realities of the world outside.

A renewed interest in seagoing pictures, triggered by the success of Burt Lancaster's buoyant *The Crimson Pirate* (1952), came just a little too late, as Stage 21 burned to the ground as part of that devastating studio fire in May of that same year.

Stages 22, 23, and 24 (Stages 1, 2, and 3)

Built in 1936–1937 as Stage 22, for $123,200.

This was the longest stage on the lot. Its dimensions were 305 feet, 3 inches long by 121 feet, 3 inches wide. It was constructed for the vast cathedral sequence in *The Prince and the Pauper* (1937) and subsequently used for other films that required very long, very narrow sets.

Stage 22, as it was called in the 1930s and 1940s, was started before, but finished after, the adjacent Property Building. Together, these two imposing structures, both fronting Olive Avenue like vast fortress walls, would change forever the look of Warner Bros. Studio from the street to the rest of the world. Today, billboards

The very long, very narrow Stage 22 was constructed in 1937.

advertising the studio's latest pictures are still painted and hung on these walls by the Scenic Arts Department.

During a 1945 labor dispute, striking workers rioted outside the gate situated between the two buildings, turned over cars, and had to be driven back with fire hoses and tear gas. At the time, the studio's motto, taken from a *New York Times* article and particularly beloved of Harry Warner, was "Combining good citizenship with good picture making." The words were even emblazoned in a triangle-shaped billboard across the street from the ongoing melée (today, on this site, there stands the aptly named "Triangle Building" studio office complex). In the midst of the riot, however, J.L. secretly ordered snipers with rifles to man the roof of Stage 22, in case things got out of hand. Nearby, in the Writers Building, Julius Epstein caught sight of one of the hidden gunmen and wisecracked "That's Warner Bros., combining good citizenship with good marksmanship."[9]

After a decade of trying to find projects that would accommodate Stage 22's peculiar shape, the building was divided into three smaller units, christened, from south to north, Stages 22, 23, and 24. These would be the last stages numbered on the lot for many years.

The 1945 labor dispute outside of Stage 22 (left) resulted in property damage, overturned cars, and nearly eighty injuries.

Tripling the stage left the Production Department with three 11,000-square-foot boxes to try to utilize—which proved to be even harder than finding a home for a single 33,000-square-foot rectangle—although the task would become easier in a few years with the arrival of television.

Sometimes they succeeded. At least part of the nail-biting merry-go-round sequence in Hitchcock's *Strangers on a Train* (1951) would be shot here. Interestingly, in the strangely circular way of these stages, Clint Eastwood, decades later, would shoot part of his own carousel sequence in *Sudden Impact* (1983) in the exact same spot—one of the few instances of his fantastically successful "Dirty Harry" series shooting on the lot.

More normal were the oddities that passed through these odd little stages, including the "prehistoric world" sequences (that's what it says on the daily production reports) for Irwin Allen's *The Story of Mankind* (1957), the counterculture curiosities *The Phynx* and *Flap* (both 1970), the very strange kiddie TV program *New Zoo Review* (1972 and 1975), Sondra Locke's bizarre *Ratboy* (1986), and the TV series *My Sister Sam* (1986–1988), whose talented leading lady, actress Rebecca Schaeffer, was tragically murdered by an obsessed fan.

Perhaps the strangest of all the many tenants in these stages would be the deservedly suppressed *Star Wars Holiday Special* (1978), which is universally renowned as the worst *Star Wars* project ever made, even though it included the entire original cast. Carrie Fisher even got to sing the heretofore unknown lyrics to the "Star Wars" title theme here. George Lucas has sworn that the project, which he produced for television, will never be released on video.

The shape of the stages and their building's proximity to the street and potential studio audiences made it perfect for situation comedies. *Room for One More* (1962) had been the studio's first sitcom. But that series had been filmed with a single camera, just like a movie. *Alice* (1976–1985), however, would be the studio's first of hundreds of three-camera sitcoms shot in front of a live audience on the lot.

A sitcom is an entirely different animal from a movie, or from a TV series shot like a movie. All sitcoms are, or at least were until very recently, shot on film (very few sitcoms have ever been "taped," despite many people's proclivity for using that phrase). Three cameras recorded the action at the same time. And three-walled sets, much like those used in the theater, allowed a studio audience to sit where the fourth wall would have been and watch the action play out like a theatrical performance. The audience is strongly encouraged to laugh at the proceedings, as that laughter is integrated into the show's soundtrack.*

Starting in 2008, a third type of TV series would also make its home at Warner Bros. And it would happen in this soundstage as well.

Actually, the first talk show to regularly film on the lot was *The Rosie O'Donnell Show* (1998–2011), which would shoot on Stage 5 (Stage 15 at the time) for much of its 1998 Hollywood-set season. Rosie was followed by *Ellen: The Ellen DeGeneres Show* (2003–), which would start shooting on this stage (Stage 2 actually, although she rented all three stages) for the 2008 season. *Ellen* would be followed by other talk shows shot on the lot featuring George Lopez (in the new Stage 29) and Conan O'Brien (Stage 5, which is now 15).

After Stage 22, no more soundstages would be constructed on the lot for sixty-two years, although a 7,000-square-foot space on the eastern side of the Flat Repair and Labor Department Building in the Scene Dock area would be known occasionally as "Stage 25" in the late 1950s.

---

*I've often heard it said that it is unethical, or a union violation, or something, to sweeten a sitcom's soundtrack with prerecorded or "canned" laughter. The truth, however, is that this practice is still in effect whenever needed. Not only is laughter added to cue audiences that something is funny, but also the laughter they use in this practice still often comes from the soundtracks of old radio dramas from the 1940s. So the next time you see an unfunny sitcom, you can perhaps find solace in the fact that the people who are laughing at it are quite probably dead now.

In 1999, the appropriate but inadvertently named Stage 23 was dedicated. At 25,116 feet, and with an unobstructed 45-foot height inside to the rafters, it would be the second tallest stage on the lot. The Clint Eastwood vehicle *Space Cowboys* (2000) was intended to be the first film to shoot in the new stage. But delays pushed the shooting back, and so Will Smith's expensive but ultimately unprofitable *Wild Wild West* (1999) slipped through the doors first and exposed the first film ever in the new stage. The TV series *The West Wing* (2000–2006) followed the tardy Eastwood feature and created a photographically realistic duplicate of the White House, complete with a reproduction of the exterior of the West Wing, which was built over the southern elephant door, allowing the production to move from exteriors to interiors in a single unbroken shot, as needed.

Stage 23 was renamed Stage 29 in 2009, when a new soundstage was constructed across the street from the Mill and next door to Stage 17 (then known, you may recall, as Stage 22). The Stage 23 appellation was then given to this new 21,600-square-foot stage because of its proximity to Stage 22. This shuffling brought the stage count, including the nine divided stages, to thirty (in twenty separate buildings—including those using A and B designations—but still minus the absent, and presumably unlucky, Stage 13). The count-up continued with five more stages, numbers 30–34, located up the road at the Warner Bros. Ranch (to be discussed in chapter 7), but Stage 29 would be the last of the Warner Bros. soundstage constructed to date on the lot.

FIVE

The Backlot—
30 Acres of Fairyland

The fading light of day still tends the California gloaming. I drive through the back lot, a curious landscape: A Mexican settlement where water sprinkles in a deserted fountain, a Tibetan village where fake cherry blossoms cling to the tips of stage trees, a Midwestern village square where a silent bandstand echoes lost and forgotten march music, the darkened western street where ghosts of movie gunslingers and cowboys seem to linger in the gathering dusk.[1]

THE ABOVE paragraph, from the book *Goodnight John Boy*, describes producer Earl Hamner's thoughts upon visiting the standing outdoor sets on the Warner Bros. backlot. Hamner, creator of *The Waltons* (1971–1981), is a successful executive who has worked in Hollywood for a long time. And yet he, like many of us who have spent time working on them, finds there is something mysterious and intangible about backlots. F. Scott Fitzgerald called backlots "30 acres of fairyland."[2] Nathaniel West referred to a backlot as "a dream dump."[3] Billy Wilder in *Sunset Boulevard* (1950) has a character mention about a backlot that they "like it better than any street in the world."

A lot of this feeling, as Hamner and others have pointed out, is due to the fact that backlots look almost exactly like real places but, except when in use, are eerily devoid of people. Backlots are recognizable even to first-time visitors not only because they evoke real streets in New York or the Wild West, but also because it's likely that this visitor has seen movies or television programs shot on these very streets. In fact, for many people, their very ideas of what New York or the Wild

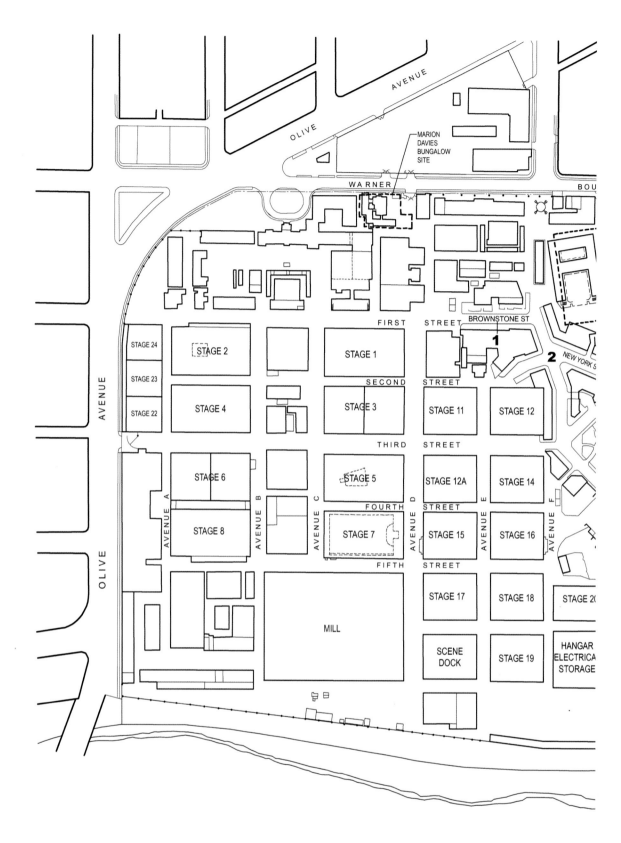

Studio map, circa 1967, with numbers corresponding to the sections in this chapter.
Courtesy of Robert Lane.

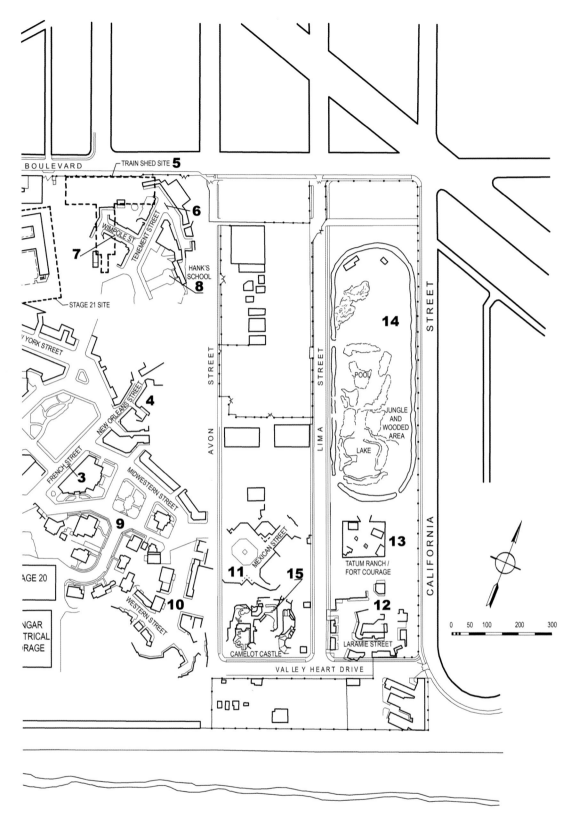

KEY:
1. Brownstone Street
2. New York Street
3. French Street
4. New Orleans Street
5. Train Shed (Site)
6. Tenement Street
7. Wimpole Street
8. Hank's School
9. Midwest Street
10. Western Street
11. Mexican Street
12. Laramie Street
13. Tatum Ranch/Fort Courage
14. Jungle
15. Camelot Castle

The Warner Bros. backlot: "30 acres of fairyland."

West looks like come not from the real places at all, but from movies made on these backlot interpretations.

Warner Bros. in the twenty-first century is one of the only studios in the world that can still boast of standing sets dating back into the 1930s and before. So many movies (perhaps 30 percent of America's total filmic output) originated on these sets, or on even older sets that stood on the same ground, that, when television, advertisements, still shoots, modeling jobs, and even amateur photography by employees and visitors are factored in, it would be possible to argue that these acres of copied reality constitute the most photographed real estate in the world.

And yet, as familiar and as overexposed as it is, the backlot quixotically refuses to show us all of its secrets. So many films have been realized in front of its weathered façades that it is impossible to list them all, although for the purposes of this book, the first attempt in history has here been made.

Part of the problem in identifying the cinematic tenants of a backlot lies in the studios' habit of rebuilding backlot sets inside of their soundstages. Often only

One of the earliest designated views of the backlot, taken before the 1934 fire that destroyed most of the mysterious worlds that are visible here. The barnlike structure, near top left, is the "theater set" slightly northwest of where Stage 12 would be constructed in 1935. The empty pool, top center, is where Stage 21 would appear in 1939. The wide boulevard between this pool and the ship set is "Viennese Street," which today is French Street. Brownstone Street is near the top left corner, and the original New York Street is just underneath it.

establishing shots of a building would be taken on the actual backlot, and then the unit would retreat to a copy of that set on a stage, where more control of sound and lighting would be possible. Even a careful study of the resultant film, and of the corresponding production paperwork, often does not reveal what exactly was shot where.

Additionally, as Warner Bros. has been plagued with several studio fires over the decades, some of the mysteries involving the backlot are theoretical. If, for example, a standing set happened to burn down but is later reconstructed in the same exact spot, from the same exact blueprints, and looks, ultimately, exactly the same, should this second set still be considered the same building as the original, or is it now an entirely new entity with a new history?

But at the end of the day, the biggest mystery inherent in a study of the Warner Bros. backlot involves not policy or logistics, but rather those intangibles that the backlot evokes, both on the screen and off. I'll always remember being told once by some old-timer about how, when Humphrey Bogart would have too much to drink, he would occasionally steal a studio bicycle and then proceed to peddle drunkenly across the backlot, shouting obscenities about his boss, Jack Warner, and then listening to those oaths dance and echo across the façades.

You know, sometimes when I'm alone out there and the sun is setting, gathering black-and-white shadows across those same façades, I feel like I can hear Bogie still.

1. Brownstone Street

One of the staples of any studio's backlot, then as today, is a Brownstone Street. The reasoning for this is that there are no authentic brownstones in California. Even today, there are Brownstone Streets in most modern studios in Los Angeles. The oldest original specimen is here at Warner Bros.

Brownstone Street in the 1940s. Note the portable dressing room near the top of the street, and Stage 21 towering beyond.

Warner Bros.' Brownstone Street seems to have grown out of a First National Picture called *Lady Be Good* (1928). The original street ran east from the Commissary and, then as now, consisted of a series of five staircases and numerous doorways and windows decorating a row of three-story brick homes, all supposedly based on a part of Manhattan's Lexington Avenue. The opposite (northern) side of the street, surprisingly, was never more brownstones, but rather a row of east coast–style small business and office-based façades, which never really matched or complemented the buildings they faced.

Through the 1930s, the street survived and was expanded upon. As the adjacent New York Street grew around the district, a large façade with rounded doorways appeared at the eastern end of the street, allowing for a much wider variety of camera angles when photographing Brownstone Street from the west. In the mid-1930s, interiors were added in back of some of the doorways, and a storage hanger for carbon arc-lighting equipment was installed on the building's backside. A complete stairway with landings was also constructed inside one of the front doorways and was used extensively for a shootout between Bogart and Edward G. Robinson in *Bullets or Ballots* (1936).

Gangster films such as this contributed to the street's white-hot résumé during this period. *Doorway to Hell* (1930) marked Cagney's first attempt at this genre. *Little Caesar* (1931) was Robinson's. Both of these pictures utilized the set. Bogart's *The Maltese Falcon* (1941) placed the exterior of Sam Spade's apartment at the end of the street. But *The Big Sleep* (1946) brazenly used the same façade as the "Holbart Arms" hotel. Years later, in *The Young Philadelphians* (1959), Paul Newman is represented as living in the very same building. This doubling and tripling up of who-slept-where-when extends to all the structures on the street. A doorway on the other end of the block has been passed off as being the home both of television's Murphy Brown and of Wonder Woman!

The set has often done service in musicals, usually as a speakeasy or a nightclub; dramas; romantic comedies; superhero pictures (a trench down the center of the street, added to remotely control the Batmobile for *Batman Returns* [1992], is still there); disaster films; and sitcoms. There seems to be no genre that hasn't floated through. Alfred Hitchcock shot sequences here twice—for *Rope* (1948) and, more extensively, for *Dial M for Murder* (1954)—as did Steven Spielberg, for both *A.I. Artificial Intelligence* (2001) and *War of the Worlds* (2005).

Unlike any other first-generation set on the lot, Brownstone Street has never been burned or bulldozed. Although it has been extensively modified, the changes to the street have not really altered its outward appearance. In 1995, the less-seen northern side of the street was demolished and the Warner Bros. Museum and Steven J. Ross Theater went into the spot. The outside of this new building did not really match the Brownstone look any more than the buildings it replaced did. But it was a beautiful structure, which has often been used as an upscale theater district set. Movie premieres, beginning with *The Bridges of Madison County* (1995), are often held at the theater, with red carpets and celebrities sweeping past the brown-stones and under the marquee into the theater.

In 2002, Brownstone Street was officially renamed Ashley Boulevard, after Ted Ashley, a late and much-liked Warner Bros. chairman.

There is one other secret that the set once possessed that might as well be acknowledged. If a visitor to Brownstone Street before the mid-1990s had chosen to enter through one of the front doors and then crawled between the flats and through a narrow and badly lit hallway created by the space between two disused set walls, this person would eventually have found themselves inside a tiny and irregularly shaped room, originally created, presumably, by a gap between the back walls of two interior sets.

Inside this room, lit by a single bare bulb, was a ragged "bachelor's pad," presumably created and then lovingly decorated by crew members to escape their employers. The room contained a cot with a ratty mattress, a tiny end table with

The original New York Street. Note Stages 8, 12A, and 11 on the left. After the 1934 fire, more soundstages were constructed on the right, and the street was pushed east. 1930.

an ashtray, and a single chair, probably pilfered in earlier decades from some long-wrapped project.

The most distinctive thing about the little room was how it was decorated. Every inch of available wall and ceiling space was wallpapered with layer upon layer of vintage pinups of vintage pinup queens. There were girls with lingerie, girls without lingerie, girls playing volleyball, girls picking flowers, girls sunbathing. The spectacle of it all was somewhat disorienting because there was no escaping it. The ladies were so numerous and so overwhelming, and were spooned together so tightly, that it all resembled some crazy, R-rated, Busby Berkeley nightmare. Peeling one pinup away made no difference in the compositions because she inevitably had a sister waiting to take her place underneath. There were so many layers of ladies that the very walls may in fact have been held together by them. Presumably, like cutting a tree open to count the rings, the older clippings would have been layers deep, while the newer ones were closer to the top. Most of the pictures were relatively innocent. The most recent appeared to be from actress Suzanne Somers' notorious 1980 *Playboy* spread—which had been printed in the magazine against her strident objections. Somers was actually shooting a TV series on the lot at the time, *Step by Step* (1990–1997). One wonders if the lady would have been flattered or horrified to know how much she was appreciated by her male coworkers on the lot.

The pinup room is no longer there. In 1993, the Fitness Center was expanded, and that part of Brownstone Street was removed.

2. New York Street

Although this most iconic of backlots is often referred to generically as having been built in 1930, its origins actually seem to go back even further, to *Outcast* (1928). The street was and is still shaped like an upside-down peace symbol. It begins with a large artery emerging out above Brownstone Street and heading southeast for approximately one city block—where it branches three times; as a fork in front of a very large, triangular-shaped city street, and into an alley behind Stage 12 (Stage 24 today). Originally the district contained a courthouse, a library building, a variety of backstreets and alleys, a theater with stage entrances, a park, an arcade, a hotel, a subway terminal, and a variety of shops and storefronts.

The first 1952 fire effectively destroyed the large city block in the center, and the district's northernmost wall, which shielded the area from Stage 21, was also destroyed. By the time of the second 1952 fire, almost the only thing left behind of the original New York Street was a single wall of façades built against Stage 12, which were themselves damaged on their northern end, and the large columned courthouse that still overlooks the entire street.

In fact, it is odd indeed that this courthouse *wasn't* burned. Several historians have assumed that it was a casualty of the fire because in the 1950s, after two decades as a building sitting serenely at street level, the entire structure, complete

New York Street in the 1940s. Note the courthouse at the end of the street before the staircase was constructed at its base. Circa 1940s.

with six 15-foot-high Greek columns, suddenly appeared at the top of a brand-new, majestic-looking staircase! The building was never just a façade; the interior was actually a dance rehearsal hall, so adding those steps under it would have been difficult and expensive. Yet surviving records indicate that the building avoided fire damage. So whether this elaborate, Hearst-worthy renovation was done when the street was being rebuilt, or later, or even before the fire is unclear and strange.

The staircase, however, whatever its origins, has certainly been a magnificent improvement to the structure. Recently, Ben Affleck and Alan Arkin were seen having lunch on those steps and discussing Hollywood politics in the Academy Award–winning *Argo* (2012). Projects that have not featured the building as part of their stories have usually used the structure to add interest to the background. One film, *I Was a Communist for the FBI* (1951), seemed so eager to show us the courthouse standing regally in the distance, as a seemingly unassailable bastion of capitalism, that it also, inadvertently, gave us a peek at the soundstage behind it at the same time. A much later film, *I Wanna Hold Your Hand* (1978), made the same mistake, although both times audience might have just wondered why it was that the city courthouse was unexpectedly situated on the edge of a warehouse district, which, to an uninitiated eye, the soundstage would have resembled.

A second courthouse, or at least a civic-style structure, was around the corner. This building, which always *did* have a staircase, was so familiar to audiences that when it burned, an entire 1952 page of *Life* magazine was commandeered to note some of its appearances onscreen. Post fire, the area remained open, with no permanent set erected on the site for many years. Sometimes studio wizards found ways to make this defect into a virtue. *The Young Philadelphians* (1959), for example, turned this open area into the construction site called for by the script. Not until 1990, for the short-lived series *The Flash*, did a permanent set appear on the site. However, these new façades, because of their distinctive art deco look, have been cast by employees giving impromptu tours to their friends as sets much older than

The May 6, 1952, fire that destroyed much of New York Street.

The TV series *ER* (1994–2009) constructed the Chicago ambulance bay and elevated train tracks seen here on New York Street's eastern end. Photo courtesy of Ronald Charles Reeves.

that. An elevated train trestle and station, as well as an elaborate ambulance bay, were successfully grafted into this district for the long-running, Chicago-set series, *ER* (1994–2009).

Between the two courthouses was a city park, which often played Central Park and, nearly as often, a cemetery. Across the street was the original triangular-shaped city block, which was originally bisected by an alley that ran all the way through the façades. When this structure was lost, something similar but slightly more upscale was constructed in the same footprint. The alley was replaced by a fancy square, called "Embassy Courtyard," which, post fire, would remain as part of the architecture from then on. In *The FBI Story* (1959), it was a South American Nazi headquarters. In *The Thorn Birds* (1983), it played a restaurant adjacent to the Vatican. In *The Man with Two Brains* (1983) and *To Be or Not to Be* (1983), the area was eastern European. In an episode of *Lois and Clark: The New Adventures of Superman* (1993–1997), it was Buckingham Palace; in *Eraser* (1996) and *Thirteen Days* (1999), it was Washington, DC.

Embassy Courtyard and the hotel set next door has also played Gotham City at least three times, in the *Batman* (1966–1968) television series, in *Batman Forever* (1995), and in *The Dark Knight* (2007), although in all fairness it is hardly recognizable in either of the features, and it is the large courthouse across the street that the television series focused on most often. It is strange, and unremarked upon by critics and commentators, that three very different interpretations of the same material should have utilized the same set, each apparently unaware of the other "Dark Knights" having ever been there.

On the northern corner of this same center structure, there is a significant office building façade fronted by two thick support columns. Because of this building's prominence on the street, it is photographed perhaps more often than any other building on the set, and perhaps the world—sometimes in creative ways to make it virtually impossible to spot onscreen. For example, *Falling Down* (1993) used the columns as support for an (optically added) freeway overpass, *Blade Runner* (1982) hid them behind a cowgirl-shaped neon sign, and *The Last Samurai* (2003) made them look like they belonged to a nineteenth-century Japanese village. More often, the same building is used undisguised and serves as a backdrop for every type of tragedy and comedy available to humankind. And to insect-kind as well, as the building has been featured as part of invasions by ants (*Them!*, 1954), killer bees (*The Swarm*, 1978), and even (the) Beatles (*I Wanna Hold Your Hand*, 1978).

Coincidences and ironies and flukes and fortuities seem to happen often on these streets. A musical echo of the last project mentioned above occurred on the occasion of a 2005 party celebrating the video release of *Concert for George*, a tribute to the late ex-Beatle George Harrison, which brought Harrison's old bandmates, Paul McCartney and Ringo Starr, along with much of the rest of the music industry, to Warner Bros. *ER* was staging a dramatic plane crash sequence for the episode "Two Ships" on the same night on New York Street, however, so the party attendees had to be led through that series' blood- and debris-strewn "crash site" set in order to attend the gala tribute inside the nearby Steven J. Ross Theater.

On the other side(s) of these same buildings are general copies of the original New York Street façades. Both sides of both incarnations of the street could be "blackened" for nighttime shooting during daylight hours by means of scaffolding across the top from which black duvetyn could be unfurled to keep the sun out. Originally rigged into the set in 1946, the scaffolding and the black dropcloths were kept in place until 1982.

Among these façades is a prominent Broadway-style theater entrance. The current structure mimics the original set, built in 1929 for *A Showgirl in Hollywood* (1929), which was lost in the first 1952 fire. In the climax of the classic musical *42nd Street* (1933), an impresario played by Warner Baxter walks out of these theater doors and into an alley, where he sits on the bottom rung of a metal staircase and listens to his audience file out onto the street talking about the triumphant show they don't know he has just produced. Today, eerily, it is still possible to retrace his ghostly steps. An interested party in the twenty-first century can exit through the theater doors (there is, need we mention, no theater inside the façades, just a few feet of lobby), walk past the box office, duck into an alley, and then sit on a stage

The rebuilt, current New York Street, looking west. Note the iconic theater front, left, and the building with the "London Music Hall" awning, which notably played the wax museum in *House of Wax* (1953), Hollywood's first 3D feature. Circa 1970s.

door staircase that is in the same spot it was at in 1933. Reenacting the setting of this scene, on its original location, is perhaps as close as it is possible to be "inside" the movies.

The same theater, need I add, also hosted Al Jolson in *Mammy* (1935), James Cagney in *Yankee Doodle Dandy* (1942), Doris Day in *On Moonlight Bay* (1945) and *April in Paris* (1952), Judy Garland in *A Star Is Born* (1954), Liberace in *Sincerely Yours* (1955), Jack Webb and Janet Leigh in *Pete Kelly's Blues* (1955), Elvis Presley in *Loving You* (1957), Rosalind Russell in *Mame* (1958), Bette Davis in *Kid Galahad* (1937) and *Whatever Happened to Baby Jane* (1962), Natalie Wood in *Gypsy* (1962), Lucille Ball and Bob Hope in *Critic's Choice* (1963), Barbra Streisand in *Funny Lady* (1975), Mel Brooks and Anne Bancroft in *To Be or Not to Be* (1983), and even George C. Scott in *Movie Movie* (1978). Is there any real theater, on Broadway or anywhere else, which can boast such alumni? Recently, the façade played several

The row of New York façades that once fronted Stage 21, as seen from the scaffoldings. Circa 1970s.

different theaters in the Oscar-winning silent film *The Artist* (2011), bringing the storied set full circle and back to its 1920s silent movie roots.

Yet an even more apt, if inadvertent, tribute came thirty-five years earlier in Peter Bogdanovich's *Nickelodeon* (1976); in that comic valentine to the early days of cinema, Bogdanovich has his cast watch *The Birth of a Nation* (1915) inside the theater. Afterward, Brian Keith, playing a producer not unlike Warner Baxter, exits the set and, instead of sitting on the staircase, crosses to beneath the marquee, where, having realized the true power of cinema for the first time, he proclaims (quoting James Stewart in an interview with Bogdanovich) that what the movies really do is give the people "little pieces of time, that they never forget."

3. French Street

The murky origins of this district go back to 1937 and a picture called *Tovarich*. For this film, a lower class French tenement street, dark and narrow and winding, was constructed slightly northeast of where the current version is. The stucco walls were built on top of a narrow and twisting property storage building constructed as a skeleton for the sets on the outside. This particular French Street was subsequently used

The original grotto-style French façades that concealed a prop storage shed. Early 1940s.

most often not as a contemporary French boulevard at all, but rather as a period, usually French Revolution–era Gallic district, and it can be seen as such in films like *All This, and Heaven Too* (1940).

Just south of this district, there already existed a very wide boulevard built in 1930 for *Viennese Nights* and named, not surprisingly, Viennese Street. The Art Department quickly figured out that this more upscale boulevard, wider and cleaner than the grottos and artists' lofts that dominated the newer French Street, could itself play a convincing Paris with only the addition of the proper signage and attitude.

Some of the most romantic moments in *Casablanca* (1943) consisted of a short flashback sequence set in Paris. The effectiveness of the sequence is partially due to the fact that it is intentionally dreamlike and is, in fact, actually a dream, a drunken remembrance by Bogart's character of old times and lost loves. The sequence is so stylized and audacious that, for perhaps the only time in cinema history, a rear screen projection of a road running behind a car dissolves into another road entirely while the car somehow stays in focus in the foreground!

A few seconds later in the same sequence, a street in Pairs is glimpsed as the German occupation is announced. Now, for decades, studio tradition has held that Viennese Street, now known as French Street, was the location used for this sequence. A close viewing of the film and a visit to the surviving set would seem to bear this out. The outline of the street, and even the shape of the second-story windows from which Bogart and Ingrid Bergman watched the Germans march in, all seem to line up fairly well. The daily production reports and the corresponding set photos, however, do not identify the location as Viennese Street, as it should have been on May 27, 1942, when the sequence was shot, but as "French Street," which was, in fact, a few hundred feet to the north at the time.

Incidentally, the street in the film appears to be built on a slightly sloping hillside, but neither street in fact is. It should also be noted that production records for that film refer to the location of the Blue Parrot nightclub as being "Moorish Street," a heretofore unknown backlot set, if it existed at all; and the exterior as seen from Victor Lazlo's window is listed as being shot on a "French Street" as well. We do know that other Moroccan street scenes identified as being recorded on the likewise nonexistent "Casablanca Street" were in fact shot on another existing set, Dijon Street, which had recently been rebuilt for *The Desert Song* (1941). Still, the slate on the set photo of the Paris scenes does say "French Street," which isn't necessarily as definitive as it sounds one way or the other, because the scene was indeed "set" in France. The same slate also refers to the film as "CASA BLANCA" (in two words), by the way. The point is that the production records, at least in this instance, cannot really be trusted.

Yet it's hard to dismiss *Casablanca*'s association with the street entirely, if only because one wants it to be true. Adding to the murkiness of it all, we know that about the time of *Casablanca*'s production, the original "French Street" as well as the property warehouse inside were removed and reconfigured, so that a storage hanger for the studio's aircraft could be constructed on the site. A rather dissimilar "English Street" eventually ended up occupying the real estate in question for the rest of the decade, so it is perhaps debatable whether the original French Street was actually even available when it was needed by the *Casablanca* production team.

So the answer to the question of where exactly this sequence was shot will have to remain as engaging, inexplicable, and ultimately irrelevant as that audaciously dissolving rear-projected road behind Bogie and Ingrid Bergman.

Another French Street myth, perpetuated in print and online, is that Viennese Street was demolished in 1947 to create an 1890s evocation of New York City for the studio's expensive production of the Broadway super-success, *Life with Father*. The truth is that half the street, the northern half, was rebuilt for that production. But the French, or Viennese, façades on the other end of the street were preserved and are visible, although altered by camera placement and matte paintings, in *Father* and in many subsequent productions. Madison Avenue, as the *Life with Father*–sector end of the street came to be known, survived until the

The cryptic and mysterious *Casablanca* set still. 1942.

second 1952 fire. It has always seemed to me that the set's similarity to the smaller and nearby Brownstone Street was so striking that it's surprising that the older set had not been considered originally for the *Life with Father* location to begin with.

After the fire, Madison Avenue was not rebuilt, leaving French Street, as it was now officially called, a boulevard with only one side. The New York park set opposite it, now visible due to the house cleanings caused by the fires, made the set look somehow even more casually Gallic than before. A New Orleans Street, built in the 1950s where those old French and later English Streets once stood, increased the available shooting space and camera placement opportunities to evoke the "French" architecture significantly.

The resultant set has seen a lot of use over the decades, and not always as France. The district has played San Francisco (*Days of Wine and Roses*, 1963); Baltimore (*Chamber of Horrors*, 1966); Galveston, Texas, (*4 for Texas*, 1963); and even Viet Nam (*The Green Berets*, 1968). It also provided a location for the New England roadhouse sequences in *Who's Afraid of Virginia Woolf?* (1966).

In the 1960s period of our tour, all of this Gallic architecture could be rented by outside producers for $1500 a day.

4. New Orleans Street

New Orleans Street had a somewhat different origin than most of the other sets on the backlot. The façades were constructed in 1951 on a soundstage for usage in the studio's controversial (and successful) *A Streetcar Named Desire*. When the film

For *Life with Father* (1947), half of Viennese/French Street was destroyed to create this Gay '90s New York tableau.

wrapped the sets, instead of being destroyed or consigned to a slow death in the scene dock, were instead towed out onto the backlot and repositioned at the end of French Street just on the other side of the lip of the nearby Midwest Street. The way the sets were positioned, one particular building placed at the junction of all of these districts improbably found itself a part of all three sets, and so was routinely called upon to be part of the Deep South, Europe, or small-town United States, depending on what was being shot near that corner at that moment. The building is still there, and it received a lot of exposure in the TV series *Sisters* (1991–1996) as Mitch's Fish Market, and *Gilmore Girls* (2000–2007) as Luke's Diner.

New Orleans Street languished badly over the course of its twenty-year lifespan, perhaps owing to its not being designed to sit outside, or to exist at all, beyond its initial appearance. As the stucco walls peeled and flaked, however, and the wrought iron banisters and rails oxidized in the sun, the set's authenticity and believability for audiences actually increased. By the time the TV series *Bourbon Street Beat* (1959–1960) made the most extensive use of the sets since *Streetcar*, it felt like the district was as old and storied as the actual French Quarter.

The set was removed in the late 1970s, although to this day, some of the landscaping and parts of the sidewalks are still visible in the parking lot behind the Producers 3 (production offices) Building. For *Point of No Return* (1993), however, the

New Orleans Street can be seen supplementing and expanding French Street's perimeters on the left. 1970.

studio found itself in the position of needing to re-create New Orleans (at Mardi Gras, no less) on the backlot yet again. They did so on the adjacent Midwest Street by using French signage, carefully selected camera angles, and a great many extras, and by judiciously intercutting footage of the real New Orleans with the backlot material.

Perhaps any one backlot set and a lot of imagination are all that an Art Department really needs to create any location anywhere.

5. Train Shed (Site)

A spectator in the later 1960s wouldn't have known it, but one of the most impressive sets on any studio lot was once this large T-shaped structure above the lake and next to the water tower. From the outside, despite its size, it was fairly nondescript. But inside was a large urban railroad station re-created in detail, complete with tracks, stations, platforms, and ticket offices. A smaller, more rural station was outside near the end of the track. The studio owned outright two regulation Pullman cars, coaches, engines, and numerous rolling stock pieces—all sawed in half to allow the camera access "inside" any of the cars. Some of rolling stock seen pulling into this "station" was authentic, and some of it consisted of partial or nonworking passenger car exteriors, all of which could be precision stopped via a towing cable on a predetermined mark for the benefit of the camera.

This set was constructed in the late 1930s, apparently not for a single movie, but rather when it was discovered that many of the studio's scripts inexplicably contained heartbreaking hellos or tearful goodbyes with a railroad station backdrop. World War II, which consisted of many a real-life equivalent of what was being fictionalized on this set, only made these scenes all the more frequent, and poignant, to audiences.

With the end of the war, and all the sentiments that the war evoked, the set fell into a period of relative disuse. The studio did nothing to preserve or repair the building during this period, and every project that used it contributed to its decline. During the production of an episode of *Lawman* (1958–1962), the entire depot partially collapsed, although it somehow continued to be used even while the rubble was being was cleared away. Some employees remember part of it still being there as late as 1965 while *F Troop* (1965–1967) was in production.

6. Tenement Street

A walk east past the Train Shed leads a visitor to one of the studio's most storied and recognizable settings. Tenement Street is a more downscale version of New York Street, horseshoe shaped, with alleys, fire escapes, and storefronts evoking a New York that was more Bowery than Broadway. The district looks like a relic left over from any of the early 1930s Cagney-style gangster pictures, although, surprisingly enough, those films actually predated Tenement Street by several years.

Aptly, the set was indeed constructed for a James Cagney film, *Frisco Kid* (1935). But that picture was not set in New York at all but in San Francisco's nineteenth-century Barbary Coast district. Frisco Street, as it was originally called, received a makeover and a new name in 1938 for another Cagney picture, which was indeed a gangster film. *Angels with Dirty Faces* (1938) was the star's return to the genre, and to Warner Bros. after a protracted contract dispute. It is possible that both the film and the set were intentionally designed to evoke that earlier cycle of crime pictures, which, with the participation of their original star, they most certainly did. That film begins with a dramatic tracking shot across the set's northeastern wall and down into the tenements and alleys of "Dock Street," where most of the story takes place. This wall, or its equivalent, fortunately survived the 1952 fires and is still there today. Likewise, *Angels with Dirty Faces'* success in turn triggered another mini-explosion of Warner Bros. gangster pictures, some of which starred Cagney, and most of which were indeed shot on these mean and evocative streets.

Tenement Street set photo; note the cobblestones added for some European-set production. 1940.

Tenement Street is among the most specific of sets on the lot. Unlike most other backlots, there is very little that is generic about the setting it evokes, specifically New York City's hardscrabble East Side. And yet, like any other backlot setting, it has proven to be surprisingly versatile. In *Strawberry Blonde* (1941), it was redressed as an appealing Gay '90s–era boulevard. *House of Wax*, Hollywood's first 3D production (1953), was set in approximately the same period, but now the façades looked sinister and foreboding. *To Have and Have Not* (1944) was set in Martinique, of all places, but used the district as successfully as star Humphrey Bogart's earlier, New York–set epics. *My Fair Lady* (1964) staged the catchy "With a Little Bit" musical number here, with the street playing a convincing Edwardian London. *Time after Time* (1979) returned to that period and its location for its foggy Jack the Ripper sequences. The *Bring 'Em Back Alive* series (1982–1983) used the district as 1930s Singapore, and *The Karate Kid II* (1986) as Tokyo, Japan. Both *Hooper* (1978) and an episode of *Sex and the City* (1998–2003) cast the set as part of a Hollywood backlot. *The Ultimate Warrior* (1975), *A.I. Artificial Intelligence* (2000), and *Minority Report* (2001) all had futuristic science fiction settings, while *The Last Samurai* (2003), with unknowing irony, brought the street and audiences back to nineteenth-century San Francisco.

In recent years the street has been the home of a great many comic book adaptations. Warner Bros.' first big budget comic book movies, *Superman* (1978) and *Batman* (1989), were not shot on the lot, but from *Batman Returns* (1992) onward until Christopher Nolan's mostly location-filmed reboot *Batman Begins* (2005), this street was Gotham City, as it was in the TV series *Birds of Prey* (2002–2003). It was also Metropolis, at least on television, for Superman, and was the comics-inspired homes of *Wonder Woman* (television, 1976–1979), *The Shadow* (1993), *Barb Wire* (1996), *Annie* (twice: in 1982 and for television, 1999), *Spiderman* (2001), and *Daredevil* (2002).

For perhaps the most interesting and literal of all comic book movies, *Dick Tracy* (1990), director-star Warren Beatty painted the entire street primary comic book colors, meaning that every red or yellow was the exact same shade of red or yellow, with no shadings or gradients. Cinematographers often limit or emphasize their color pallets for dramatic effect. For example, art director Tom Duffield painted the entire set green for *A Little Princess* (1995) to set off leading lady Liesel Matthews' green eyes. But *Dick Tracy* took the comic book esthetic and followed it to its most literal extreme ever.

A very different esthetic is presumably on view in *Bukharin: Enemy of the People* (1990), a Russian film shot at the very end of the Cold War. The picture, apparently never released in the United States, should rate at least a footnote as a curiosity in world history because it was the first, and last, Soviet picture shot on "location" in Hollywood. Surprisingly, considering the economic and political roadblocks inherent in mounting such a project during such a period, when the Russian crew arrived in the United States, it was not to shoot on America's real city streets but on reproductions of those streets here on a backlot.

In 1981, for Columbia's expensive adaptation of the comic strip–via-Broadway hit *Annie*, most of Tenement Street's aging inner façades were replaced or resurfaced by production designer Dale Hennesy. The most significant results of these rebuilds were an imposing orphanage façade that survives today, and a new name for the set, "Hennesy Street." A plaque in the sidewalk in front of the orphanage commemorates the rechristening in honor of Hennesy, whose last film this was.

Annie was also the last that project director John Huston would shoot at the studio; Huston's involvement with the company went back to 1938, at least. Employees on the lot in 1981 remember him still, seventy-six years old, sitting in a director's chair, barking orders, and sucking oxygen out of a bottle while smoking a cigar.

In the 1960s, south of Tenement Street and east of New York Street, there stood a large, open swath of real estate. Today, Parking Lot H is at the center of this open area. But most of the employees who park their cars on this property every morning probably will never know of the strange and romantic real estate that once stood on this site.

New York . . . or Burbank?

One of the largest sets that inhabited this area and in fact predated Tenement Street by half a decade was Dijon Street, sometimes known as Dijon Square. Created in 1929 for the lamentably lost *Kismet* (1930), the set was later reused as assorted Eastern and European villages, often with the Arabian architecture disguised by wartime damage, for pictures like *Sergeant York* (1941) for World War I and *Desperate Journey* (1942) for World War II. European-based period films like *The Private Lives of Elizabeth and Essex* (1939), set in 1601, and *The Miracle of Our Lady of Fatima* (1952), set in 1917, also managed to find a use for the district. At the very end of Dijon Street was the original French Street, discussed earlier in this chapter, and its "sequel," English Street.

Nearby and slightly to the east was the large and beautiful Bonnyfeather Street, which was erected for *Anthony Adverse* (1936) as the eighteenth-century "Casa da Bonnyfeather." The set was distinguished by a large town square with a stone fountain and courtyards, balconies, and storefronts.

Anthony Adverse was something of a departure for Warner Bros. Its literary origins, toney period settings, and lavish production values were more indicative of an MGM picture than any of the gritty salacious melodramas the studio was producing at the time. When producer Mervyn LeRoy asked J.L. if he had read the lengthy book (by Hervey Allen) that the property was based on, Warner reportedly wise-cracked, "Read it? I can't even lift it," [4] one of the producer's better one-liners. The resultant picture was part of a concerted, and ultimately successful, stab at respectability. The film was nominated for a Best Picture Oscar, which it lost. The studio would not receive its first Academy Award in that category until two years later, for the similarly highbrow *The Life of Emile Zola* (1937).

Bonnyfeather Street terminated in front of the outdoor lake that first was a predecessor and later was a supplement to Stage 21. Both period and contemporary scenes set in ports and shipyards utilized this district. Although the fuselage of a metal freighter-liner was incongruously parked for many years in an open area across from Stage 16, where a shallow basin in front played the "ocean," most of the outdoor port scenes for most Warner Bros. movies prior to 1952 were filmed in this larger area next to Bonnyfeather Street instead.

On the opposite end of this vast backlot lake, before Stage 21 rose castle-like over the district, was another cluster of backlot real estate. Most prominent was a

Bonnyfeather Street as used in *Anthony Adverse* (1936). The numbers at the bottom of this still reference individual buildings for the convenience of future productions.

replica of the Venice canals, probably constructed for *Broadway Gondolier* (1935). The lake continued to be used even after 1940, when Stage 21 moved many of the studio's aquatic spectacles indoors.

All of these sets, and much of the original Tenement Street as well, burned in the second 1952 fire.

7. Wimpole Street

Wimpole Street was an annex or spur street that jutted out from the western wall of Tenement Street for about a block and terminated at the base of where the bottom of the Train Shed once stood. The set consisted entirely of townhouse units that had been constructed on Stage 8 for *My Fair Lady* (1964) and that, upon completion of filming, were moved out onto the backlot, *Streetcar Named Desire* like, for continued usage. A 1965 memo about the general condition of the backlot grumbled that these buildings "have never been roofed, or backed up, and as a result, they are not yet shootable." Eventually these needed modifications were made, although the set was always something of a second choice for producers. Except for Lucille Ball's ill-conceived *Mame* (1974), the district made few prolonged appearances on camera.

Incidentally, in *My Fair Lady*, Henry Higgins lived at 27A Wimpole Street in London, which is not a real address, except apparently on *this* Wimpole Street.

Lucille Ball walks, or skates, or something, down Wimpole Street as *Mame* (1974). © ImageCollect.com/Globe Photos

8. Hank's School

The rear of the center Tenement Street façades consisted of a "U"-shaped alcove that originally only offered a view of the telephone poles and plywood that usually constitute the back side of a backlot. In the early 1960s, a school set was constructed on top of these telephone poles only because it was more economical to build these façades on the already existing scaffolding than to start from scratch. Records note that the project these sets were created for was an unnamed "television pilot." No matter: having a school façade on the lot seemed to encourage productions to find ways to use it. *The Music Man* (1962) cast the building, which had two front entrances, one adjacent to the other, as River City High, and featured it in that film's toe-tapping "76 Trombones" number. *Hank* (1965–1966), another TV series set at a high school, used the set extensively and gave it its commonly used name, "Hank's School." Hank's School was later adapted for use in the independent science fiction film *Village of the Giants* (1965) and as Boatwright University for the TV series *The Waltons* (1971–1981).

In 1995, the set was removed during a rebuild of Tenement Street that was undertaken for the film *Batman Forever*. By this point, the Operations Department at the studio had been trying to budget a new, modern backlot set for several years, in the belief that a contemporary-looking façade would be a successful alternative to the other standing sets on the lot, all of which were now decades old. In 2000 they unveiled "Downtown Plaza," which, like its immediate predecessor, was built onto the back wall of Tenement Street. The set was designed to resemble a contemporary office complex, with a silver atrium, revolving glass doors, a businessman's café, four-story glass walls, and a broad staircase leading from the street to the lobby. It overlooked a grassy lawn with a driveway and a broad disc of concrete with a water hookup that could accommodate a fountain, if required.

Unfortunately, Downtown Plaza looked too much like any number of real offices in the neighborhood, some of which were already owned or leased by Warner Bros. There was no compelling reason to use a backlot to replicate something so readily available anywhere else. Except for some low-budget features and television commercials, the set's only memorable moment onscreen was a funny scene involving a Godzilla parade float for *Austin Powers in Goldmember* (2002). In 2005, Downtown Plaza was extensively rebuilt to play the front of Al Pacino's Las Vegas casino in *Ocean's 13* (2006) and then, in tried and true fashion, replaced by more New York–style storefronts and townhouses and renamed "Park Place" in 2007.

9. Midwest Street

The most influential, beloved, and recognized set at Warner Bros., and probably anywhere in the world, is also the least exotic, glamorous, or flamboyant sector on the lot. In fact, Midwest Street's significance comes from the fact that it is so achingly familiar. It is the small town we all feel like we grew up in, but in which none

The current Midwest Street. Circa 1970.

of us really did. It is the small town that not even Norman Rockwell really grew up in—in fact, the popular illustrator was raised in New York City, and he was probably influenced by movies made on the WB Midwest Street, rather than the other way around.

The shadow this street has cast on American popular culture is so far reaching that people watching this real estate on TV today have no idea that the same set was watched by their parents and by their parents' parents as well. Or that each generation probably assumed against all logic or evidence that their parents or grandparents had probably lived in such a place. Paradoxically, the further away we get from such a reality, the more important and cherished it seems to become. The stereotype is still very much alive, from Mayberry, North Carolina, to River City, Iowa, to Stars Hollow, Connecticut; none of these are real small towns, but they are all part of the same small-town set at Warner Bros.

Warner Bros. was, without a doubt, the most urban of all the major studios. Their pictures were designed to play in cities for city audiences and were primarily set in cities. Jack Warner in particular liked to think of himself as a sharpster, a city slicker quick with a wisecrack and resplendent in his white spats and loud ties. He apparently did not share the reverence for small-town America that was already prevalent even before that way of life had vanished. J.L.'s idea of wistful nostalgia was of the more urban, Gay '90s variety, on display in his productions of *One Sunday Afternoon* (1933), *Strawberry Blonde* (1941), and *Life with Father* (1947). Nevertheless, it was hard to deny that there was a more or less constant need for a small-town set on the lot, if only for contrast with the crime and vice running amok on the other backlot locations.

Dr. Socrates (1935), about a racket-busting small-town physician, was the film for which what had previously been only a town square of sorts was reorganized into an actual district that would come to be known as "Midvale Street," inexplicably, because the town in the film was Big Bend, Indiana. This district lasted for only four years, and after *Socrates*, it seems to have been primarily used for westerns. A "Small Town Street" used concurrently, and later known as "Canadian Street" close to where Parking Lot W is now, served a similar purpose.

Warner Bros.' original "Midvale Street" as Big Bend, Indiana, in *Dr. Socrates* (1935).

Warner Bros. had a surprise success in 1938 with *Four Daughters*, which was set in a small-town America that would have been familiar to many who lived in similar towns, or at least had visited similar towns through non–Warner Bros. productions. So popular was the musically inclined family that the film was centered on, the Lemps, that a sequel, a much rarer occurrence then than now, was immediately commissioned. The entire cast returned, with the exception of John Garfield, who had made his film debut in the first film as a cynical composer, and whose character appeared to have wandered over from nearby Tenement Street anyway. Actually Garfield did make a cameo appearance, as a sort of ghost. Studio records show his much-abbreviated role took only six hours to shoot.

Four Daughters had primarily been shot inside soundstages, with perhaps a few contributions from Midvale Street, but the script for the sequel *Four Wives* (1939) called for more of the town to be seen, enough to justify rebuilding Midvale Street from the ground up. Many of the original buildings were moved, and sidewalks and landscaping were installed. A house, somewhat matching the original Lemp family home from the original film, was constructed, which is still there today.

This new set, originally called "Mid-West Street" or "New Midvale Street," cost an estimated $40,000. A press release at the time trumpeted that "outstanding among the sets constructed for *Four Wives* was a 23 home Midwest town residential section covering two and a half acres and including a park." The mention of "23 homes" was a rather impudent exaggeration. There were originally eight houses in the district. Six of them, or their equivalents, are still there today.

Three years later, the set was improved upon significantly with additional house detailing and new businesses and landscaping for *Kings Row* (1942). For that film the original Lemp house was utilized as the "Drake" home, where Ronald Reagan had his "Where's the rest of me?" moment. That same house has, over the decades, also played James Dean's home in *East of Eden* (1954), the Boyd home in *Damn Yankees* (1958), Marion the Librarians' house in *The Music Man* (1962), and even Michael Jordan's house and yard in *Space Jam* (1996). The back side of the same façade sometimes doubles as the front side of a second house, as it did in television's *The Dukes of Hazzard* (1979–1985) and *Gilmore Girls* (2000–2007).

The other houses on this street, which curves so that a visitor, or camera, cannot see that it only contains but six, are equally storied. If the street can be said to belong to any one individual, that person would probably be Doris Day. It has been estimated that Day made enough movies at the studio to have lived in every house on the street at least once (indicating that the lady was perhaps not so virtuous as her reputation would suggest?). Unforgivably, the houses have not been given permanent names, so surviving records have never indicated exactly which house on the street was being used for which picture. A viewing of the films is helpful, but often the houses were combined both with other residences on the street and with soundstage-constructed duplicates, and the geography of the street itself was constantly altered through editing and via camera angles, and by painted backings that sometimes reflected a conflicting geography, making verification difficult indeed.

It is a fact, however, that Miss Day did use one particular house at least four times. The house on the western corner, closest to the courthouse, was her family homestead in *On Moonlight Bay* (1951) and its sequel, *By the Light of the Silvery Moon* (1953). And it was also her residence in the otherwise unrelated *Young at Heart* (1954)—unrelated except that this film was actually a remake of *Four Daughters*, with Frank Sinatra playing the John Garfield role—and the house where Day marries Errol Flynn in *It's a Great Feeling* (1949). The same house, without any assistance from Doris Day at all, also portrayed the disreputable Lute Mae's Tavern in *Flamingo Road* (1949), the disturbed Plato's home in *Rebel without a Cause* (1955), Julie Harris' house in *Rebel without a Cause* (1955), The Justice of the Peace's residence in *A Summer Place* (1959), Robert Mitchum's boardinghouse in *The Good Guys and the Bad Guys* (1969), and even the Seaver house in the long-running series *Growing Pains* (1985–1992), to name but a few.

None of the houses, it should be noted, are or ever were real. No one, outside of film or television, has ever lived or slept in any of them. Some of them have backs, and some of them even have limited interiors. But they were created, unlike any other homes anywhere, only to be photographed. They elicit emotion, and somehow they provide reassurance and comfort through their familiarity, but paradoxically they are uninhabitable, with no working appliances, furniture, or amenities inside. The entire block influences the real world, without being a part of it. Even the squirrels that live in the trees in the yards in front of these houses appear to be performing a role, rather than living a life. One wonders if they realize it.

The district is crowned by a church on one side of the business area and a courthouse on the other. Façades that can play a variety of small businesses are on the northern side; the residential "Kings Row" area, discussed above, is opposite it. A green park area, with a (removable) gazebo, stands in the center. People visiting the set *always* claim to recognize the gazebo from *The Music Man* (1962), although for that film the gazebo was not there and had, in fact, been replaced with a statue.

The courthouse was damaged in the 1952 fires. It was rebuilt with a second municipal entrance on one side and a fire station door on the other. The back side was, and is, the alleged *Casablanca* wall facing French Street—which again makes one wonder how much of the current set could have been there in 1942. Studio maps from before and after the fire tell us that the shape of the street was also reconfigured slightly this time, although presumably original façades were retained whenever and if ever it was practical to do so.

The courthouse front entrance is often seen on camera; probably its appearances rank in the thousands. However, it seldom got to be the center of attention, except on television, where for example it was the primary setting for *Inherit the Wind* (1999), which contained the last performance of famed Academy Award

The Midwest Street courthouse has a police station on its left side, a firehouse on its right, and part of French Street on the back. 1996.

refuser George C. Scott, and the last episode of the legendary sitcom *Seinfeld* (1990–1998). The side entrance on the south is often a police station entrance, as in *The Chase* (1966), where Robert Redford was shot on the steps leading to the front door, and *Rebel without a Cause* (1955), where James Dean is taken after his arrest for drunkenness.

The origins of the church opposite the courthouse are somewhat mysterious. It has often been referred to as the *Johnny Belinda* (1948) church. And it does seem to date from that period. But production records and a viewing of the film prove irrefutably that the actual church used was the Mendocino Presbyterian Church in Northern California. Furthermore, publicity materials for the picture even tell us that Reverend J. W. Kooyers and his congregation were paid $15.56 each per day to work as extras—plus an additional $6.67 for singing onscreen in the church choir.

Studio records regarding the backlot church are not so definitive. Before 1948, storefronts (some of them the backsides of nearby Norwegian Street façades) occupied the space, but about that time, it is irrefutable that a white-steepled church façade, which still survives today, rose on the street and ultimately proved to be the right and perfect addition to the set, to the point where it is hard to imagine how the street ever worked without it. The church is actually only a church from the front. One side entrance is often redressed to play a town meeting hall; and the opposite side, with the proper signage, can be another storefront. From the back, when the camera is placed in just the right spot, the line of the roof perfectly obscures the

The iconic Midwest Street church and James Dean. 1954.

steeple, and the building can ingeniously double for a one-room schoolhouse. What all this means is that, in theory, this one building could play four different roles in the same project, or in four different projects.

Examples? For *The FBI Story* (1959), James Stewart married Vera Miles in the church. In the television reunion movie *A Walton Wedding* (1995), John-Boy tied the knot here as well. In the original *Ocean's Eleven* (1960), the film's church-funeral climax was staged in the building (which has a working interior). In *Blazing Saddles* (1974), it was the Rock Ridge Church; and most exotically, for an episode of *Lois and Clark: The New Adventures of Superman* (1993–1997), an onion-shaped dome was placed on the steeple so that the church could play part of a Russian village!

The business district contains a turnoff into a pleasant alley or side street (no Tenement Street film noir darkness here), a bank building with columns, changeable

The Midwest Street church as dressed with snow for *Gremlins* (1984).

storefronts (including a small-town movie theater façade, which was replaced in the 1980s), and at the very end, opposite the church, a beautiful Victorian building with a tower on its roof.

This last building anchors the street from its corner just as the church and the courthouse do from theirs. As the "Metropole Saloon," this structure found cinematic glory in 1976's *The Shootist*, when John Wayne, with blazing guns, finished his cinematic career here. Interestingly, the same set, with the expensive addition of a railroad line, had been a primary location for legendary director John Ford's last western *Cheyenne Autumn* (1964), one of his few sound films in that genre *without* Wayne.

Midwest Street was also a location for *Yankee Doodle Dandy* (1942), where James Cagney's character was born during an Independence Day parade; for *East of Eden* (1954), where James Dean takes a Ferris wheel ride with Julie Harris; and *Cool Hand Luke* (1967), where Paul Newman cut the heads off of a row of parking meters and was sent to a chain gang. The street was even the location of an annoyingly catchy Dr. Pepper commercial from 1980 ("I'm a Pepper, you're a Pepper").

Midwest Street has continued to be the most popular backlot location at the studio right up to the present, averaging 125 working days a year. Recently, the

Coen brothers used the set in the George Clooney vehicle *O Brother, Where Art Thou?* (2000); Eddie Murphy clowned on it in *Norbit* (2006); Clint Eastwood used it to double for Centralia, Washington, in *J. Edgar* (2011); and *The Muppets* (2012) staged a musical number on the street, which played the berg of "Smalltown." The casting was perfect.

10. Western Street

It's somewhat surprising that Warner Bros. didn't have a permanent western street on their lot until 1956. The reason for this isn't that Warner Bros. didn't make westerns, as the stereotype would imply. In fact, they made almost as many "oaters" (as *Variety* insists on calling films of the genre to this very day) as any other studio, including some undisputed classics of the genre, such as *The Searchers* (1956), *Rio Bravo* (1959), *The Wild Bunch* (1969), and *Unforgiven* (1992) (as if examples are required). The explanation is that many of their westerns were made on distant locations, and many of the local ones were shot on a very long, very detailed western street at the studio ranch in Calabasas. Interiors for Warner westerns were indeed shot on the lot, inside the soundstages. Oftentimes, exteriors were shot inside these stages as well. Canadian Street or Midwest Street could be used for westerns not desiring to go off-lot as needed.

In December 1956, however, with usage of the ranch falling into disfavor due to industry-wide belt-tightening measures, and with television and television's quicker production methods becoming the norm rather than the exception at all the majors, a permanent western street was finally constructed beneath Midwest Street for *Shootout at Medicine Bend* (1957).

The set rose on the site of the old Philadelphia Street, which consisted of a colonial-style row of shops and storefronts that had been erected for *Alexander Hamilton* (1931), a vehicle for the prestigious, but aging, stage star George Arliss. Occasionally, Philadelphia Street itself would be subsequently referred to as "Hamilton Street."

Eventually Western Street grew to encompass Canadian Street as well. Canadian Street, sometimes known as Small Town Street, was basically a western set anyway. The district had been constructed in 1930, probably for *River's End*, which was hardly the first of a surprisingly large subgenre of Warner Bros. films concerning themselves with the frost-bitten adventures of the Royal Canadian Mounted Police. The roots of this interest in the Mounties probably originated with one successful Rin Tin Tin adventure or another, several of which had successfully mined "northern" themes and settings. Canadian Street was still being used as late as the 1950s for the TV series *The Alaskans* (1959–1960). When Western Street was first erected, the hill that part of Canadian Street had been built into had to be leveled. Another nearby set, Norwegian Street, constructed in 1942 for *Edge of Darkness*, vanished or was incorporated during this period as well.

Western Street was constructed on the site of the old Philadelphia Street, which dated from 1931.

Originally the set followed a slightly curved line behind the residential section of Midwest Street. Eventually it assumed an "L" shape as it expanded into the footprint of the Canadian and Norwegian sets. It also absorbed an old property shed, a fighting ring set, and the battleship fuselage mentioned earlier. Western Street eventually ran all the way down into the edge of the scene dock area bordering the Los Angeles River.

Midwest Street and Western Street, because of their similarities and proximity to one another, were able to share several buildings and could be used simultaneously. The Midwest Street church, in particular, could be used as part of either setting. In fact, most of the houses on the eastern side of Kings Row had western façades built into where their back yards should have been. One of them represented a rural tack shed and farmyard that is still there today.

As expected, the new set was a successful location from the very start. Westerns, before this, had been popular mostly with children and rural audiences. Big-budget westerns by major directors like John Ford and Cecil B. DeMille had been successful but comparatively rare until the 1950s, when the Cold War and its ramifications made the concept of a lone cowboy, a horse, and an endless horizon seem appealing to suburbanites and to their families.

Western Street as dressed for *Blazing Saddles* (1974). Note the Midwest Street church on the left.

Tellingly, Warner Bros.' first TV series consisted of a revolving wheel of adaptations of their feature films *Casablanca*, *Kings Row*, and *Cheyenne*. Only *Cheyenne* (1955–1963) was a success. That series' star, Clint Walker, who only a few years before had been a security guard at the studio, epitomized on the small screen the same qualities of self-reliance and fortitude that John Wayne was embodying in Cinemascope and Technicolor on the big screen, and at a fraction of the cost. Astonishingly, the 6-foot, 6-inch Walker, a lifelong fitness buff, used to enjoy jogging off-lot during his lunch break to the top of the very formidable Hollywood hills, which were often visible on camera from Western Street, before returning to the studio to complete his day's work.[5]

The success of *Cheyenne* led, in rapid succession, to other Warner Bros. television westerns in the 1950s and 1960s, including *Sugarfoot* (1957–1961), *Maverick* (1957–1962), *Colt .45* (1957–1960), *Lawman* (1958–1962), and *Bronco* (1958–1962), all of which contributed to the remarkable total of twenty-six westerns crowding the prime-time schedule in 1959 alone. No other genre has ever dominated the medium to this extent. Eventually Warner Bros. had to build two more western districts on their backlot in order to accommodate all this production. And still crews kept bumping into each other, gunshots fired for one program would be recorded on the soundtracks of the units shooting down the street, a chase scene for *Maverick* would spill over into a saloon brawl being staged for *Bronco*, and so on.

As was perhaps inevitable, the western had largely become self-reflective and nostalgic about its own saddle-worn conventions by the 1970s—sentiments that the laconic and non-introspective cowboy heroes of these programs would not have understood. *Kung Fu* (1972–1975), about a half-Chinese martial arts expert adrift in the west, was just the sort of oddity that the genre needed at the time. But that series' success would mark the last time a Warner Bros. western would survive more than a single season of production on the backlot.

The conventions of the genre as a theatrical medium were changing as well. Familiar sets that had represented the frontier for decades, and that had been long unquestioned by audiences because of their very familiarity, were suddenly considered unacceptable for the same reason. In 1968, producer Phil Feldman wrote a memo to studio head Kenneth Hyman regarding director Sam Peckinpah's refusal to use Western Street for his upcoming *The Ballad of Cable Hogue* (1970). "One of the fetishes Sam and I have is that buildings look like real buildings and not like sets," he complained. Hyman must have listened, because ultimately the film was shot in Arizona and Nevada and not on Western Street.

In its last years, with the near death of westerns on both big and small screens, most of the films that utilized Western Street were either satirical or not westerns at all. *Blazing Saddles* (1974) was an outrageous and successful send-up of the genre, made all the funnier, and richer, because it was made on the site of some of that genre's greatest and most straight-faced triumphs. The film concludes with a raucous fistfight involving the entire cast and climaxing with the camera pulling back from street level to bird level, where it is revealed that the entire film, and perhaps life itself, is actually and in fact taking place on the Warner Bros. backlot.

Westworld (1973) was a science fiction picture about a Disneyland-style amusement park where guests could live out their Wild West fantasies in a western town populated by robotic cowboys. The film was produced by MGM, which had demolished their own western street three years earlier. The barn where the gunshot robots were taken for repair every night was the back of the Midwest Street home, already referenced above, which survives today.

That structure is all that does remain. On July 20, 1983, a fire once again started on the backlot. This fire was farther south, and ultimately not as devastating as the twin 1952 blazes. But the 125-foot-high flames, which took forty-five minutes for the studio and Burbank City fire departments to extinguish, destroyed all of Western Street and partially destroyed the houses on the eastern side of King's Row as well. As the TV series *The Dukes of Hazzard* (1979–1985) was constantly utilizing those homes at the time, and a feature film, *Gremlins* (1984), was shooting on that street as well, new sets had to be immediately, and exactly, rebuilt to match the originals. Unfortunately, Western Street was unused at the time and so the studio decided there was no call to rebuild those façades. At least not right away.

That call to rebuild the street never came. Today the spot where a thousand bad guys greeted cinematic oblivion is the site of studio parking lot W.

The site of Western Street in 1998. Parking lot W.

11. Mexican Street

Until the 1950s the real estate east of Avon Street (a largely residential avenue that currently funnels into Gate 5) was never used for permanent backlot construction. The area was largely an open, grassy pasture upon which flats were stored and temporary sets were constructed, photographed, and then disassembled. The lath house and the Greens Department claimed the northern part of the area, so industrial sheds and greenhouses were the only part of the parcel that had been developed at all.

It is surprising that this real estate, originally leased by the studio, was so little used. During an era when the studio's output approached or even exceeded a picture a week, one would assume that every acre, every yard, would be vital indeed. Actress Joan Leslie, who was there during this period, has said that things were so hectic and frantic that there was little time for expanding the infrastructure of the lot, however beneficial it may have ultimately been to do so. "It's a myth that those were golden days at Warner Bros.," she has remarked. "We worked six days a week! The place was a big, noisy, industrial site. The streets were muddy and dirty and crowded, and everyone was stressed and tired and overworked. The studio lot is much prettier, and more genteel, now than it ever was back then."[6]

In the 1950s, however, the pace slowed and permanent, or at least more permanent, sets started to appear on this real estate. Mexican Street was constructed in the early 1960s on the real estate parcel between Avon and Lima Streets. Along with Western Street and the nearby Laramie Street, the set was a primary location for most of the westerns the studio was helping to saturate the television market with at the time.

Mexican Street's viability was not restricted to south-of-the-border locations, however. It was medieval England in *Camelot* (1967); a Greek village in *America, America* (1963); and Albania in *Mrs. Pollifax—Spy* (1971). In 1965, the entire set was rebuilt and enlarged for Frank Sinatra's *Marriage on the Rocks*. The studio continued to use the setting, often as a rental set for independent producers, until it was dismantled in 1984 in order to construct a horseshoe-shaped 31,000-square-foot office complex (which today is known as Building 136, or Producers 8).

An earlier Mexican Street, "Mexican Plaza," stood, for a brief period, slightly west of its younger brother discussed above, in the 1930s.

12. Laramie Street

In September 1957, an employee reading the in-house newspaper *The Warner Club News* may have noticed some photos of a new western street being constructed only a year after the last one. The reason for this second set was cited as being the four western programs scheduled to shoot on the lot the following season. Interestingly, this article also mentions one of the shows, *Maverick*, as starring James Garner as "one of two brothers,"[7] although people associated with the show have always maintained that Garner was not given a brother until eight episodes into production, when it was realized that a single lead would prohibit multiple units from shooting at the same time, and so slow down production.

The new western town was to be constructed on the farthest reaches of the backlot on the southern tip of the parcel of land between Avon and California Streets. The district, designed by art director Perry Ferguson, was to be called the "TV Western Street," but the name was immediately changed to Laramie Street instead when it was realized that no respectable feature film would want to shoot on a set designated for television, although some early lot maps included the original name.

Laramie Street was named for the town of Laramie, Wyoming, which was the primary location for the series *Lawman* (1958–1962) and the set's most constant tenant in the early years. It consisted of a wide and dusty boulevard running north-south, with a smaller street running parallel to it on the east and a couple of cut-throughs to move from one street to another. The way the street was segregated enabled more than one unit to shoot on the set at the same time, a near necessity considering the amount of product being produced in the late 1950s, but definitely problematic; Will Hutchins, the star of *Sugarfoot* (1957–1961), recalls that he once drove several cattle into a nearby *Maverick* set.[8]

Watching any of these early westerns, it's difficult to believe how little location work was involved in their production. Little was needed. If the camera was required to be more than a few feet back from the action and the actors, stock footage, culled from thousands of hours of Warner Bros. features, would be intercut to expand the scope of the scene. Usually a similar architectural feature from the older film would be replicated on the newer set—a pair of swinging saloon doors, for example. A viewer's eye would accept both sets as being the same, because of the similarity of those doors.

Actors were used the same way. Costumes from feature films were re-created (or the originals pulled from storage) and worn by the television casts, so that Errol Flynn's twenty-year-old fall from a horse, for example, could now be attributed to James Garner, wearing Flynn's hat and coat, and presumably riding a younger horse. Even the scripts were from stock. For example, a 1955 *Cheyenne* episode, "The Argonauts," is actually a not-so-disguised remake of the feature film *The Treasure of the Sierra Madre* (1949). And because much of Laramie Street's physical makeup came from the studio's well-supplied scene docks, the only thing new was the actors—when in close-up, anyway.

The street was built on the cheap. Those initial stock buildings came close to fulfilling the movie studio cliché about backlots consisting of single walls facing a street and supported by rickety two-by-fours. Unlike most of the backlots constructed by the majors, there was little electricity available on the set. Portable generators had to be driven in as if the unit was shooting on a distant location somewhere. When the street needed to be changed or visually altered, new walls were nailed on top of the existing ones, eventually creating a fascinating archeological record of what had shot on the set.

By the mid-1960s, another district, slightly isolated from the rest of the set and consisting of a row of clapboard houses along the studio's eastern berm, was being rented out as yet another set, "Mining Town," although this new "set" was really just a Laramie Street annex.

The remarkable glut of television westerns did not last, of course, although surprisingly, Laramie Street survived them all by decades, and by studio standards became both permanent and venerated. In 1981, amid great fanfare, James Garner returned to Warner Bros. and his best known character for *Bret Maverick* (1981–1982). For the occasion, and because, unlike in the original, this series was going to be set almost entirely in a single western town in Arizona, the studio decided to give the street a major rebuild. Rickety buildings, or building fronts, including several damaged in yet another (October 1980) studio fire, were knocked over or shored up. Interiors were constructed on many of the structures, including an ornate saloon and brothel with a long bar, and even a second floor with rooms for conducting business. A jail, a second saloon, a watchtower, a blacksmith's shop, and a courthouse all added to the district's comparative realism. An adobe church was also part of the reconstituted set, but that structure was one of the few backlot sets ever damaged in an earthquake, so it was ultimately replaced with yet another saloon.

In 1981, this rather ornate saloon was added to Laramie Street for the series *Brett Maverick*.

Unfortunately, *Brett Maverick* failed to capture the quirky magic of the original series and only lasted one season. With the long-ago demolition of their Western Street at the Warner Ranch, and the studio fire that destroyed the studio's other western street in 1984, Laramie Street, what it stood for, and, yes, the money that had so recently been spent on it took on a new air of importance. Studio employees new on the lot in the 1980s assumed that the street went back to the 1930s at least, and told their gullible visiting relatives that the street was the longtime home of every western icon from John Wayne to Clint Eastwood, although it's debatable whether either of those venerable actors ever worked on the set. Wayne, or at least a Wayne film, *The Cowboys* (1972), apparently shot something on the street somewhere. But most of Eastwood's westerns were shot in Europe or distant locations, although Clint was certainly familiar with the set and posed for an amusing Annie Leibovitz photo on the street once.

But as fewer westerns were made and more studios demolished their western street sets, Laramie Street became more and more of a beloved anachronism, although, in the 1990s, when westerns made a bit of a comeback with the duel Oscar winners *Dances with Wolves* (1990) and *Unforgiven* (1992), the studio was able to make some coin with television movies, commercials, documentaries, music videos, and even corporate parties on the street.

One of these projects was the first new television series to shoot on the street in many a year, *The Adventures of Brisco County Jr.* (1993–1994)—which kept the street busy every day for what, lamentably, would only be a single-season run. Another was a feature film, *Wild Bill* (1995), from MGM, with Jeff Bridges as Wild Bill Hickok. For this later project, the Art Department playfully painted "Cable Television" on one of the set windows as a joke on director Walter Hill. No one noticed, however, and there was talk of painting another sign, this one labeled "Sushi Bar." At the last minute, Hill, or someone, realized what was going on and had the window changed.

Yet another project, this one more nostalgic, was the television documentary *Big Guns Talk: The Story of the Western* (1997), which happily brought James Garner back to the set for the last time, dressed in his *Maverick* costume and standing on the street reading cue-card platitudes about the whole genre. When the director called "cut," Garner would be led inside one of the façades to a portable air conditioner to cool off for a minute before being called back onto the street and its authentically brutal temperatures.

In 2000, the street's southern tip was chopped off in order to set up storage space for production trailers. Dutifully, the impact of such a compromise to the set's viability as a location was taken into account first, and it was discovered that by building a western-style wall of storefronts along the edge of the compromised area, the sightlines would not be permanently impacted.

It didn't matter. The mini-western boom of the 1990s had burned itself out, and there was so little production during this period that the street ended up being used as a scene dock. The studio's single major western of the period, *Wild Wild West* (1999), made little use of the set, although Will Smith's accompanying music video gave whoever might have cared a last look at the location.

It wasn't quite the last look. Very sharp-eyed viewers may also have recognized the set out of context in its very last appearance. A sequence for *The Last Samurai* (2003), set in nineteenth-century Japan, was shooting in an adjacent lake set when someone noticed that through the camera viewfinder, the façades of some of Laramie Street's rooftops were visible at the very top of the frame. Quickly, someone was dispatched to the Staff Shop and Asian-style tile was pressed out of plastic and nailed to the offending structures. It's fortunate that they did so because some of these buildings are indeed visible onscreen in the finished film.

Clearly something had to be done. Gary Credle, executive vice president of administration and studio operations, found himself faced with a serious dilemma. On the one hand, the set was basically "sitting there fallow,"[9] as he put it. And yet, because this was one of the last western streets in Hollywood (of all the major lots, only Universal still maintained such a set at the time), he realized that he was in danger of stripping away what made his studio feel "like" a studio, as opposed to a collection of offices with a fence around it. He realized that there was value, and even branding opportunities, in cliché. Additionally, the set was a very popular stop on the studio tour, and with fans who sometimes made pilgrimages from all over the globe for a look at the dusty street. Studio employees, as well, many of whom were inordinately proud of Laramie Street, had complained loudly when the edge of the set had been removed, and had threatened an all-out revolt if the street were compromised further.

But Credle had always insisted that the studio was to be used for production, first and last, and that any other usage of the property, for tourism, historical context, or sentiment, would be a violation of the lot's ultimate purpose and its very reason for existence. He decided to remove the set and replace it with a row of two-story production offices that could double as Cape Cod–style homes—in other words, a front lot and a backlot on the same property.

Cannily, he deflected public outrage by not announcing to the press what he was doing until the deed was already done. He realized this tactic would not work with his own employees, however. So he bought them off by inviting the whole lot to a "Goodbye to Laramie Street" party on Tuesday, May 13, 2003—with a free barbecue! The food succeeded in quelling any internal dissent, but Cradle wisely also arranged that the actual destruction took place very quickly, and over the following weekend, when few would be on the lot to watch the carnage.

I remember walking through the entire set many times in those last days. I took a friend from out of town, not involved in show business, to the studio a couple days before the party. We walked across the lot to the now-abandoned location, even though, atypically, the sky was black, a cold wind was blowing, and it was pouring rain. We sloshed through the muddy streets and into the comparative shelter of one of the condemned saloons, which itself was half flooded with water and mud. Neither of us wanted to stay long, for different reasons. And I don't think my friend had any idea why I was so upset.

Not surprisingly, the following week I found myself battling a persistent flu. But I returned to Laramie Street again and again in those last days to try to decide what to save for the company before the Caterpillars arrived and made the decision for me. In the end, a few windows, the ornate saloon bar (although it only dated from 1981), and, of course, the iconic western swinging doors were salvaged. On the day of the party, I'll always remember walking forlornly with a raging fever and a plate full of barbecue, and listening to my fellow employees talking about the street and what it meant to them.

At the last minute, calls were made to the owners of Melody Ranch, an independent western location in Newhall, to see if they wanted any of the structures themselves, but it was quickly determined that the aged buildings could not be safely, or feasibly, transported. And so over the weekend the Caterpillars took them all instead.

At the party, an employee contest had been held to determine what the name of the new set would be. The rather unimaginative but decidedly accurate moniker "Warner Village" was the eventual winner. The houses that made up this new set, because of their responsibility to satisfy as both production space and production offices, are—contrary to the legend about backlot structures being smaller than full scale—actually somewhat too large and too uniform to look like actual residential homes. But productions, mostly television productions, have taken repeated advantage of the set all the same.

So Laramie Street, the studio's last period-specific set, now survives only as a pair of swinging saloon doors, a bar, and a few panes of glass. To film fans and to a few aging employees it is still a lot more, however. "Laramie Street was just like home to me," one of those employees, James Garner, recalled. "I don't think you could walk three feet in any direction . . . that I haven't done a scene on."[10]

13. Tatum Ranch/Fort Courage

Adjacent to Laramie Street from the late 1950s onward, a grouping of three farm-style buildings stood in a triangular clearing with the western set as a backdrop from one side and a forested area, the "Jungle," on the other. The origins of the name "Tatum Ranch," as the set was called, have since been forgotten.

In 1965 the studio sold a pilot for a rather unusual western, *F Troop* (1965–1967). Promotional materials have always stated that the show was set in Kansas, but although there were occasional references to "riding up to Dodge City" in the series itself, no location was ever specified.

Wherever the show was set, however, a U.S. cavalry fort, somewhere out west, was to be the series' location. Unfortunately, no similar set existed on the lot, although *Charge at Feather River* (1953), *Fort Dobbs* (1958), and *Cheyenne Autumn* (1964) all had cavalry settings, so there were probably stock units and painted backdrops representing such a location to be found on the lot at the time. The *Fort Dobbs* outpost was actually a standing set in Kanub, Utah, built for the earlier *Fort Yuma* (1955) and rented to the production, but it isn't inconceivable that pieces of the set were duplicated in Burbank as well. In fact the daily production reports indicate that a "fort wall" was re-created on the backlot, although how extensive it was, or where on the backlot it stood, can no longer be determined.

But even with the assistance of these cavalry-picture leftovers, it quickly became obvious that a rather substantial amount of construction was called for, something that the tightfisted Mr. Warner had never before approved for television. For Jack Warner, an example of an expensive television location had been the awning he had ordered constructed for the successful *77 Sunset Strip* (1958–1964)—and that had been on a soundstage. What's more, *F Troop* was a lowly situation comedy. Sitcoms had been shot on the lot before, but this was the first to utilize feature-film-sized sets.

Ultimately, it was decided to construct these sets next to Laramie Street on a five-acre parcel at the Tatum Ranch location. The original farmhouse was converted into the C.O.'s headquarters, the barn into a barracks, and so on. The walls of the compound, and even the famous, always-falling-over watchtower, matched those same settings on *Fort Dobbs* so closely that whenever there was an Indian attack, stock footage from the earlier film, still the best friend of Warner Bros. editors, could be inserted for the wide shots. Although the Utah desert terrain from the feature hardly lined up with the forested real estate on the lot, the editors heedlessly spliced the two locations together anyway and let them fight it out.

The fort opened from the front into the Warner Bros. Jungle set and from the back into the town of Fort Courage (Laramie Street). There was allegedly some complaining in the Administration Building about how much of the backlot was being taken up by a single thirty-minute series. James Hampton, who played the world's most inept bugler, recalled that the series' budget also managed to support a "combination golf cart and wet bar, owned and operated by series star Forrest Tucker, which was driven onto the set every afternoon for a pick me up."[11]

F Troop ultimately lasted only two seasons, after which the fort was eventually disassembled. The current whereabouts of the golf cart are likewise unknown.

14. Jungle

The most unique set on the Warner Bros. backlot is this combination of hundreds of real trees, vines, shrubs, and plants, most of which, including vast thickets of

Forrest Tucker's well-remembered *F Troop* combination wet bar–golf cart, surrounded here by a most appreciative cast: Ken Berry, James Hampton, Tucker, and Melody Patterson. 1965.

bamboo, would not grow in Burbank otherwise, and carefully imported, or created, rocks, caves, ponds, and lakes.

Although the set was crafted specifically for the Alan Ladd vehicle *Santiago* (1956), art director Edward Carrere was instructed to create a permanent setting to be utilized by other productions after his own, "thus effecting large savings in time and transportation to far locations,"[12] as the studio newsletter put it at the time. Therefore, unusual detail was incorporated into a set that otherwise would have probably consisted of a few potted plants and plaster rocks in a corner of a sound-stage. Dirt-moving equipment created berms, which encircled three-quarters of the set and themselves were landscaped with thick foliage in order to make the area seem much larger and more isolated than it was.

A 250,000-gallon lake, with a 4-foot asphalt bottom, was designed with the capability to be refilled for other productions. Its unusual shape was cleverly plotted out to always evoke the illusion that the lake continued beyond where one could see from any single vantage point along its shores. The TV series *The F.B.I.* (1965–1974) later added a shack to one corner of the shore that, surprisingly, is still there, and was utilized by Clint Eastwood for the very last scene in his Oscar-winning *Million Dollar Baby* (2004).

In some ways, naming this set a "jungle" does the place a disservice, since it is, in fact, suitable for any outdoor, natural setting. Very few people notice what sort of plant is standing behind an actor if the actor is a good one. "A tree is a tree, a rock

The studio Jungle and lake dressed for a Budweiser commercial featuring some very talkative frogs. 1995.

is a rock. Shoot it in Griffith Park," as MGM's Louis B. Mayer allegedly said. And so very often, although vast outdoor sequences would in fact be recorded in the vast outdoors, closer scenes, often involving stars or animals, could be shot in the controlled settings available here. No matter if the trees didn't quite match up with the ones on location. Will Hutchins once remarked how funny it was to have to report to a "jungle" to shoot a western.[13]

The studio also maintained wooden A-frames on wheels with real branches stapled onto the sides, which could be rolled into position to provide "portable jungle" for backgrounds. Interestingly, when the branches on these frames would dry up and turn brown, they could be painted green and reused, apparently forever.

The set at one point included a lot of boulders, sometimes known as the "B-52 Rocks" after *Bombers, B-52* (1957), which could be stacked or arranged as needed for scenes involving cliffs or Anthony Mann–style rock shootouts. As the jungle filled in, many of these pieces were moved south to a district called "Devil's Gulch." An abbreviated cave set and a cluster of rocks constructed on wheels remained behind, however, and were still being used into the mid-1990s. The wheeled rock formation had the *Bonanza* logo stenciled into its (hollow) interior, which indicated its probable origin and vintage.

In the northern end of the jungle stood a farmhouse set, sometimes referred to as "Doonevan Flats," which started playing ranches and rural homes when the "Tatum Ranch" set was conscripted into the U.S. Calvary. The house, with an adjacent barn, first achieved some recognizability on television as the home of *F Troop* alumni Ken Berry for the later years of the series *Mayberry R.F.D* (1968–1971). Almost immediately afterward the same set, with scant modification, was converted into the family farmhouse for *The Waltons* (1972–1981) when that series' creator, Earl Hamner Jr., noticed its resemblance to his own family home in Schuyler, Virginia.

The Waltons, based on Hamner's own life growing up during the Great Depression, would be a tenant on the lot for more than a decade, and television reunion movies would extend its influence over the lot even further. The jungle lake would often be seen as Grucilla's Pond; Midwest Street would be Charlottesville, Virginia; another corner of the jungle would include Ike Godsey's General Store; and at least two Walton children would get married in the backlot church. The house itself had sides, but no back, explaining why the backyard was never glimpsed in all those years; it became so familiar that it was difficult for at least two generations of employees or guests to walk up the unpaved lane leading to the house without hearing Hamner's voice drawling, as it did in every episode, "When I was a boy growing up in the Blue Ridge Mountains of Virginia . . ."

Those mountains were actually played, usually, by the nearby Hollywood hills of Burbank, and the greenery that viewers thought they were seeing was actually sage and scrub trees, with a pine tree branch or two in the foreground to obscure that fact.

I visited the set of one of the *Walton* reunion movies once. The original cast was all in front of the house (a very strange sight), waiting for their cue. I happened to walk by two of the now adult Walton sons (I don't remember which ones) and overheard one of them asking where the bathroom was at. "Just go in back of the house, like we used to," the other replied. I remember making a mental note about taking care in exploring that part of the set in the future!

The Waltons ended its original run in 1981. But no one quite had the heart to remove the family farmhouse. It stood for ten years until Friday, November 22, 1991, when someone, apparently a disgruntled employee, set fire to the set. Almost all of the house and part of the nearby barn, as well as some trees, were destroyed in the blaze.

In 1992, however, the series' continuing success in syndication encouraged Hamner to reassemble the cast for a television movie, *A Walton Thanksgiving Reunion* (1993). The house was as key a factor in the series' popularity as that cast was, however, so there was nothing to do but rebuild the house practically from the ground up on the original site, which was done. The same year a feature film named *Sleepwalkers*, based on a Stephen King story, rather ironically used the home as the scene of several grisly murders. Afterward, it was partially rebuilt yet again to play a rustic ranch cabin in *The Adventures of Brisco County Jr.* (1993–1994).

The next year, management decided that they would chop the jungle in half in order to build a parking lot for the adjacent Warner Records Building. This meant that the house, as well as the cave, the rock formations, half the trees, and even Ike Godsey's Store, would have to be sacrificed in the name of . . . parking.

The previous *Walton* reunion movies had been ratings winners, and the studio was eager to keep the franchise alive, if at all possible. A new TV movie, *A Walton Easter* (1997), had already been greenlit. But they most definitely did not want to have to rebuild the house for a third time. With the demolition date approaching, they decided that the solution was to transport the house up the road a half mile to the Warner Ranch property. In one corner of that auxiliary backlot, there was a tropical area, densely forested, where, ironically, the set for Hamner's *Apple's Way* (1974–1975) had once stood. The house was moved there.

As of this writing, the much traveled, and much rebuilt, Walton house is still standing in a clearing in the trees at the Warner Bros. Ranch. It has most recently been seen as the Dragonfly Inn (in Connecticut) in the TV series *Gilmore Girls* (2000–2007).

15. Camelot Castle

Castles are a rarity in California. Except for the Disneyland castle in Anaheim, most California castles have been of the backlot variety. (The Disney castle is arguably of that species as well.)

Warner Bros. constructed several castles on this property and at the ranch in Calabasas over the decades. This one was the most elaborate and detailed, although miraculously, it came at the very end of the studio era and was constructed almost as a rebuttal to the rapid encroachment of new techniques and new realism in cinema at the time. What, after all, could be less practical, less realistic, and more old-fashioned than a medieval castle in suburban Burbank?

In 1966, Jack Warner was seventy-four years old. One of the films the old tycoon was proudest of had been *My Fair Lady* (1964)—which, in spite of its eventual critical and box office success, had been a risky and unusual product for a studio never known for making highbrow musicals, British drawing-room comedies, or adaptions of George Bernard Shaw. *My Fair Lady* was all of the above, and its success proved, at least to J.L., that his studio could make a classy, MGM-style picture and do it during a risky period when MGM, or any other studio in Hollywood, might not have been able to pull it off.

For a follow-up, Warner again looked to the stage. *Camelot* had, like *Lady*, been a smash hit on Broadway and in London; had a musical score by Alan J. Lerner and Frederick Loewe; and had "class" in a British sort of idiom that appealed to his striving American sensibilities in a way that J.L. probably wouldn't have admitted to or understood.

It probably never occurred to Warner *not* to make his film at his studio, although a location trip to Spain for some backgrounds eventually supplemented the massive sets he constructed within the gates of his fiefdom. These sets included the castle, which by itself cost $2.5 million to erect; an adjacent village; and corresponding interiors, as well as exterior forests and snowy meadows to be created in the Jungle and inside soundstages.

Most impressive was the castle itself. Art director Eugene Lourie, who scouted the then derelict set in 1972 for television, and in fact did use the set as a Chinese temple in the series *Kung Fu* (1972–1975), remembered that "the set was strange indeed. A large, flagstone paved yard was flanked on one side by a high crenelated wall; on the other side was a cloister-like colonnade, and on the third side, high rocks. The roughly U-shaped set was open on the fourth side, probably for the best long shot camera angle. The set had many terraces and stairs, and this multi-leveled construction was fitted for spectacular stagings."[14]

Lourie probably didn't know that the rock wall was adapted from the earlier Devil's Gulch set, or that the village under the set partially consisted of elements of the adjacent Mexican Street. But he was right that the set was "strange indeed." It was constructed more or less full scale, but like the lake in the jungle it looked even bigger than it was because its battlements seemed to continue beyond where a spectator or a camera could see. Because it was impossible to take in the whole set from any one vantage point, it was difficult to determine what specifically the set looked like, architecturally. All of this undoubtedly made it easier to intercut the Burbank

The storied battlements of the *Camelot* castle—here dressed to play an Asian temple in the TV series *Kung Fu* (1972–1975).

castle with the several actual European fortresses whose likenesses were secured on location. So the final impression that Camelot, both the castle and *Camelot* the film, gives us is of a castle that looks different and suggests different imagery every time we see it and wherever it is glimpsed from. Art director Edward Carrere perhaps was working under instructions to make the edifice vague and nondescript so that it could be reused (a most optimistic conjecture, considering how little production was going on in Hollywood at the time). Or perhaps he wanted the castle to be indistinct and somewhat dreamlike, in keeping with the transient, fleeting feeling that the film itself, with all of its talk of a world moving on, evokes.

But neither audiences nor critics were impressed with whatever it was the movie or its sets, or its producer, were trying so hard to visualize. Many reviews concentrated on how cheap the film looked, although the budget had been colossal—almost $15 million. In the face of withering reviews, the film's director, Joshua Logan, complained publicly about having to shoot the picture on a backlot—although the realism of location shooting would have probably crushed the fantasy elements even quicker than the dried-out California hills visible in back of the castle ultimately destroyed any sense of being in an authentic medieval setting. Logan had earlier been in consideration to direct My *Fair Lady*, but had fumbled the opportunity when he had tried to convince Warner that the movie should be done on location in England.

Camelot would mark the end of large-scale backlot production in California. Never again for a top-shelf feature film would a major studio try to evoke a distant location using the smoke and mirrors and tricks and crafts that had convinced audiences for decades that Southern California could be anywhere and play anything. In the future, with some notable exceptions, backlots would be used for television. Standing sets, when used for feature films, would supplement real locations, not the other way around.

But *Camelot* marked the end of an era in a more personal sense as well. The film opened on November 26, 1967. On the same day, Albert Warner died in Miami Beach, Florida. He was eighty-four years old.

Jack Warner, then, was the last Warner brother standing. But time was running out for him as well. *Camelot* was to be his last film at the studio. While it was in production, he sold his interests in the company for $32 million to Seven Arts, an operation that previously had primarily financed and sold films to television.

On a hot day in July 1967, Jack spent his last hours as boss of the company he and his brothers had created. At some point early in the day, he probably realized the futility of trying to work and went home. Ironically, this was the same day that a twenty-two-year-old film student from the University of Southern California, George Lucas, arrived at the studio to begin a paid internship as winner of the Sam Warner scholarship. Lucas remarked to an associate about how quiet and somber the studio was, and was informed that Jack L. Warner had left the lot just about the same time that Lucas had arrived. Neither man knew it, of course; history doesn't work that way; but apparently on that day old Hollywood drove out the gates just as New Hollywood drove through them. The first half of film history folded into the second. One era became another.

It was all a little like something out of *Camelot*.

SIX

....

Into Hollywood's Future

THE IDEA was that J.L. Warner would initially produce films independently for the company. But Jack quickly discovered that he had no real duties and that every idea he pitched to the new management was rejected. He quickly tired of being a figurehead.

Perhaps the Seven Arts kingpins, Elliot Hyman and his son Kenneth, should have listened to the old tycoon, because after less than two years, in July 1969, the floundering company was sold again, at a significant profit, this time to Kinney National Company. Steven J. Ross, the dynamic founder of that company whose rags-to-riches life story was similar to that of the Warners, installed Ted Ashley, a former agent, of all things, in Jack's old office. From his window, Ashley could still see the ivy that Warner had insisted upon clinging to the wall of Stage 1, although he never, as far as anyone could remember, remarked upon it. In 1972 the parent company would be renamed Warner Communications.

Ashley and Ross were apparently aware of the rather unceremonious way in which Jack Warner had been forced out by the Hymans. As an atonement gesture, they organized a dress dinner as a salute to Jack Warner, scheduled to be held on that same stage, the one tented with ivy, on November 22, 1969; and they must have been gratified when J.L. himself , as well as most of the surviving stars Warner had created, agreed to show up for the tribute.

Unfortunately, the evening, which should have been an unforgettable epilogue to an indelible career, turned out instead to be a rather morose affair. A wonderful, forty-minute montage of film clips that was projected on a big screen behind the podium only seemed to make the studio's current efforts look more pallid than they were. And the endless speeches in J.L.'s honor eventually felt more like eulogy than tribute. Frank Sinatra, whom Warner still admired above all others, was inexplicably not in good form as master of ceremonies that evening. At a Friars roast for his boss and drinking buddy only four years earlier, Sinatra had been at his irreverent best: "Mr. Warner and his partners have shown this town the true meaning of brotherhood: They were brothers and they were hoods."[1] But in 1969 Sinatra seemed subdued and intoxicated, as if even he couldn't believe that the game really was over this time.

The game wasn't over. But it would never be played the same way again. Jack Warner rented offices in Century City, offices that, ironically enough, were built on the site of the old 20th Century Fox backlot that had recently been bulldozed. He independently produced an unsuccessful play, *Jimmy*, and two unsuccessful movies, *Dirty Little Billy* (1972) and *1776* (1972)—both released by Columbia Pictures. He died on August 13, 1978. As far as anyone can remember, the 1969 tribute was the last time Warner ever visited the lot—although in 1972, he came very close indeed.

During this period, life on that lot was in a constant state of flux. There was talk of selling off the studio outright, of selling part of it, or of repurposing the property somehow. The move was not unprecedented. Fox and MGM had both recently sold off most of their property. And at Paramount, Chief Operating Officer Stanley R. Jaffe boasted to *Life* magazine that "as for the studio, we're going to get rid of it. That delights me personally."[2]

Television paid some of the bills during this era, but as historian Gene Fernett put it at the time, "in the California of today, where space is at a premium, and taxes overwhelming, the Burbank Studios and nearby ranch seem an almost unbelievable luxury."[3] The same sentiment was echoed almost word for word in the *Los Angeles Times*, which upon the occasion of Warner's exit mused that "chances are that the vast studio complex will not survive intact, for the vast number of stages and the large backlot are expensive luxuries in a day of rising land costs and declining production."[4] Unfortunately, this luxury was one that the new management could ill afford. Although Ross and Ashley scored hits with *Bullitt* (1968), *The Wild Bunch* (1969), and the documentary *Woodstock* (1970), none of these films were shot on the lot.

Salvation for the facility would come about because of another studio's misfortune. Columbia Pictures had been operating nearly since their inception out of a cramped, one-city-block-long studio in Hollywood proper, located on the corner of Sunset Boulevard and Gower Street. In the 1970s, however, Columbia, like the other six sisters, was suffering from severe financial issues. Noticing that Warner Bros. up the road in Burbank had the exact same issues, it was proposed by one company or another that the two studios combine some of their assets and create a third company, to be known as "The Burbank Studios," which would operate the Warner Bros. studio lot independently for both companies to utilize. In a press release (dated June 3, 1971), Ted Ashley was quoted as saying that he welcomed "Columbia not as a tenant but as a joint owner and occupant of the new studio facility," although actually Warner would keep 65 percent of the new company and the property. Columbia, for their part, announced that they would sell off both their lot in Hollywood and a separate backlot, the so-called Columbia Ranch, which they had maintained since 1935 and which, coincidentally, was also in Burbank, although they eventually ended up keeping, and sharing, the latter.

In 1973, on a largely undeveloped area on the backlot, a new administration building for Columbia Pictures was dedicated. The building was, and is, a squat, white abomination, which evokes the post-Watergate and pre-disco era in which it was constructed better than any set could hope to do. Similar offices for Columbia Pictures would follow in 1979, in 1984, and—off-lot, facing Gate 5—in 1988.

On the face of it, this merger was a wise decision, and it was a decision that almost certainly kept Ross and Ashley from selling the property outright or piecemeal as other studios were doing. But the union, which began so hopefully, had several fissures in it almost before Columbia's first trucks pulled onto the lot. For one thing, suddenly nearly doubling the manpower at the surviving studio meant that many positions would be duplicated. An announcement in the press warned that the "technical staff for the combined facility would be drawn from both companies."[5] Everyone knew that this meant that there would be downsizing and layoffs from the ranks—not the best way to start a harmonious business relationship. Columbia employees, not without some justification, immediately suspected that Warner Bros. employees were being favored in this regard. And longtime Warner Bros. staffers resented another studios' employee base being pigeonholed into their departments.

Even worse, it soon became evident that The Burbank Studios, as a company, had no particular autonomy or muscle, and was in no position to dictate policy to either of the two larger entities operating inside its gates. Subsequently, the property itself suffered because neither of the tenants would agree to spend anything for its upkeep, often because they each believed that the other wasn't doing their fair share of the work, which in many cases was probably true. The result of all this buck-passing and finger-pointing was that in no time at all, paint was peeling and sets were crumbling away on the backlots. In the production offices, there never seemed to be anyone around to take out the trash, and both carpets and tempers were often threadbare.

An industry joke at the time was that the "TBS" logo on the water tower, designed to look like a film magazine but actually resembling nothing so much as a set of Mickey Mouse ears, had been engineered to cause just such confusion by employees of the nearby Disney lot. Why, or how, Disney would have wanted to do this was never explained to the satisfaction of anyone at either studio, although, oddly enough, the Disney Studios had their company name, but no mouse ears,

Potholes and peeling paint. The Burbank Studios never had adequate funds to maintain the facility, as this study from 1980 illustrates all too well.

painted on their own water tower during this period. So disoriented visitors wishing to tour the Disney lot often ended up harassing the guards of The Burbank Studios instead.

If nothing else, this perceived rivalry between Warners/Columbia and Disney was illustrative of another problem that would have been inherent anytime any two of the Seven Sisters were forced to operate within a single property. After all, Warner Bros. and Columbia, just like Coke and Pepsi, were *supposed* to be long-standing rivals (an off-point but interesting note: from 1982 to 1989, Columbia would be owned by Coca-Cola). According to legend, the original movie moguls used to occasionally play *very* high-stakes poker among themselves, which apparently served to keep their inherently competitive natures ever honed for the kill. It was always understood that beating Fox or Universal at the box office or in the acquisition of a star or a story property was an important, even healthy, part of the dynamics of the business. Further down the food chain, almost every issue of the *Warner Club News* is filled with articles about rival studio bowling or softball teams dueling to the death. Combining any two of these rivals on one property inadvertently compounded petty resentments and rivalries, which before the merger had been harmlessly encouraged by the management of both companies.

"Thieves and Perverts!" a longtime Warner Bros. employee said when asked, decades later, about the staff at Columbia Pictures. "Every last one of them. They robbed us blind. Anything that wasn't nailed down, those bastards would just take."[6]

Because of the three-way stalemate, there would be few improvements on the lot during this era. Soundstages were doubled up by putting an internal wall between them, and the chaotic numbering system would be junked in 1972 in favor of a more orderly north-south consecutive grid of numbers (although Stage 13 would remain MIA). On the backlot, fires and neglect would rob the facility of several iconic sets, none of which, with the exception of the Midwest Street residential district, would be rebuilt. The only significant addition would be the renovation and additions to Tenement Street for *Annie* (1982)—paid for by the production, not the facility.

On the plus side, because money and cooperation between the pertinent parties were so scarce, the studio lot eventually hunkered down into a sort of mummified, unchanging freefall—which effectively preserved it during a time when either relative success or outright failure would have probably led to change and renovations. Consequently, the studio remained frozen in time. Except for the signage on the gate and the confusing logo on the water tower, the lot inadvertently ended up looking very much the same in 1989 as it had in 1969.

By the mid-1970s, Hollywood's transitional period of family-run fiefdoms evolving into vast and integrated corporations was nearly complete. The studies had mutated from almost feudal family businesses into conglomerates managed by lawyers or ex-agents like Ashley or Universal's Lew Wasserman. With new blood came new talent. Young filmmakers like George Lucas and his contemporaries, who had learned their craft not apprenticing at the studios but in film school, brought new ideas and new talent onto California's movie lots. With younger people making movies for younger audiences, the eventual result was that movies started making money again.

The effect of this trend was not immediately apparent on the lot. Although successful movies were again being made by Warner Bros.—*Dirty Harry* (1971), *Enter the Dragon* (1973), *The Exorcist* (1973), and *Superman* (1978), for example—none of these pictures had any significant amount of their actual production done in Burbank. The perceived trend toward realism, and the expenses and overhead of shooting in Hollywood, had largely turned the studios into corporate headquarters, or places to grab pickup shots that no one had remembered to capture on location. Postproduction, scoring, and editing, as well as all television production, were still largely done on the lot and in-house, but this was probably only because the infrastructure for such work did not yet exist outside of Los Angeles.

Part of the problem was Hollywood's new accounting system, which now involved paying residuals to talent in perpetuity. As a response to this inconvenience, the studios began to charge for services that in the past would never have been tacked onto an (in-house) picture's budget. Suddenly utilization of the backlot,

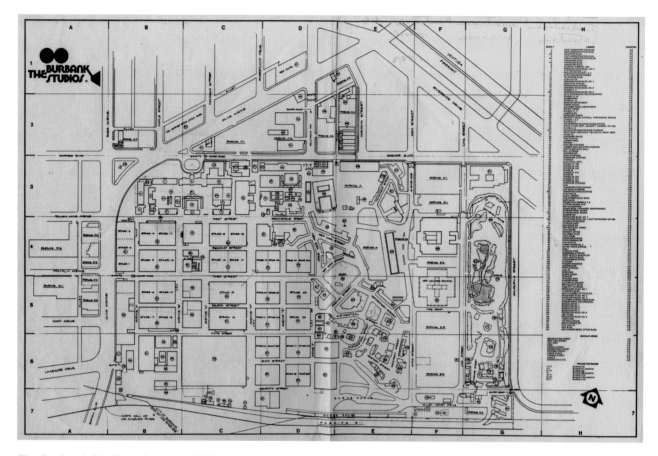

The Burbank Studios plot plan. 1983.

or a soundstage, or a Maltese Falcon statue, or a costume, or postproduction services was billed in real dollars against a picture's budget. Admittedly, in some cases, for some Warner Bros. or Columbia movies, the money would actually be traveling from one pocket to another in the same pair of pants. But more and more "in-house" productions were actually being developed outside, and less of the people involved in these projects actually worked for the studio, which often was now only operating as a co-financer or distributor. So there was no longer an incentive to shoot a Warner Bros. movie *at* Warner Bros. at all, or to utilize any of the studio's peerless technical departments either—not if these services could be purchased elsewhere and at less expense.

With different people often on hand to produce every movie with which the studio was involved, a new assembly line had to be created for every single project. Even if it was the exact *same* people for every project, everyone had to be hired fresh each time. And when that project was completed, this new, just-up-to-speed assembly line now had to be broken down, and its staff on the sets and in the offices all had to be laid off and sent home. This process had to happen for every film the studio made during this period, even though for the next movie many of the same people would have to be rehired so that the entire wasteful, inefficient process could ramp up all over again. The only thing more ridiculous than accepting that this is how the industry operated during this period is realizing that this is exactly the system by which Hollywood still operates today.

Politics and economics aside, from the physical look of the Warner Bros.–Burbank Studios lot during this era, it was obvious that the system of sharing facilities was not working well. Successful television programs like *The Dukes of Hazzard* (1979–1985), *Wonder Woman* (1975–1979), and *The Waltons* (1972–1981), however, were a constant and lucrative presence. And both features and television rentals from other studios, many of which were forced to use the studio because they had, by this time, disassembled their own facilities, certainly did help to pay the bills. Columbia also undeniably brought a bit of its own colorful history, and its own success, into the studio mix. Some of Columbia's most successful movies of the period, such as *Close Encounters of the Third Kind* (1977) and *Ghostbusters* (1984), filmed on the lot and irrefutably became part of the studio's history. And yet there was constant dissent as to which company should pay for what, and The Burbank Studios management team was usually unable to untangle these problems to anyone's satisfaction.

Yet what no one knew was that by the mid-1980s, a perfect storm was brewing outside the gates that would change the landscape around which the studio operated once gain.

Lorimar Telepictures had been formed in 1969 to produce television product. So successful were they to this end, with hits like *The Waltons*, *Dallas* (1978–1991), and *Knots Landing* (1979–1993) on their résumé, that in the 1980s they started to produce lower-budget feature films as well. *The Waltons* originated at Warner Bros., but many of their series were shot on the old MGM lot in Culver City. In 1986 Lorimar went from tenant to landlord when, for $100 million, they purchased that property outright.

Back in Burbank, Warner Bros. had for several years secretly felt that with the relative upswing in business, they could once again support their entire facility financially. But there was one problem. What to do with Columbia?

In 1989 Warner Bros., whose parent company, Warner Communications, had just merged with Time Inc. and would hereafter be known as Time Warner, purchased Lorimar, which was subsequently rolled into Warner Television and effectively shut down. With this piece removed from the chessboard, Warner Bros. now found themselves in control of two major studio lots, yet sharing one of them with another, rival studio.

The obvious solution turned out to be amenable to everyone. Columbia had just been purchased by the Sony Corporation, and the new owners were agreeable to surrendering their 35 percent ownership in The Burbank Studios in exchange for the Culver City studio. The Columbia Ranch, for which no suitable buyer had ever been found, also went to Warner Bros. as part of the arrangement.

A Warner Bros. employee with no love for Columbia recalled his favorite memory of the entire eighteen-year marriage with the following anecdote: "When

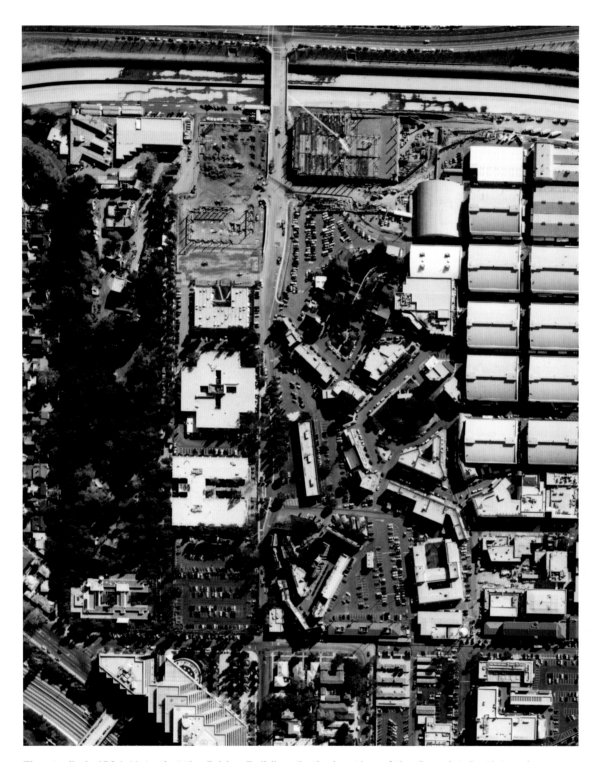

The studio in 1994. Note that the Bridge Building (in the location of the Camelot Castle) and a new Costume Department/parking lot are both under construction. The oddly shaped Cartoon Building (chapter 3) can be seen at top left.

Columbia's trucks were driving off the lot for the last time, after 18 years, I couldn't help myself; I gave some of 'em the bird as they pulled away."[7]

Gary Credle, who came to the studio in 1983 and in 1992 became the president of studio facilities after The Burbank Studios had been dissolved, had a background in (television) production, which led to his standing dictate that every inch of the newly rededicated lot was to be available for filming. Therefore, soundstage walls peeking out from behind standing sets were painted to extend those sets, and offices and office buildings were made available to play offices and office buildings. Jon Gilbert, who replaced Credle after his retirement in 2000, has continued and expanded on the same policy.

Bob Daly and Terry Semel, who replaced Ted Ashley's appointees Frank Wells and John Calley in 1980, provided the stability and continuity for the studio to rebuild itself. The only setback during this period was the death of the well-liked Steve Ross in 1992. In 1999, Daly and Semel stepped down. Their retirement was marked with a footprint ceremony at Grauman's Chinese Theater and a rededication of the Administration Building, hereafter to be known as the Daly-Semel Building. Allan Horn and Barry Meyer replaced them in that building, and in fact in Jack Warner's old office, Horn would leave to become the chairman of the Walt Disney Studios in 2012. Meyer would follow in 2013, replaced as chief executive officer by nineteen-year studio veteran Kevin Tsujihara.

In recent years, out-of-state tax incentives and cheaper material and labor costs have led to Hollywood exporting some of its projects to other markets. This so-called runaway production, as well as the advent of "digital backlots" (virtual sets created inside a computer), has left many to question the long-term viability of a traditional movie studio in the twenty-first century. These concerns are legitimate. And yet, if the era of the backlot is truly in eclipse, how to explain the large amounts of money and resources that are still spent annually by Warner Bros. and other studios in upgrading their facilities? In 2008, Universal suffered a major lot fire that burned most of their New York Street. They immediately replaced it with another set that was even larger. Likewise, Sony (Columbia) constructed their own modest New York Street during the same period, the first permanent backlot set erected on that lot in decades. Disney outdid them both, starting construction on new soundstages as well as an extensive backlot on their ranch property north of the studio in 2009. At Warner Bros., there is now talk of a new European Street and vague plans for other outdoor sets as well. Audiences and even many filmmakers fail to realize just how much production actually still happens on Los Angeles backlot locations. Watching a recent Super Bowl, I counted three commercials whose locations originated on the WB backlot alone.

Call it wishful thinking if you must, but it appears that backlots, either on screen or on lot, used either for production or for inspiration, either created in a studio or on a computer, are, just maybe, not going anywhere.

SEVEN

Shadow Lots

THE PURPOSE of this book has been to illustrate that the Warner Bros. story is not a name or a logo, but rather the narrative of a specific geographic *place*. Yet that name and that logo have both appeared above other gates of other studios many times. Some of the pertinent details regarding these other "Warner Studios" have been recounted in the context of their relationship with the Burbank plant. But a complete history of these previous, concurrent, and post-Burbank "shadow lots" is beyond the scope of this narrative, and, in fact, would undermine its central tenet: that Warner Bros. Studios is in fact *this particular* studio.

Yet these other lots are not without their own lore and history. And some of the company's most notable films have been crafted on these alternate properties. So, for the sake of context and completion, and just because information up till now on these facilities has been so elusive, here is the story of those "other" Warner Bros. studios.

Sunset Boulevard Studio

The first actual Warner Bros. studio, all 10.1 acres of it, still exists and is still used for film and television production. But its story represents both the highs and lows of its industry and of Hollywood as a physical place. The lot, once it was supplemented by the much larger studio in Burbank, suffered rare indignities, even before it was sold off by the men who built it, and even as it was venerated as the birthplace of talking pictures.

Production continued at a brisk clip on the lot even as the company and the company's management abdicated to Burbank. But it was obvious to employees even at the time that an era was passing. The 1934 Burbank fire briefly caused a surge in production on Sunset, but by the mid-1930s the entire operation had largely been relocated, with the notable exception of Leon Schlesinger's Looney Tunes unit, which was still owned by Schlesinger, meaning that Warner Bros. was in no hurry to relocate a mere tenant to their other lot. In fact, even after Schlesinger sold most of his interest in the company to Warners in 1944, Termite Terrace would not be relocated to Burbank for another eight years!

In 1937, someone—J.L. perhaps—realized that the profits generated by the property no longer justified the expenses of keeping the lot staffed. The obvious thing to do would have been to either shift more movies to Sunset, or rent any underutilized stage space to other studios or to independent productions. Poverty Row was just up the street, after all, and many of these mini-producers often rented soundstages that they could not yet afford to own. But perhaps not wanting to see another major like Columbia Studios rise out of this situation, and wanting to consolidate production rather than funnel it out of Burbank, J.L. decided to lease the bonus space to a recreational company whose management team included someone with lucky nepotistic ties to the Warners; this company arranged to build the "Sunset Bowling Center" inside the Historic Stage 1. With fifty-two lanes operating inside its cavernous interior, the center would become the largest bowling alley in

In the late 1930s, the Sunset lot ended up parodying itself. In *You Ought to Be in Pictures* (1940), Porky Pig tries to renegotiate his contract on the lot, and in *Hollywood Hotel* (1937), seen here, the studio played "Miracle Pictures," where "if it's a good picture it's a miracle."

SKATE YOUR
DATE WITH
THE STARS
hollywood
ROLLERBOWL
1452 No. BRONSON AVE. - Near Sunset
WORLDS
GREATEST
SKATING
RINK

"Rollerbowl" on the stages of Warner Bros.

the world. To add to the indignity, shortly thereafter, Stage 2 was converted into a roller rink and Stage 7 into a badminton court.

Although KFWB would continue to utilize the lot for their offices, and for pre-broadcast recordings, most of the other buildings, including the mill and Sam Warner's remarkable film lab, would stand largely vacant for decades. In fact, Warners would keep these unleased buildings, including the large (118 by 132 feet) Stage 6, maintained, if empty, for nearly twenty years! It can only be speculated if someone in the organization was being sentimental. Or if Jack or Harry ever visited the lot during these lonely decades and walked its dark streets, perhaps seeking out, or trying to avoid, Sam's ghost?

On December 30, 1953, the lot was finally sold to Paramount, which intended to use the facility for their burgeoning television unit. The administration building–bowling center was at the time earmarked for a permanent motion picture industry "exposition" designed in association with the Motion Picture Relief Fund. Apparently this was to be an early version of a long-planned Hollywood museum, which, like all of its other incarnations has, as of this writing, still not become a reality.

Klaus Landsberg, general manager of KTLA, Paramount's local subsidiary, decided that many of the original buildings were no longer worth saving. A *Los Angeles Times* reporter was on the lot the day that the screening room atop Sam Warner's lab was being decimated. The paper described how "hands jerked down the rotting, faded red velvet drapes that still hung from the walls." Walls where the "words that first revolutionized an industry . . . the first spoken words of the first successful talkie" were first uttered.[1]

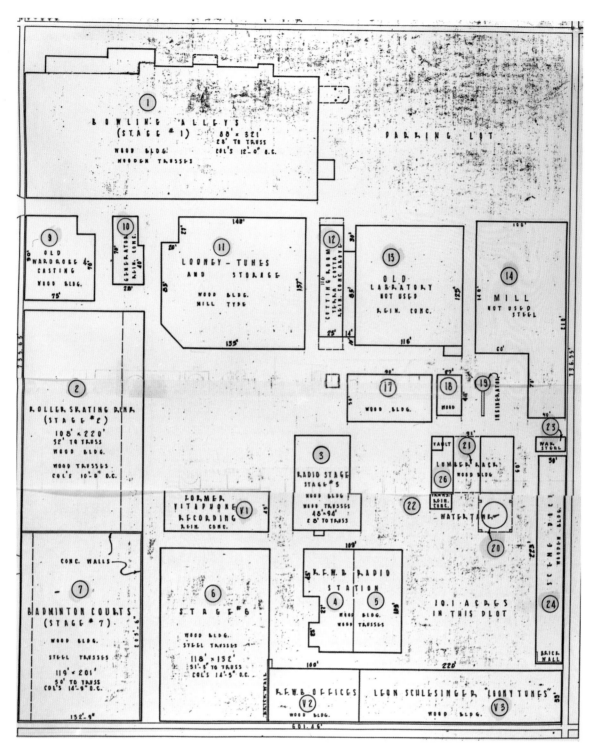

A 1949 Sunset Studio lot map, with the bowling alley, skating rink, and badminton courts notated.

In 1953, the lot was finally put up for sale. Paramount would be the eventual buyer.

In 1967, cowboy star turned millionaire businessman Gene Autry purchased the studio from Paramount for $5 million. Autry had previously been leasing much of the lot for his radio and television company, Golden West Broadcasters. He would own the lot, and eventually KTLA as well, until 1982, when it would be sold to an investment company and eventually to media conglomerate Tribune Broadcasters.

In 1995 Tribune and Warner Bros. created an all-new broadcast network, "The WB." Ironically, the local affiliate was KTLA, which was still broadcasting from the lot, meaning that once again the Warner Bros. logo would hang over the administration building—at least until 2006, when the WB network became "The CW" (the initials representing CBS and Warner Bros.). In 2008, Tribune sold its interest in the studio to another investment group for a reported $125 million. This time, the lot was renamed for the cross streets on which it stands: Sunset Bronson Studios.

The Sunset lot in 1987.

Those working on the lot at night, even today, sometimes report hearing strange noises, thunderous and mournful, coming from inside the stages, even when those stages are empty and locked. Some unimaginative souls claim these disturbances are only the Santa Ana winds rustling an unsecured sheet of tin siding. Those of a more romantic bent, however, believe that these noises somehow represent the storm created by the first talkies that were made inside. Still others believe these sounds are actually the spectral echoes of a bowling ball, firing across the stage floor and knocking off one lucky strike after another.

Vitagraph Studios

As would later be the case with First National, Warner Bros.' 1925 purchase of Vitagraph was an attempt to bulldoze into the center of the film industry by purchasing a larger, more established, but less aggressive rival company. Vitagraph's origins went

The Vitagraph Brooklyn lot in 1926.

back to 1896, nearly to the beginning of motion pictures. In fact, Vitagraph was one of the production companies that was licensed to legally produce movies using Edison's patented equipment. The founders, James Stuart Blackton, Albert Smith, and William "Pop" Rock, somehow decided that the word "vita" meant life and "graph" stood for pictures, in one language or another, and together they constructed both a company name and an early movie empire.

But by 1914, that empire was already on the decline. Harry purchased it for $800,000 and an agreement to take over the additional $980,000 in debt the company was in. For his (borrowed) money, he received a studio in Brooklyn, New York; another in Hollywood; and, most desirably, Vitagraph's substantial distribution network.

The studio in Los Angeles had possibilities, but the New York Vitagraph lot, 2.3 acres across, although boasting a laboratory, a proto-backlot, and glass stages to utilize natural light, was hopelessly antiquated, especially for the purpose of the Vitaphone talking shorts that Sam tried to produce there.

Brooklyn, or at least the corner of Brooklyn where the studio was located (14th Street and Locust Avenue), although spacious by east coast standards, was just too noisy. Part of the problem was that there was a busy, thunderously loud railroad spur just outside the gates. Sam eventually ended up shooting most of those early shorts at the Manhattan Opera House on West 34th Street instead—although, after much

The old Vitagraph Brooklyn lot as it looks today. Photo courtesy of Bill Elliott and Jim Stathacos.

retrofitting and renovation on the building there, it was discovered that similar audio problems, this time caused by a subway being constructed under the building, existed at this second site as well.

The Brooklyn lot was eventually soundproofed, and Warners continued to use it sporadically for short subjects—which, because of the talent involved, usually had to be shot near Broadway. In 1939 the lot was sold, although the studio continued to use the lab until as late as 1952. Today a smokestack, with the name Vitagraph still visible on its side, survives, tombstone like, to mark the spot.

The California studio, sometimes referred to as the Warner East Hollywood Annex, was (and is) located on 4151 Prospect Avenue, at the corner of Prospect and Talmadge (apparently the street was named after actress Norma Talmadge, who was in fact a Vitagraph star). The studio was constructed in 1915, although some sources place the date as 1918. Regardless, it was one of the first from-the-ground-up film production plants constructed in Hollywood. Originally there were two stages, both made of glass after the style of its east coast sister. The lot also included twenty-three support buildings and an open area that quickly filled up with exotic backlot settings. The 18.7-acre studio also contained an elaborate dump tank used for pouring vast amounts of water, which would see impressive, and fatal, use shortly.

Noah's Ark (1929) was a rare attempt by the studio to make a DeMille-style spectacle. The final cost was probably somewhere close to $2 million, an enormous sum indeed. Most of the film was shot on the Vitagraph Los Angeles lot, including the flood sequences, which utilized a reported forty-five hundred extras and the large dump tank. According to cinematographer Hal Mohr, the tank was set up above a collapsible temple set with large columns that were rigged to come down upon the extras when the water was released. "I objected, not as a cameraman, but as a human being, for Christ's sake, because it seemed to me . . . that they were going to kill a few people with those tons of water and huge sets falling on them,"[2] Mohr told Bernard Rosenberg and Harry Silverstein in the 1960s. His objections were basically ignored, and so Mohr walked off the set and consequently didn't work for Warner Bros. again for four years. Reportedly, three extras did die and several more were injured when the *Noah's Ark* water and cameras finally rolled.

Other, less tragic WB films shot, or partially shot, on the lot include *The Jazz Singer* (Stage 5 is where they shot the interior club scenes), *Glorious Betsy* (1928), *Public Enemy* (1931), *42nd Street* (1933), *The Gold Diggers of 1933* (1933), *Captain Blood* (1935), and *The Lady with Red Hair* (1940).

In 1948, Jack sold the studio, or at least what was left of it, to ABC television as their West Coast studio and home of their flagship local station, KABC (known as KECA until 1954). In 1999, the station would move to Glendale, but

An aerial view of the Vitagraph East Hollywood studio. The ultimately fatal *Noah's Ark* sets and dump tank are visible near the center of the lot. Circa 1930.

The Vitagraph East Hollywood studio gate in 1929 . . .

ABC continued to operate the lot, both as a production center for their own product and as a rental facility.

In 1996, ABC became part of the Walt Disney Company. Disney had built its first real studio in nearby Silver Lake, and wanted to continue to run the plant as part of ABC. But someone pointed out that few features were being shot on the lot because of the perceived television "bias" implied by the name on the gate. So the "Prospect Studios" were created, and that name was put on an all-new semicircular-shaped sign that was a reasonable duplicate, save for the name, of the old Vitagraph signage from decades earlier.

Warner Hollywood Studio

In the 1990s, Lara Scheunemann worked the main switchboard at the so-called Warner Hollywood Studios. "It was the hardest job on the entire lot," she remembers.

> We had to keep more people on staff to answer the phones than anywhere else in the plant. From all over the world every day, people would call directory assistance and ask for the main number for Warner Bros. Studios, Hollywood, California. No one ever thought to ask for Warner Bros. in Burbank. So they would get

. . . and in 2013.

our number instead. Some of the calls were sweet, some were weird. Some of the callers barely spoke English. Many wanted to get in touch with a star or to get a job. But they all wanted to talk to someone at Warner Bros., in "Hollywood," so it was us they called.[3]

The confusion was understandable. In 1919, when it opened, it was known as the Jesse D. Hampton Studios. After that (in February 1922), it became the Pickford-Fairbanks Studios. In 1926 it officially became the United Artists Studio, although "Pickford-Fairbanks" remained the name on the gate. In 1939, Samuel Goldwyn became the controlling shareholder in United Artists and renamed the studio after himself. In 1951, United Artists changed hands again, but Goldwyn retained the studio.

The stories about the lot are legion. Composer Aaron Copeland, under contract to Goldwyn, once admitted that he wrote his masterpiece "Appalachian Spring" on the lot while being paid to write the score for *The North Star* (1943). He spoke once about walking the empty studio streets late at night alone with his inspirations. Howard Hughes and Frank Sinatra long maintained offices on the property. Sinatra used to play football with his buddies on the studio streets on Sunday afternoons. Hughes maintained his office there even after he had purchased nearby RKO Studios outright! And Laurence Olivier, in the sort of coincidence that seems to

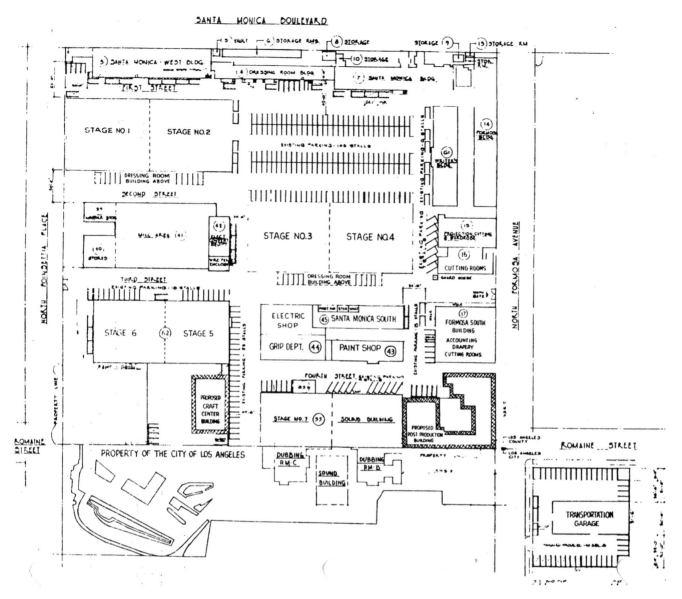

A Goldwyn lot map of the future Warner Hollywood Studio. Note the unidentified backlot in the lower left.

happen only in Hollywood, and in Hollywood movies, bookended his movie career on the lot. His first studio film, *Wuthering Heights* (1939), was nearly sidelined when a severe case of athlete's foot made it difficult for the actor to walk, and he had to be carried onto the set by production assistants. Decades later, an aged and infirm Olivier again had to be carried through the cables and equipment onto another set on the exact same soundstage to shoot his scenes for an ill-advised 1980 *Jazz Singer* remake.

When Samuel Goldwyn's wife, Frances, died in 1976, the twelve-acre lot at the corner of Santa Monica and Formosa in West Hollywood was bequeathed to the Motion Picture and Television Fund, which conducted a sealed-bid auction for the property. The minimum bid was set at $18 million. But Warner Bros. acquired

The "Howard Hughes tower" at the Goldwyn lot—from which the billionaire used to watch the outside world. 2013.

the property for $35 million, reportedly outbidding even Samuel Goldwyn Jr. The younger Goldwyn did win a battle to force a name change on the studio to avoid confusion with his own Samuel Goldwyn Company. Thus, the equally confusing "Warner Hollywood" tag was born.

Over the decades, such classics as *Robin Hood* (1922), *The Thief of Bagdad* (1924), *Stagecoach* (1939), *The Pride of the Yankees* (1942), *The Best Years of Our Lives* (1946), *Marty* (1955), *Some Like It Hot* (1959), *The Apartment* (1960), *West Side Story* (1961), *The Manchurian Candidate* (1962), *Basic Instinct* (1992), *Se7en* (1995), and *L.A. Confidential* (1997), as well as countless television shows, such as *Dynasty* (1981–1989) and *The Love Boat* (1977–1986), historically have shot on the lot. So the studio had a very lively and distinct identity even before Warner Bros. put their name above the gate. Perhaps this is why, in their almost twenty-year tenure as landlords, Warner Bros. often seemed unsure how best to exploit the property. The intention was to use the studio as a rental lot, but having the WB shield in front made it difficult for Senior Vice President Norm Barnett to brand the property as part of a larger Warner Bros. while still making that same property competitively available to budget-conscious independents and outside producers.

To his credit, Barnett and Warner Bros. lavished a great deal of money and good judgment in updating the property to the needs of late-twentieth-century Hollywood, while still retaining the lot's historical heart. This is a tradition that the current owners of the property have lamentably failed to maintain. Barnett built a commissary in the old Grip Department building, retaining the original structure's footprint and even the original tin roof top from the Goldwyn era. He spent millions of dollars updating aged postproduction and sound facilities by replacing the original analog equipment with state-of-the-art digital technology. And he and his staff took pleasure in presenting an office door arch to guests that had been built by Harrison Ford, then a carpenter, who was cast in *Star Wars* (1977) by tenant George Lucas while Ford was installing it.

In 1999, the facility was sold to an independent investment group who renamed it "The Lot," a moniker that gets points for being perhaps the only possible studio name more confusing than "Warner Hollywood."

It—The Lot, that is—continues to be used for motion pictures and television production to this day.

Warner Bros. British Studios

Teddington

England's Teddington studios were known from 1931 to 1946 as "Warner Bros. First National Productions Ltd." But the plant itself went back a good fifteen years before that.

Murder on the Second Floor (1932) was the first Warner Bros. film shot on this lot. During this period, Warner Bros. and its American dollars (which for tax reasons needed to be spent on British quota pictures) improved the property significantly, building additional soundstages and support buildings. "We could have come to England and rented a stage, made a picture any time we saw fit. But instead we came here and became a part of the British industry and employed several hundred British workers continuously," Jack Warner pointed out, truthfully, to the *Daily Film Renter Express* in 1937.[4] The films he made at Teddington were, quality-wise, little different from other British films of the period and had little Hollywood-style production gloss.

Murder at Monte Carlo (1937) was one of the most significant productions to come out of Teddington as far as the American studio was concerned, because it introduced a young actor named Errol Flynn.

After devastating World War II bombings, the lot was rebuilt, largely without any of those American dollars this time, although the reconstructed studio very closely approximated its prewar look, as was required by British government

Stage 2 at Teddington Studios after it had been destroyed by a German buzz bomb. 1944.

regulations. In 1948 another American, comedian Danny Kaye, purchased the studio, although within a few years aircraft rather than cinema would be the factory's main product. The ultimate salvation of Teddington Studios would not be a wealthy American, however, but television. From 1968 to 1992, Thames Television would be based on the lot and would produce within its walls *The Benny Hill Show* (1969–1989), *The World at War* (1973), and *Man about the House* (1973–1976), among many others. Since 2005, Pinewood studios, Britain's preeminent studio facility rental company, has owned the lot.

Warner Bros.' next venture into British studio ownership would end much more happily for the company.

Leavesden

In the 1930s the town of Watford, eighteen miles north of London in the United Kingdom, appropriated a 118-acre parcel of land to be used as an airfield. Ironically, one of the proposals that the township had considered before going with the aviation concept was to develop the land as a film studio. Unfortunately, the advent of World War II cut these plans short before significant construction could be completed. In 1940 the same real estate, as well as an additional 180 acres, was instead converted into a factory for the Ministry of Defence by the de Havilland Aircraft Company, which had been founded by Geoffrey de Havilland. Interestingly, Olivia de Havilland, one of Warner Bros.' great stars back in Hollywood, was Geoffrey's maternal cousin.

During the war years, the plant was the birthplace of some seven hundred Halifax bombers and hundreds of other military aircraft. After the conflict, commercial aircraft corporations continued to use the plant for aviation purposes. In 1959, de Havilland developed the property as a commercial airport and manufacturer of aviation engines and accessories. In 1961, Bristol Siddeley Engines acquired de Havilland. In 1966 they, in turn, were swallowed by Rolls-Royce, which continued to operate the property for the assembly of aircraft engines until 1992, when they closed the plant. In 1994, the property, with its vast hangers and heavy-industry assembly lines, started to be used for film production by Hollywood companies, which were the only ones who could afford to retrofit the property to this end. The James Bond picture *Goldeneye* (1994) was apparently the first project to use the land for this purpose, although the airfield had been used as a set as far back as 1959, for the British TV series *H.G. Wells' The Invisible Man* (1958–1960).

In 2001 Warner Bros., which had originally intended to film the bestselling *Harry Potter* book series in Hollywood, instead decided to shoot the film adaptations in England. The books were set in England, of course, and director Chris Columbus mentioned publicly how he wanted to shoot on location for the sake of authenticity, although he never elaborated how a soundstage in the United Kingdom was more "authentic" than one in California. Another factor involved in the decision to shoot overseas was when the parents of Daniel Radcliffe, the eleven-year-old who signed to play the lead, stipulated that they wanted their son to be able to attend school at home in the United Kingdom. That decision to shoot in the United Kingdom, wherever it came from, would change the history of Leavesden, and Warner Bros., forever.

Post *Potter*, Warner Bros. proceeded to spend millions of dollars turning the studio into a permanent production center. Not surprisingly they purchased the property outright in November 2010, even as they developed the studio, a process that continues as of this writing. When completed, Warner Bros. Leavesden will include an eighty-acre backlot and a quarter of a million square feet of soundstage space.

Warner Bros. (Calabasas) Ranch

Considering that the studio owned this property for approximately thirty years, it's interesting that so few details have ever been published regarding their major movie ranch and its history. This is particularly regrettable when one considers how many famous movies were partially shot at the Warner Bros. Calabasas property and how recognizable this much-photographed real estate is onscreen in so many of these films. Yet the story of the Ranch, its layout, its physical size, and even its actual

Leavesden Studios Stages J and K (named in honor of *Harry Potter* author J. K. Rowling) under construction. 2011.

location are all part of a story that has never been revealed to the public before—until now.

In the late 1920s, as the studio was expanding and buying up property and companies as fast as they could secure the loans to do so, Harry started leasing real estate in the western San Fernando Valley for the purpose of production. He apparently liked the neighborhood, because in 1936 he purchased 283 acres outright. Harry's intention at the time was to eventually raise horses, build a personal home, and make pictures on the property, so he continued to buy land in the neighborhood, eventually acquiring 510 acres in Calabasas and nearby Woodland Hills.

Most people assume that this property is now the site of the current Warner Center, a business complex north of the 101 Freeway constructed in the 1980s. This is not true. Warner Center was indeed named after Harry, but it was built on the site of a second "personal" ranch property the mogul did not purchase until 1946. Warner Center was built on this property and donated by the family in 1967, for the purpose of creating a "cultural center."

Meanwhile, the official "studio" ranch continued to be added to. Starting in 1937, the company began purchasing what amounted to another 250 acres from surrounding property owners. In 1949, Harry sold his personal stake in part of the property (670 acres) to the company for $431,000. During the same period, another 1390 acres came from the Dubrock and Stahlman families—two local property owners.

Whether this twenty-year buying spree was a result of the needs of production for ever more varied locales, some sort of an investment in local real estate, or even a tax shelter of some sort, the results would have impressed even a Texas cattle

The sprawling Warner Calabasas Ranch. Ventura Boulevard runs across the top. Mulholland Drive is on the right. The compound near their juncture is the then-new Motion Picture County home. Beneath that is where the majority of the standing sets were located. Harry Warner's Ranch is slightly to the left above the mountain range. 1940.

baron. By 1959, the final "Warner Ranch" would be bordered by Mulholland Drive on the east and Las Virgenes Road on the west. Even discounting Harry's personal fiefdom, the Warner Ranch real estate would total 2775.84 acres!

What stood on all these acres was an ever-changing collage of sets. Some of the studio's best work, architecturally speaking, was created for structures, or whole towns, built not at the studio but on the ranch property. Most of these sets were in the eastern section of the ranch, close to the junction of Ventura Boulevard and Mulholland Drive, slightly to the west of the current Motion Picture Home in Woodland Hills, and to the south of Harry's personal ranch property (known internally as the W.L. Ranch). The rest of the Ranch was kept fairly pristine for the purpose of outdoor filming, most often for westerns and war films. Errol Flynn, as Custer, met his maker, and a lot of angry Indians, in front of the ranch's vast rolling hills in *They Died with Their Boots On* (1941), for example.

"Juarez Street" was built in 1939 for the Paul Muni biopic *Juarez*. Harry Platt of the Staff Shop admitted he copied much of the architecture for the Mexican-themed village from Orange County's Mission San Juan Capistrano. The set, which could double as any western, European, or Mediterranean-style district, was perhaps

Ross Alexander, Olivia de Havilland, Dick Powell, and Jean Muir, probably wishing they were in their comfortable dressing rooms on the lot, rather than in dusty Calabasas, for *A Midsummer Night's Dream*. 1935.

the longest-lived backlot on the ranch and was still usable as late as 1958. A less prolific "Swiss"-themed set stood nearby.

The Ranch included two western streets. The smaller one was constructed in the early 1930s for a short-lived series of B-westerns. It included a dude ranch with stables, barns, cattle pens, and at least one ranch house. Nearby was a "Colonial Street" set, a small town, and a much-used plantation home. A cavalry fort and an Indian village were also adjacent tenants.

The second western set was much larger. In fact it may well have been, at the time, the largest backlot of its type in the business. Most of this remarkable T-shaped street was created for *Dodge City* (1939), a rare big-budget western for that period— although United Artist's *Stagecoach* would be released the month before *Dodge City* and Cecil B. DeMille's *Union Pacific*, and thus forever claim the credit for returning A-budget, adult-themed westerns to prominence. *Dodge City* also, remarkably, managed to make the Tasmanian-born Errol Flynn into a credible western star. Flynn would return to the genre, and the set, many times in coming years.

For *Anthony Adverse* (1936), a "Convent of the Holy Child" was constructed on the property. A French chateau supplemented it nearby, although the *Adverse* set was intended to be of Italian origin.

The formidable, and long-lived, *Juarez* set at the Warner Ranch. 1939.

Most of the sets on the property were partial, however. An employee who visited the Ranch once in its waning days remembered the vivid sight of doors with no walls around them swinging on their hinges in the wind, and ground floors of castles and churches and skyscrapers standing forlornly amid the sagebrush and scrub.

In the 1950s, with Harry out of the way and production greatly diminished, Jack commissioned a detailed appraisal of the property to see what it all might be worth. The answer came in at $6,985,000. The appraiser rather unimaginatively noted, however, that the vast standing sets on the acreage added "no value" to the property.

The lot was retained, however, until May 1959 when a sale was arranged for $10 million—which no doubt added considerably to the otherwise meager $13 million profit the studio reported that year. The original buyer was Associated Southern Investment Company, a subsidiary of California Edison, which intended on building a "planned community" subdivision on the site. It didn't happen.

The Miracle (1959) was the last film to shoot on the storied sets there, which, according to film historian Jerry L. Schneider, were in 1961 torched for practice by the Los Angeles Fire Department.[5]

In 1969, Warner Bros. returned to the location, which had since been converted into the Calabasas Park Country Club, to shoot some golf course exteriors

The Warner Bros. (Burbank) Ranch. 1966.

for *Once You Kiss a Stranger*. Longtime studio employees probably didn't recognize the place.

Warner Bros. (Burbank) Ranch

The current "Warner Ranch" is less than a mile up Hollywood Way from the main lot. The property's association with Warner Bros. was tenuous until 1972, however, although an occasional Warner Bros. picture did shoot on the property (the oil rig sequences from John Huston's masterpiece *The Treasure of the Sierra Madre* [1949] were allegedly shot at the ranch, although visual evidence from the film does not support this). Yet the property, more than any other except for the Burbank studio itself, is a reflection of American popular culture, good and bad, throughout the twentieth century and beyond.

This facility is the most recognizable of all surviving studio backlots. Not because it is the most photographed, but because the projects that used it were, from the late 1950s onward, primarily domestic-themed American situation comedies. As these series tended to run on television for years, sometimes decades, their standing sets, usually suburban homes, became as familiar to viewers as those viewers' own suburbs and their own homes within these suburbs. Actually visiting the lot, for a baby boomer or beyond, is often unexpectedly nostalgic, even if one has never been there before.

It wasn't always that way. The property was originally the site of either a horse stable or a dairy farm (depending on which account one chooses to believe), which, in any case, was occasionally appropriated as a location for silent westerns. During this same period, six miles up the road, near the corner of Sunset and Gower in the center of Hollywood's poverty row district, two brothers, Harry and Jack Cohn, were busy trying to transform a grubby start-up studio, Columbia Pictures, into a major force in the industry. That they succeeded—first with profits, then with respectability, and finally with Academy Awards and genuine, if begrudging, prestige—is one of the industry's genuine success stories.

The physical lot they did this on certainly reflects the company's hand-to-mouth origins. The Cohn plant was the smallest, physically, of the seven sisters. Even at its largest, it was only a city block deep by half a block wide. Columbia Studios always looked like a hodgepodge ghetto of squalid little offices and, eventually, fourteen overworked and mostly closet-sized soundstages.

Any sort of significant backlot there was nearly impossible; consequently, in 1934 Harry Cohn purchased the property in Burbank. The Warner Bros. movie Ranch, as noted, encompassed thousands of acres. Fox's, RKO's, and Paramount's ranches were of a similar size. The Cohns' cut-rate equivalent was a whopping forty acres (a second, largely undeveloped forty-acre parcel was purchased in 1949 and sold off in 1959). So confined was the property that in 1952's *High Noon*, it is possible to spot the telephone poles and postwar tract houses spiraling across the "western" landscape during the famous crane shot near the climax.

Columbia's spread, however, did evolve into one of the more interesting satellite backlots. Perhaps because space was so limited, and budgets so low, many of the façades constructed there saw an inordinate amount of duty over an inordinate number of years. A single curved block of residential homes, which either had no backs or had two "fronts," so as to be eligible for double duty, started appearing in features from the mid-1930s, but really reached iconic status from the 1950s onward, when Screen Gems, Columbia's television division (started in September 1948), began shooting their domestic-themed sitcoms there.

Any tour of this amazing property, highlighting places that were there when Warner Bros. arrived in 1972, would have to begin with this street. So that's what we will do. Feel free to consult the Warner Bros. Ranch map as we explore the property.

1. The Skeffington House

This impressive-looking suburban edifice was constructed as Spencer Tracy's home for John Ford's beautiful and melancholy *The Last Hurrah* (1958). Less ambitious, but enjoyable, was its transformation the following year into mad scientist Vincent Price's domicile in *The Tingler*. But since the 1970s, when the structure regularly played the dotty Baldwin sisters' plantation in *The Waltons* (1971–1981), the Skeffington house's appearances have been so scattered that the studio once commissioned a survey to determine if the shell was even worth preserving. To their surprise the executives discovered that the home, although seldom featured as a primary set, tended to appear

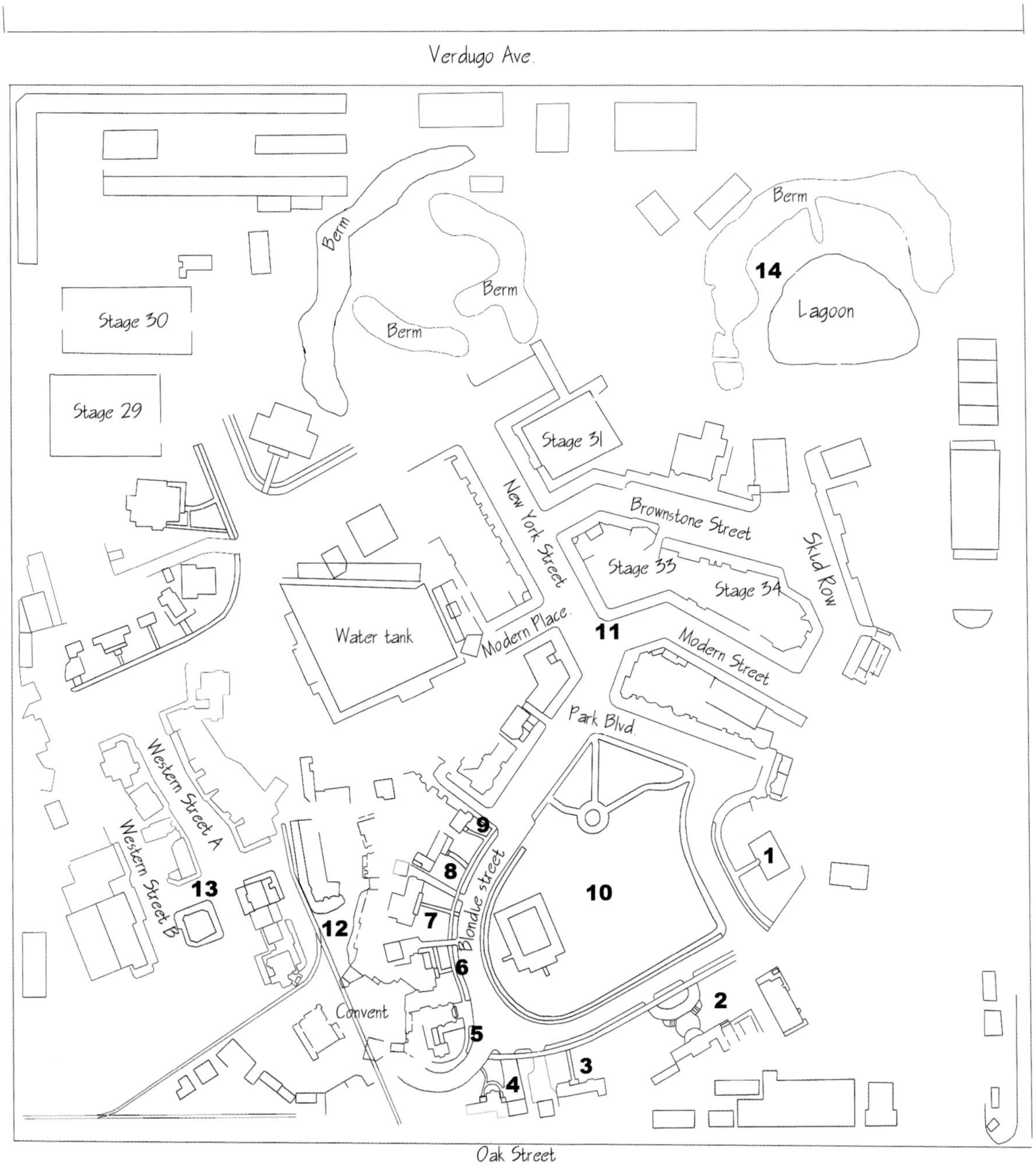

Verdugo Ave.

Berm

Berm

Berm

Berm

Lagoon

14

Stage 30

Stage 29

Pass Ave.

New York Street

Stage 31

Brownstone Street

Skid Row

Stage 33

Stage 34

Water tank

Modern Place

11

Modern Street

Park Blvd

Park And Pool

Hollywood Way

Western Street A

Western Street B

13

9

8

12

7

6

1

10

2

Convent

5

4

3

Oak Street

Warner Bros. (Burbank) 1960s ranch map. Courtesy of Mischa Hof.

KEY:

1. The Skeffington House
2. The Deeds House
3. The Lindsey House
4. The Bewitched House
5. Bel-Air House
6. The Partridge House
7. The Blondie House
8. The Oliver House
9. The Little Egbert House
10. Park And Pool
11. Park Boulevard and City Streets
12. English Street and Covenant
13. Western Street
14. Jungle and Lagoon

in the background on virtually every project shooting anywhere on the block. And removing it would have decreased significantly the number of available camera angles open to a production. So the house was saved and is still on the lot.

2. The Deeds House

The Deeds house was a magnificent mansion, large enough to double as a town hall or hospital. It was constructed in 1936 out of three smaller buildings for the Frank Capra classic *Mr. Deeds Goes to Town*. Somehow it survived a myriad of Three Stooges shorts, including *3 Dumb Clucks* (1937), *Tassels in the Air* (1938), and *Violent Is the Word for Curly* (1938), long enough to, decades later, play a high school for both *Gidget* (1965–1966) and *The Partridge Family* (1970–1974).

In 1989, the aged Deeds home was removed and replaced by the Chester House and the Griswold House. The later was named after Chevy Chase's family name in the *Vacation* series (starting with 1989's *National Lampoon's Christmas Vacation*), in which this was his hapless character's home. In *American Beauty*, the same house belonged to the equally frustrated Kevin Spacey. This later film won the Academy Award for Spacey and for Best Picture of the year in 1999.

3. The Lindsey House

Moving down the street, one comes across a two-story structure (with actual, if limited, interiors beyond the front door and upstairs) that was constructed in 1938. Its name comes from the character that Edward G. Robinson played in *I Am the Law*

The Deeds House was actually not so much a house as a mansion—a mansion with no servants, electricity, running water, or even a rear wall. Photo courtesy of Mischa Hof.

(1938)—although in the film the character was named "Lindsay." The misspelling is apparently an error dating from the original set blueprints, and it has been perpetuated ever since. In 1949 the serial *Batman and Robin* used the structure as a not-so-stately Wayne Manor, making this the only cinematic Batman story to date to be set in suburbia.

In the 1960s, the home came into its own as the Baxter family home in the TV series *Hazel* (1961–1966) and the Lawrence house in *Gidget* (1965–1966).

In the blockbuster *Lethal Weapon* (1987) and its sequels, this was the "Murtaugh home," populated by Danny Glover and his family. In *Lethal Weapon 2* (1989), a gag in which a toilet is blown out of a second-floor bathroom, through the roof, and onto the street forced production to repair part of the roof after the sequence was in the can (no pun intended). The patch is still visible on the set and can be seen in subsequent films using it.

Across the street in the 1970s was a grassy lawn. But in 1998, a rather eccentric Victorian style home, the Alan house, would be constructed on the site for the feature *Small Soldiers*. It has since been used in the cult comedy *Pushing Daisies* (2007–2009) and the feature *Project X* (2011).

Incidentally, *Small Soldiers* was a DreamWorks SKG picture. Because that "studio" does not have a physical lot of its own, producers were instead forced to construct their set on someone else's—in this case, that of Warner Bros., which has retained the set for subsequent productions.

The Lindsey House is familiar from the *Lethal Weapon* film series. Photo courtesy of Mischa Hof.

The beloved *Bewitched* House. Photo courtesy of Mischa Hof.

4. The Bewitched House

The most recognizable house on the lot began life as a freestanding garage for the Lindsey House next door. In 1962, for the series *Our Man Higgins* (1962–1963), a distinctive two-story A-frame residence was created that would soon become the home of the Stephens family for *Bewitched* (1964–1972), 1164 Morning Glory Circle. Until 2000, when a corrugated metal back was added, the house was a front only.

This set has had a rather remarkable afterlife in spite of its high recognizability factor (which often unfortunately translates to a decrease in commercial viability for a backlot set). Even while *Bewitched* was still on the air, the house landed a returning role in the "rival" sitcom *I Dream of Jeannie* (1965–1970) as Dr. Bellow's home. It also played the doomed Brian Piccolo's home in the TV movie classic *Brian's Song* (1971).

The Bewitched House can also be seen in the legendary TV movie *The Night Stalker* (1972), and assorted episodes of *The Monkees* (1966–1968), *Charlie's Angels* (1976–1981), *The Wonder Years* (1988–1993), *Home Improvement* (1991–1999), *Step by Step* (1991–1998), *The Geena Davis Show* (2000), and even a Barenaked Ladies video, "One Week" (1998).

One place where the house cannot be seen, however, is the place where one would have most expected to find it. Inexplicably, the producers of the feature film reimagining of *Bewitched* (2005) either did not know, or care, that the original set for the TV series was still standing and available. So they shot elsewhere.

5. Bel-Air House

Our street veers east here, where the next house long stood above the sidewalk in back of a 2-foot stone wall. The so-called Bel-Air House was built where a church set stood from 1953 to 1970. Recently, the house itself has been extensively remodeled, and it can currently be seen in the TV series *The Middle* (2009–). In its previous incarnation, however, the set's most notable and sustained appearance was in the Richard Pryor vehicle *Moving* (1988), a film about which Pryor notoriously told the press, when asked what it was about, "It's about two hours too long."[6]

6. The Partridge House

This set was built in 1953. A fire destroyed the original house in August 1970 after *The Partridge Family* (1970–1974) had already used it for their first five episodes. After the fire, the house was rebuilt, although a tree in the front yard that also burned was not replaced. This second house, different from the first only because of this landscaping error, continued to be used throughout the run of that series, even reprising its role in a TV movie, *Come On Get Happy* (1999), which was, aptly enough, about the making of the *Partridge Family* TV series.

Other tenants have "lived" in this building as well. They have included the nosy neighbor Mrs. Kravitz in *Bewitched* (1964–1972), Mrs. King in *Scarecrow and Mrs. King* (1983–1987), and the Thatcher family in *Life Goes On* (1989–1993).

7. The Blondie House

The Blondie House was, of course, named after a long-running series of feature films that were in turn based on an even longer running syndicated comic strip. In fact, the entire street is still referred to as "Blondie Street" as a tribute to this film (and later television) series.

Actually, the early entries in the *Blondie* film series (which ran from 1938 to 1950) were shot at a very similar home on Agnes Street in Burbank. In 1941, to avoid continuing these expensive location shoots, a very similar but not quite identical house was built here on the backlot, to be utilized for the remainder of the series and beyond.

The set's second claim to immortality came with *Father Knows Best* (1954–1960), the classic baby boomer sitcom that cast the residence as the Anderson House. *Dennis the Menace* (1959–1963) also used the set as Mr. Wilson's home during this era, and later the same structure became familiar to yet a third generation when it played Major Anthony Nelson's Coco Beach, Florida, home in *I Dream of Jeannie* (1965–1970).

Sadly, the house was badly damaged by the same 1970 fire that destroyed the Partridge home. Actually, the unlucky structure was almost completely destroyed twice in two out of the three tragic fires that plagued the Ranch that year. It was

The Blondie House. Photo courtesy of Mischa Hof.

ultimately rebuilt with an interior, which today furnishes office space for the Warner Bros. Ranch Operations Department.

8. The Oliver House

The last significant house on the block is a comfortable-looking suburban home that was named after Jean Arthur's character in *Party Wire* (1935)—a film notable as the first ever to be shot at the Ranch—although this particular set, while used in the film, stood elsewhere at the time and was moved to its current location later on.

Again, it was through television that this house became most familiar. *The Donna Reed Show* (1958–1966) used the setting as the domicile of the perfect Eisenhower-era American family. *Dennis the Menace* (1959–1963) showcased a less perfect, but still idealistic, representation of nearly the same period. And finally, *Once and Again* (1999–2002), with its cast of variously divorced, estranged, or at least neurotic family members, showed us how far audiences, and television, had changed over the decades—without ever leaving the confines of this single ordinary, and yet somehow quite remarkable, set.

9. The Little Egbert House

This small, Tudor-style residence, at the very end of Blondie Street, was once at the lip of an entire British-themed Little Egbert Street set, built for *A Feather in Her*

The Oliver House, home of both Donna Reed and Dennis the Menace. Photo courtesy of Mischa Hof.

Hat (1935). Today, much of the British architecture has been stuccoed over, and the house today looks like yet another mid-twentieth-century tract home, which is exactly what it usually plays.

In 1999 this house and the entire, surreal city block starred in the feature film *Pleasantville*. The plot concerned a strange place inside a black-and-white television world where old sitcoms flower magically to life. The same year, an X *Files* (1993–2003) episode, "Arcadia," cast Blondie Street as an all-American suburb, complete with pink plastic flamingos, which turned out to actually be a television-inspired recreation in Russia, of all places.

In both cases, the casting was perfect.

10. Park and Pool

Blondie Street is bordered by several acres of green lawn, landscaped with trees, a rather ornate city fountain, and a swimming pool.

The pool goes back to 1948 and is a conventional swimming pool with a twist. Portholes have been carved into various points along its sides. Removable metal plates allow a crew to access these windows to shoot underwater sequences through them. Films like *The Fugitive* (1993) have used it for underwater inserts—allowing it to be said, quite truthfully, that Harrison Ford was able to jump off a dam in North Carolina and splash into the waters of a pool in Burbank!

The pool. Unlike real pools in the real world, this one includes underground portholes. The Partridge House can be seen in the background. Photo courtesy of Mischa Hof.

Across from the pool, the fountain, which dates from 1935, will be immediately recognized as the setting of the opening credits for the TV show *Friends* (1994–2004), but it can be seen on the big and small screens many times. Most notably, it appears in the science fiction favorites *20 Million Miles to Earth* (1957) and *The Omega Man* (1971), where it, or rather an octagon-shaped duplicate, was the setting for Charlton Heston's dramatic, Christ-like death scene.

11. Park Boulevard and City Streets

The façades currently being used by Warner Bros. are actually but a small portion of the original sets constructed here beginning in the 1930s. Originally, the area was the southern entrance to a large urban backlot with New York, Brownstone, Skid Row, and Modern Street sections. Some of these districts were actually built over the top of three rather oddly shaped soundstages. (Columbia maintained five stages on the Ranch, and two of them, along with three newer Warner Bros.–constructed stages, are still in use today.) At one time, this area included a theater, department store, elevated train, nightclub, and apartment complex.

Sadly, most of this was destroyed in a September 1974 fire. Only the Bostonian townhouses facing the park survive today.

The so-called *Friends* fountain. The Skeffington House is in the background. Photo courtesy of Mischa Hof.

These townhouses once led into a vast hive of city streets and tenements. Photo courtesy of Mischa Hof.

12. English Street and Convent

The backside of several of the Blondie Street houses were once part of a European-Latin-Asian-Arabian district, which was built in the 1940s but once again received a lot of exposure in those Screen Gems sitcoms. This was particularly the case in *Bewitched* and *I Dream of Jeannie*, for every time anyone was transported back in time or to Baghdad or London or Naples, this street was put to use.

Although part of the set burned down on the January 30 and September 8, 1970, fires, I was lucky enough to be able to explore what was left just before it was removed in 1996. I vividly remember the odd sight of yet another V (1984–1985) spaceship shell; it was parked alongside a robotic killer whale, used in the then-recent hit *Free Willy* (1993), beached in the middle of the cobblestone streets and with hydraulic cables spilling out of its belly.

A rather elaborate convent set, much used in the series *The Flying Nun* (1967–1970), stood at the street's far end.

13. Western Street

Constructed in the early days of the Ranch for the studio's Charles Starrett B-westerns, Columbia's Western Street(s) were among the best in the business and

Leftover props from the TV series *V* (1984–1985) and the feature *Free Willy* (1993) rather surreally sharing space on English Street. 1995.

The legendary Columbia Studios Western Street. Photo courtesy of Mischa Hof.

were versatile enough to be adapt to Midwestern, southern, and modern-set pictures as well. Marlon Brando's legendary biker film *The Wild One* (1953), for example, used the street right after Gary Cooper shot up the same streets in the classic western *High Noon* (1952).

Again, much of the set was destroyed in the January 1970 fire. It was largely rebuilt, although its days were numbered. Sharp-eyed film historian Tinsley Yarbrough tells us that Western Street's last big-screen appearance was not in a western at all, but in the Hollywood-set *Guilty by Suspicion* (1991), in which Robert De Niro played a director shooting a *High Noon*–inspired picture on the set.[7]

The last of Western Street was removed on June 25, 1993. A truck parking lot stands on the site today.

14. Jungle and Lagoon

The northeastern corner of the lot was for many years an open area where some of Columbia Pictures' most notable sequences were created. For *Lost Horizon* (1936), the temple of Shangri La was constructed on a section of real estate at the corner of Verdugo and Hollywood Way. This set, the most expensive in Columbia Studio's history, was reused and reconfigured for many subsequent pictures needing an "exotic" setting. In 1965, landscaped berms were added and a lake was created, all for a short-lived TV series, *Camp Runamuck* (1965).

After *Runamuck* received its cancelation, the area was reconfigured to resemble a southern California beach area for *Gidget* (1965–1966). The district retained this look for almost a decade, with the forested berms also doing duty in *Here Come the Brides* (1968–1970) and *The Young Rebels* (1970–1971).

Today that real estate is a shopping center, thanks to a 1974 deal that sold six acres of the ranch to a development company.

In 1977 the studio, which was TBS by this point, developed a series to be titled *Code R*. The setting was, again, a 1977 California beach community. So a new "ocean," along with a beach and boardwalk village, had to be created south of the original era, which was by then a CVS Drug Store.

Unfortunately, *Code R* was no more successful than *Camp Runamuck* or *Gidget*. And although the studio tried to find more ways to use the set, it was eventually removed and landscaped over.

Today only part of this wooded area and those berms still survive. Until 1998, when much of it was removed to install some satellite dishes, a tropical pool with an adjustable waterfall stood in the area. This waterfall was last used as a Hawaiian

The series *Fantasy Island* (1977–1984) originally shot its exteriors outside this mansion at the Los Angeles Arboretum in Arcadia, California.

For convenience, a duplicate of the mansion in the previous photo was constructed on the Ranch. Notice how few similarities there really are. Yet audiences never noticed. 1995.

location in the *Lois and Clark: The New Adventures of Superman* (1993–1997) series. Nearby was a clearing where a house with a paddlewheel was constructed for another series, *Apple's Way* (1974–1975). This house was later converted into the familiar *Fantasy Island* (1977–1984) Queen Anne's cottage, and became the site for the Walton family farmhouse and barn in 1997, both of which are still there as of this writing.

Since taking sole control of the property in 1990, Warner Bros. has constructed new offices, including a home for Warner Bros. Animation, a day care center, a restaurant (since closed), and a new gate and guard shack facing Hollywood Way. But when they originally took co-control of the property in 1972, there were several other sets, structures, or departments operating at the Ranch. These included an aquatic dump tank, one of the largest at any studio, with a painted sky backing; a commissary, which doubled as a house exterior; three gas station sets, of which one survives today; the Smith House set, which was seen (rather briefly) in the Columbia classic *Mr. Smith Goes to Washington* (1939); a cabin, once part of one of the Western Streets, and now used by the WB Greens Department; and a scene dock, mill, commissary, and first aid shack. Some of these departments or structures are still in use today.

Later the Walton house was reconstructed on the same site, minus the tropical vegetation. Photo courtesy of Mischa Hof.

Also in 1972, at the same time that Columbia was moving up to Burbank, another refugee who had fled Burbank for offices in Century City found himself pulled back to very near where he had been ensconced for close to fifty years.

At the time, Jack Warner was eighty years old. As an independent producer, he was free to take any film project wherever he could make a deal. Yet when he chose to make a film version of the Broadway hit *1776*, it was still surprising, as it had been for the same year's *Dirty Little Billy*, to see the Columbia pictures logo in front of a film produced by Jack L. Warner.

Dirty Little Billy had been shot on location in Arizona and New Mexico. But *1776*, a period musical about the signing of the Declaration of Independence, virtually demanded a backlot setting, which in Columbia's case meant Burbank. What's more, with the merger with Warner Bros. only months away (it was scheduled to happen officially in April 1972), the old mogul discovered he would have to shoot his picture quickly or end up, once again, part of a company he had renounced forever. Warner never commented publicly on the irony of his situation, as *1776* was to be his last picture. With his past literally catching up with him, Warner and his director, Peter H. Hunt, shot interiors at the old, soon-to-be-forsaken Columbia Lot on Sunset, and then moved north to Burbank, where an elaborate recreation of Philadelphia's Independence Hall had been constructed on Little Egbert Street for the production. When production ended, J.L. returned to his offices in Century

An illusion-shattering view of the rear of the Walton farm. Photo courtesy of Mischa Hof.

City. Not long after that, a new generation of Warner executives drove onto the Columbia Ranch, or rather the Burbank Studio Ranch, as it had just been renamed, to have a look around. When they arrived, they found a most mysterious and ironic surprise waiting for them.

Stored in a scene dock in a corner of the lot, the Warner people discovered a set of two life-sized prop statues. Both of them depicted a man in a suit standing next to a podium. And in both cases, the person depicted in the statue was none other than that of their own, very recently departed independent producer and founder, Jack L. Warner.

At the time, and for years later, it was assumed that these statues had probably been commissioned for some sort of party welcoming J.L. to Columbia Pictures. The problem was, however, that no one on the Columbia side could remember any such party ever taking place. But if these effigies predated Jack's appearance at the studio, then where had the statues originally come from? And what had a monument to a Warner Bros. film executive been doing in a scene dock at Columbia Studios?

This Easter Island–style mystery only gets more perplexing. Leith Adams, Warner Bros. corporate archivist, recognized the statues as depicting Jack Warner and saved them both, assuming that maybe J.L. had owned the statues personally and had been storing them at the ranch while working for Columbia. I believed this story was a possibility myself and accepted it. I well remember seeing both statues standing, sentinel-like, seemingly watching me from their home in a studio warehouse many times. And I was there when Jack's daughter Barbara took a tour of the archive and was able to tearfully confirm their identity, if not their origin.

Then I met Mischa Hof, a preeminent scholar of all things Ranch related. I told Mischa about the mystery. He listened attentively, but instead of offering a solution to the mystery, he told me that he had something very interesting to show me. True to his word, he produced a still from an episode of *Gidget*. Sure enough, one of the Jack Warner statues could be seen in front of the Deeds home, which was playing that program's Westside High School. That show was filmed at the Ranch, making the statue's cameo interesting but not extraordinary—at least not until it is taken into account that that particular series had run in 1965–1966, a full five years before the beginning of Jack Warner's gig there.

And it gets better. More research on Mischa's part showed that one of the statues also appeared, this time standing inside the *Friends* fountain, in a Columbia feature, *We Were Strangers*, shot at the Ranch in 1949. The same statue also makes at least one more appearance onscreen, in Columbia's *Together Again*, which was shot, again at the Ranch, in 1944!

This all is a mystery without an answer. And anything beyond the facts outlined above can be merely speculative. One theory, favored by no less an authority than Leith Adams, is that, at some point, a Warner Bros. employee who worked in the Staff Shop was laid off and managed to pick up a few days working at the equivalent department over at Columbia. Perhaps this employee, called upon to construct a prop statue, remembered J.L. and sculpted the statue to resemble his old boss. Or maybe the resemblance was some sort of a slight by someone at Columbia who wanted to mock a rival studio head, although the statues were treated, from all available evidence, with respect during all of their onscreen appearances. Or perhaps the statue's resemblance to J.L. *is* simply coincidental, despite what Barbara Warner and many others who have seen them believe. I showed them to a fellow employee once, who thought that they actually rather resembled actor Rolland Young!

Perhaps because it is a mystery with no immediate solution, I've often wondered about those statues, and their origins, and all that they must have seen, standing sentinel at the Ranch for all those decades. I've also wondered if, just maybe, when he was on the lot for those frantic months in 1972, Jack Warner himself ever made their acquaintance and wondered the same thing.

In my mind I can see the old man, having been somehow apprised of their existence, journeying out to a remote corner of an unfamiliar backlot to have a look for himself. It's interesting to imagine Mr. Jack L. Warner, impresario, empire builder, last of the moguls, creator of Hollywood's ultimate backlot, his gait now slow and deliberate, picking his way through a crowded scene dock to take a look at, perhaps, his own younger self.

One wonders if, in that moment anyway, the man who created a world, a thousand worlds, all on a backlot, would have been able to appreciate the mysterious irony of becoming part of one himself.

APPENDIX

....

Productions Shot on the Backlot

A COMPLETE ACCOUNTING of the productions shot on the Warner Bros. backlot would be both impossible and redundant. But, at the same time, part of the fun of enjoying the vast Warner Bros. library is in identifying the locations where those pictures were created. No one, including the studio, has ever attempted this before at any level. So let's consider the following lists, which I've been compiling on my own for almost twenty years—a good start on a trip down an endless road.

A couple of notes. Each set is identified here as it was on your studio map at the beginning of chapter 5. Earlier sets referenced in the text only are not included, although I have tried to include films shot on an identifiable street, even when that street might have had an earlier, different, or contradictory identity. The dates here, as throughout the book, indicate the year of the picture's release, not of its production. Films for other studios are noted as such. Projects made for television are also notated as such, although individual TV episodes and outside TV production companies are not always accounted for.

Some of these listings indicate locations that may have ultimately been cut from the finished project, so if you can't always spot a particular set in a particular movie, don't blame me. Specifics as to how each project used the set, or what it played, are noted whenever possible. A warning: Some of this material is taken from the production records and tends to be idiosyncratic, to say the least.

That said, I hope you enjoy the lists of films that follow. Do feel free to add more titles to them yourself, as films yet unmade and films made decades ago come to light. I feel compelled to warn you, however, that as these sets become more familiar and more recognizable to you, it will ultimately become impossible to ever watch film or television quite the same way again.

This list will never be complete, will never be definitive. What follows is no more than an entrance ramp onto a celluloid road: endless in both directions, rolling backward into the dark and forward into the future.

Enjoy the journey.

Brownstone Street

Lady Be Good (1928) — as New York

Show Girl in Hollywood (1930) — used for drive up street toward the commissary

Doorway to Hell (1930)

Public Enemy (1931) — Cagney's friend is shot from the window

Bought (1931)

Little Caesar (1931)

Blondie Johnson (1932) — as New York

Central Park (1932) — as New York

The Kennel Murder Case (1933)

Havana Widows (1933)

42nd Street (1933) — Ruby Keeler's apartment

Bureau of Missing Persons (1933)

The Mind Reader (1933)

Upperworld (1934)

Dames (1934) — "Laundry number"

Kansas City Princess (1934) — Joan Blondell's home

The Big Shakedown (1934)

Dangerous (1935) — "cheap apartment"

The Girl from 10th Avenue (1935)

Bullets or Ballots (1936) — Bogart and Edward G. Robinson shootout

Marked Woman (1937) — "Club Intimate"

The Sisters (1938) — "Frisco Street"

Three Cheers for the Irish (1940)

All This, and Heaven Too (1940) — "Mrs. Haines School for Young Ladies"

A Dispatch from Reuters (1940) — "Benfey Bank" and "Bender Bank"

The Maltese Falcon (1941) — Spade's apartment

The Strawberry Blonde (1941) — James Cagney in 1890s New York

Background to Danger (1942)

Mr. Skeffington (1943) — as 1914 New York

Never Say Goodbye (1946)

Three Strangers (1946)

The Time, the Place and the Girl (1946)

The Big Sleep (1946; shot in 1945) — "Holbart Arms"

Always Together (1947) — boardinghouse

The Voice of the Turtle (1947)

Rope (1948) — under opening credits

Winter Meeting (1948) — Bette Davis apartment

My Dream Is Yours (1948) — "Green Room Exteriors"

The Damned Don't Cry (1950)

Young Man with a Horn (1950) — "Galba's Club"

Come Fill the Cup (1951)

I'll See You in My Dreams (1951) — "Yes Sir That's My Baby" number

Lullaby of Broadway (1951) — Hubbell house

I Was a Communist for the FBI (1951)

Stop, You're Killing Me (1952)

The Winning Team (1952)

Dial M for Murder (1954) — as New York

A Star Is Born (1954) — in front of commissary

Pete Kelly's Blues (1955) — Kansas City blues club

I Died a Thousand Times (1955) — Jack Palance stalks the street

The Steel Jungle (1956)

Marjorie Morningstar (1958)

Too Much, Too Soon (1958)

The FBI Story (1959)

The Young Philadelphians (1959) — Paul Newman's family home (northeast end of street)

A Majority of One (1961)

That Touch of Mink (1962) — rental/Universal — as New York

Critic's Choice (1963) — traffic jam with Lucille Ball

Dear Heart (1964) — as New York

Robin and the 7 Hoods (1964) — Frank Sinatra's Chicago speakeasy

The F.B.I. (television, 1965–1974) — episode: "Special Delivery" (1966) and others

Chamber of Horrors (1966) — as Baltimore

Any Wednesday (1966) — New York apartment

Wait until Dark (1967) — as New York

The Out-of-Towners (1970) — as New York

Portnoy's Complaint (1972) — "Chinese Street"

Lady Sings the Blues (1972) — rental/Paramount

Wonder Woman (television, 1975–1979) — assorted

Funny Lady (1975) — rental/Columbia

Won Ton Ton: The Dog Who Saved Hollywood (1976) — rental/Paramount — pie fight

Two of a Kind (1983) — rental/Fox — as Chicago

National Lampoon's Vacation (1983) — as St. Louis
Pee Wee's Big Adventure (1985) — as a movie studio
Bird (1988)
Murphy Brown (television, 1988–1998) — Murphy's apartment
Harlem Nights (1989) — rental/Paramount — Eddie Murphy
Postcards from the Edge (1990) — rental/Columbia — as a studio
Batman Returns (1992) — as Gotham City
Lois and Clark: The New Adventures of Superman (television, 1993–1997) — Lois' apartment
The George Carlin Show (television, 1994–1995) — some of street duplicated on Stage 3 (now 17)
ER (television, 1994–2009) — assorted
Friends (television, 1994–2004) — assorted
Batman Forever (1995) — as Gotham City
Executive Decision (1996) — theater exit
Suddenly Susan (television, 1996–2000) — as San Francisco
Midnight in the Garden of Good and Evil (1997)
Ally McBeal (television, 1997–2002) — used once, in 2000
Two of a Kind (television, 1998)
Annie (television, 1999)
A.I. Artificial Intelligence (2001)
The Time Machine (2001) — rental/Dreamworks
The Drew Carey Show (television, 1995–2001) — used in 2001
The West Wing (television, 2002–2006) — assorted
The Court (television, 2002) — used once
The Practice (television, 1997–2004) — used once, 2003 season
Cold Case (television, 2003–2010) — used twice, November 2003 and January 2005
"Best Buy" commercial (television, November 9, 2004)
Looney Tunes: Back in Action (2004) — as itself
War of the Worlds (2005) — rental/Paramount
I Could Never Be Your Woman (2007) — rental — as a movie studio set
Valentine's Day (2010)

New York Street

Outcast (1928)
A Showgirl in Hollywood (1929) — theater
Fifty Million Frenchmen (1931)
Public Enemy (1931)
A Soldier's Plaything (1931)
I Am a Fugitive from a Chain Gang (1932)
Three on a Match (1932) — courthouse

Footlight Parade (1933)
Gold Diggers of 1933 (1933) — store window, alley
Wild Boys of the Road (1933) — courthouse
42nd Street (1933) — theater
Baby Face (1933) — courthouse was Gotham Trust Bank, where Barbara Stanwyck "works"
The Big Shakedown (1934)
Dames (1934)
Mammy (1935) — as "Prosperous Street"
The Girl from 10th Avenue (1935)
Dangerous (1935) — Metropolitan Street
I Found Stella Parrish (1935)
Bullets or Ballots (1936)
Colleen (1936) — 5th Avenue, public park
Gold Diggers of 1937 (1936)
The Life of Emile Zola (1937) — as Paris
Green Light (1937) — Errol Flynn drives up street
Black Legion (1937) — traffic signal
Talent Scout (1937)
Marked Woman (1937)
Kid Galahad (1937) — "Shelton Arms" and theater staircase (last shot)
She Loved a Fireman (1937)
They Won't Forget (1937) — Lana Turner's walk
Hollywood Hotel (1937) — Callahan's drive-in
Men in Exile (1937)
The Patient in Room 18 (1938) — Patric Knowles sleepwalks here
Mr. Smith Goes to Washington (1938) — rental/Columbia — as Jackson City
Lovely Lady (1938)
The Amazing Dr. Clitterhouse (1938) — courthouse
Four's a Crowd (1938)
The Sisters (1938) — as San Francisco
The Roaring Twenties (1939) — as New York
Each Dawn I Die (1939) — car crash in town of "Banton"
Four Mothers (1940) — courthouse
A Dispatch from Reuters (1940) — House of Commons and Hyde Park
Virginia City (1940) — deserted mansion
High Sierra (1941) — hotel
They Died with Their Boots On (1941) — as Washington, DC
Sergeant York (1941) — New York park parade
The Maltese Falcon (1941) — hotel exterior
All through the Night (1942) — theater played "Hotel Marquis"
Yankee Doodle Dandy (1942) — parade at end and theater exteriors
The Gay Sisters (1942) — courthouse
Gentleman Jim (1942) — theater staircase

Thank Your Lucky Stars (1943) — theater alley

The Hard Way (1943) — alley

This Is the Army (1943) — "This Time Is the Last Time" number

Northern Pursuit (1943) — courthouse covered with snow

The Constant Nymph (1943) — as London

Hollywood Canteen (1944) — soda fountain and "Hollywood and Vine"

Mr. Skeffington (1944) — Embassy Courtyard site

Uncertain Glory (1944) — courthouse

Musical Movieland (1944) — short subject studio tour

Mildred Pierce (1945) — as Los Angeles

Rhapsody in Blue (1945) — theater lobby and Grand Hotel

Humoresque (1946)

The Big Sleep (1946; shot in 1945) — bookstore, Brody's apartment, and "Fulwider Bld."

Deception (1946)

The Time, the Place and the Girl (1946)

My Wild Irish Rose (1946)

Dark Passage (1947) — Bogart at bus depot

Always Together (1947) — Chicago cab stand and theater

Escape Me Never (1947) — theater alley and stairs

Love and Learn (1947)

The Unfaithful (1947) — outside of Los Angeles nightclub

Winter Meeting (1948) — as New York

Romance on the High Seas (1948) — travel agency next to theater alley

My Dream Is Yours (1949) — newsstand, Hollywood street, and music store

Beyond the Forest (1949) — as Chicago

Flamingo Road (1949) — newspaper office

Always Leave Them Laughing (1949)

Night unto Night (1949; shot in 1948) — as Florida

So You Think You're Not Guilty (1949) — "Joe McDoakes" short subject

The Damned Don't Cry (1950)

The Daughter of Rosie O'Grady (1950) — Debbie Reynolds dances on courthouse steps

Two Million Dollar Bank Robbery (aka *Highway 301*) (1950)

Force of Arms (1951) — as Italy

I Was a Communist for the FBI (1951) — courthouse

Tomorrow Is Another Day (1951) — as New York

Painting the Clouds with Sunshine (1951)

Force of Arms (1951) — as Rome

The Enforcer (1951) — beauty salon

Strangers on a Train (1951)

I'll See You in My Dreams (1951) — as "Wabash Avenue," also theater

A Streetcar Named Desire (1951) — "cemetery"

On Moonlight Bay (1951) — theater

Come Fill the Cup (1951) — "Blue Pencil Bar" and "Hurricane Club"

Stop, You're Killing Me (1952) — New York Park

April in Paris (1952) — theater as "Knickerbocker Theater"

The Winning Team (1952) — alley

The Iron Mistress (1952) — park

This Woman Is Dangerous (1952)

House of Wax (1953) — wax museum set is still on set's northern wall

She's Back on Broadway (1953)

So This Is Love (1953)

Dragnet (1954) — feature version of TV show

Young at Heart (1954)

Lucky Me (1954)

A Star Is Born (1954) — Judy Garland's movie opened in theater

Them! (1954) — giant ants

Jump into Hell (1955)

Sincerely Yours (1955) — theater alley

Pete Kelly's Blues (1955) — Jack Webb and Janet Leigh on top of marquee, also theater staircase

I Died a Thousand Times (1955)

Illegal (1955)

Battle Cry (1955)

Serenade (1956) — Embassy Courtyard

The Girl He Left Behind (1956)

Giant (1956) — nightclub

Miracle in the Rain (1956)

The Helen Morgan Story (1957) — nightclub at Brownstone Street–New York Street junction

Loving You (1957) — rental/Paramount

Damn Yankees (1958)

Darby's Rangers (1958)

Too Much, Too Soon (1958)

Lafayette Escandrille (1958) — Embassy Courtyard, with subway station in front

Marjorie Morningstar (1958)

Auntie Mame (1958) — theater

77 Sunset Strip (television, 1958–1964) — assorted

The Young Philadelphians (1959) — Flannigan construction site

The Ice Palace (1959)

Hawaiian Eye (television, 1959–1963) — assorted

The FBI Story (1959) — assorted

The Rise and Fall of Legs Diamond (1960)

The Bramble Bush (1960) — Cape Cod, Massachusetts

A Fever in the Blood (1961) — courthouse

Elmer Gantry (1962) — rental/UA

Gypsy (1962) — theater

The Incredible Mr. Limpet (1962)

Whatever Happened to Baby Jane? (1962) — theater

Island of Love (1963)

Palm Springs Weekend (1963) — park

Rampage (1963)

Critic's Choice (1963) — theater for Lucille Ball's play

My Fair Lady (1964) — park as Covent Gardens, also exterior of opera house

Kisses for My President (1964)

Ensign Pulver (1964) — park

Sex and the Single Girl (1964) — police station exterior

The System (1964)

Robin and the 7 Hoods (1964) — Frank Sinatra's "My Kinda Town" at courthouse

The Great Race (1965) — start of race

Brainstorm (1965) — park

None but the Brave (1965) — park as country club

The F.B.I. (television, 1965–1974) — "The Assassin" at Embassy Courtyard, and others

An American Dream (1966)

Batman (television, 1966–1968) — assorted

First to Fight (1967) — New York park

High Chaparral (television, 1967–1971) — "Obligations of an Honorable Man"

I Love You, Alice B. Toklas (1968) — as Los Angeles

Assignment to Kill (1968)

The Big Bounce (1969) — park

The Learning Tree (1969) — theater in Kansas

Flap (1970) — Indian rally

The Phynx (1970) — Embassy Courtyard

The Out-of-Towners (1970) — rental/Paramount

The Omega Man (1971) — courthouse and park

What's Up Doc? (1972) — as San Francisco

The Way We Were (1973) — rental/Columbia — as New York

For Pete's Sake (1974) — rental/Columbia

Mame (1974) — courthouse steps

Funny Lady (1975) — rental/Columbia

The Black Bird (1975) — rental/Columbia — theater as "Rhythm Room"

The Gumball Rally (1976) — road race

Won Ton Ton: The Dog Who Saved Hollywood (1976) — rental/Paramount

Nickelodeon (1976) — rental/Columbia — theater and courthouse

Wonder Woman (television, 1976–1979) — assorted

Movie Movie (1978) — theater and street

I Wanna Hold Your Hand (1978) — Embassy Courtyard

The Swarm (1978) — killer bees

Hooper (1978) — as a studio backlot

The Cheap Detective (1978) — rental/Columbia

Love at First Bite (1979) — rental/AIP — as New York

1941 (1979) — rental/Universal — John Belushi lands plane on street

Moviola: The Scarlett O'Hara War (television, 1980) — as Atlanta

Private Benjamin (television, 1981–1983) — assorted

Blade Runner (1982) — as futuristic Los Angeles

Bring 'Em Back Alive (television, 1982–1983) — New York's Raffles Hotel

The Big Chill (1983) — rental/Columbia — "J.T. Lancer" credits — Embassy Courtyard

Hotel (television, 1983–1988) — St. Gregory hotel

To Be or Not to Be (1983) — rental/Fox — Warsaw, Poland

The Man with Two Brains (1983) — as Eastern Europe

The Thorn Birds (television, 1983) — Embassy Courtyard

Ghostbusters (1984) — rental/Columbia — but most exteriors actually shot at Ranch

Night Court (television, 1984–1992) — courthouse

Explorers (1985) — rental/Paramount

Nuts (1987) — courthouse

Murphy Brown (television, 1988–1998) — assorted

Family Matters (television, 1989–1998) — assorted

Harlem Nights (1989) — rental/Paramount

Gremlins II (1990) — New York

The Flash (television, 1990) — assorted

Gabriel's Fire (television, 1990–1991) — assorted

Sisters (television, 1991–1996) — assorted

The Rocketeer (1991) — rental/Disney — as Hollywood Boulevard

Naked Gun 2½ (1991) — rental/Paramount

Reasonable Doubts (television, 1991–1993) — assorted

Class Act (1992)

The Mambo Kings (1992) — as New York

Mad about You (television, 1992–1999) — once; used courthouse as art museum

Falling Down (1993) — as Los Angeles

Lois and Clark: The New Adventures of Superman (television, 1993–1997) — assorted

Double Dragon (1993) — rental/Greenleaf Prod.

ER (television, 1994–2009) — assorted Chicago locations

The Mask (1994) — rental/New Line Cinema

Friends (television, 1994–2004) — assorted

Batman Forever (1995) — Embassy Courtyard

The Drew Carey Show (1995–2004) — "Music Videos" and flying sequence

The Client (television, 1995–1996) — assorted

Eraser (1996) — Embassy Courtyard

Suddenly Susan (television, 1996–2000) — assorted

Contact (1997) — courthouse

Mad City (1997)

Father's Day (1997) — as Reno, Nevada

Prey (television, 1997) — assorted
Why Do Fools Fall in Love? (1997) — courthouse
Vengeance Unlimited (television, 1998) — assorted
Brimstone (television, 1998) — assorted
Lethal Weapon IV (1998)
"American Express" commercials with Superman and Jerry Seinfeld (television, 1998)
Introducing Dorothy Dandridge (television, 1999) — HBO movie
Hyperion Bay (television, 1999) — assorted
Annie (1999) — rental/ Disney — Embassy Courtyard
Angle (television, 1999) — rental/20th Century Fox — unaired pilot
Wild Wild West (1999)
Opposite Sex (television, 1999) — assorted
Thirteen Days (1999) — rental/New Line Cinema — Embassy Courtyard
Annie (television, 1999) — rental/Disney
Hype (television, 2000)
Fail Safe (television, 2000) — live special
Bull (television, 2000) — assorted
Dead Last (television, 2001)
Nikki (television, 2001) — dance sequences
Swordfish (2001) — ball bearing explosion
Birds of Prey (television, 2002) — pilot; as Gotham City
Gilmore Girls (television, 2000–2007) — Embassy Courtyard, 2003; others
The Last Samurai (2003) — as Japan
Without a Trace (television, 2003–2009) — assorted
Cold Case (television, 2003–2010) — assorted
Wanda at Large (television, 2003) — December 2003 shoot
West Wing (television, 1999–2006) — Embassy Courtyard (2004 season)
The Prestige (2006) — Embassy Courtyard
Batman: The Dark Knight (2007) — December 13, 2007: Embassy Courtyard, courthouse, and park
The Unit (television, 2007) — rental/Fox — Embassy Courtyard
Pushing Daisies (television, 2007–2009) — Pie Hole restaurant
World According to Barns (television, 2007) — Embassy Courtyard
The Big Bang Theory (2007–) — park, 2013 season
Opposite Day (2009) — rental/Anchor Bay — courthouse and park
The Artist (2011) — rental/Weinstein — theater
Argo (2012) — courthouse
The Incredible Burt Wonderstone (2013) — Embassy Courtyard
The Jersey Boys (2014)

French Street

Viennese Nights (1930) — original French street, north of current one
Grand Slam (1932) — original French street, north of current one
Captain Blood (1935) — original French street, north of current one
Stella Parrish (1935) — original French street, north of current one
Little Big Shot (1935) — original French street, north of current one
Outcast (1935) — original French street, north of current one
The King and the Chorus Girl (1936) — original French street, north of current one
Mazurka (1937) — original French street, north of current one
Tovarich (1937) — original French street, north of current one
The Life of Emile Zola (1937) — original French street, north of current one, "French tenement"
Juarez (1938) — original French street, north of current one, "Grand Hotel"
All This, and Heaven Too (1940) — original French street, north of current one
A Dispatch from Reuters (1940) — original French street, north of current one, "Brussels Street"
One Foot in Heaven (1941) — original French street, north of current one, "Church"
Casablanca (1942)
Desperate Journey (1942)
Devotion (1942)
Uncertain Glory (1943)
The Constant Nymph (1943)
Life with Father (1947) — 1883 New York
So This Is Love (1953) — as Paris
A Star Is Born (1954)
Battle Cry (1954)
Phantom of the Rue Morgue (1954) — "Paris street festival"
Jump into Hell (1955)
Lafayette Escandrille (1958)
Bourbon Street Beat (television, 1959–1960)
The Rise and Fall of Legs Diamond (1960)
Days of Wine and Roses (1963) — as San Francisco
Get Smart (television, 1965–1970) — occasional rental
Chamber of Horrors (1966) — as Baltimore
Who's Afraid of Virginia Woolf? (1966) — roadhouse
The Green Berets (1968) — redressed as Viet Nam village
Suppose They Gave A War and Nobody Came? (1970) — rental/ABC

The Omega Man (1971) — "car lot"
Eight Is Enough (television, 1977–1981) — assorted
The Dukes of Hazzard (television, 1979–1985) — as Georgia
Kenny Rogers as The Gambler (television, 1980)
China Beach (television, 1988–1991) — as Saigon
Murphy Brown (television, 1988–1998) — assorted, as Washington, DC
Life Goes On (television, 1989–1993) — assorted
Sisters (television, 1991–1996) — George Clooney's character "blown up" near restroom (1994)
Point of No Return (1993) — as New Orleans
Lois and Clark: The New Adventures of Superman (television, 1993–1997) — assorted
ER (television, 1994–2009) — Noah Wyle graduation scene, 1996
Ally McBeal (television, 1997–2002) — used once
Suddenly Susan (television, 1996–2000) — assorted
Small Soldiers (1998) — rental/Dreamworks — constructed toy shop
Brimstone (television, 1998) — assorted
Jack Frost (1998) — as Medford, Colorado
Hyperion Bay (television, 1998) — assorted
Vengeance Unlimited (television, 1998) — assorted
The Little Richard Story (television, 1999)
Jack and Jill (television, 1999–2001) — assorted
West Wing (television, 1999–2006) — as Georgetown
Everybody Loves Raymond (television, 1996–2005) — used once, in 2000
Dead Last (television, 2000)
For Your Love (television, 2000)
Gilmore Girls (2000–2007) — as Stars Hollow
Nikki (television, 2000–2002) — dance sequence
The Yellow Bird (2001) — Faye Dunaway short
The Drew Carey Show (television, 1995–2004) — used once, in 2001
Citizen Bains (television, 2001) — used once
Maybe It's Me (television, 2001–2002) — used once
Torque (2003)
Cold Case (television, 2003–2010) — used once, on March 11, 2005
Moonlight (television, 2007–2008) — assorted
Ghost Whisperer — (television, 2005–2010) — used once, on June 23, 2008
Terminator: Sarah Connor Chronicles (television, 2008–2009) — assorted
Mirrors (2008) — rental/Fox
Without a Trace (television, 2002–2009) — used once, on May 13, 2008
J. Edgar (2011) — as New Orleans

New Orleans Street

A Streetcar Named Desire (1951) — as New Orleans, built on stage and moved here
The Iron Mistress (1952) — as New Orleans
Band of Angels (1956) — as New Orleans
Maverick (1957–1962) — episode "Pappy" (1959)
The FBI Story (1959) — assorted
Bourbon Street Beat (television, 1959–1960) — as New Orleans
The Gallant Men (television, 1962) — as Italian village
4 for Texas (1963) — northern end
My Fair Lady (1964) — northern end, as London
The Green Berets (1968) — redressed as Viet Nam village!

Train Shed

Colleen (1936) — taxi
Four Daughters (1938)
The Sisters (1938) — "train station"
We Are Not Alone (1939)
The Maltese Falcon (1941) — "taxi process"
Sergeant York (1941) — "Crossville Railroad Station"
Now, Voyager (1942)
Casablanca (1943) — "Gare De Lyon" station
Night and Day (1943)
Uncertain Glory (1944)
Hollywood Canteen (1944) — "train shed and platform"
Rhapsody in Blue (1945) — "train #234"
Young Man with a Horn (1950)
I'll See You in My Dreams (1951)
Young at Heart (1951)
Lullaby of Broadway (1951)
Come Fill the Cup (1951) — "Boyd's car"
The Story of Will Rogers (1952)
The Winning Team (1952)
About Face (1952)
Retreat? Hell! (1952)
By the Light of the Silvery Moon (1953)
Battle Cry (1955)
The Big Trees (1956)
The Spirit of St. Louis (1956)
I Was a Communist for the FBI (1956)
Darby's Rangers (1958) — as Europe, James Garner
Lafayette Escandrille (1958)
Lawman (television, 1958–1962)

Tenement Street

Frisco Kid (1935) — as Barbary Coast of 1852
Angels with Dirty Faces (1938) — as "Dock Street"

Racket Busters (1938)

Each Dawn I Die (1939)

Dust Be My Destiny (1939)

Off the Record (1939)

The Roaring Twenties (1939)

Confessions of a Nazi Spy (1939)

Three Cheers for the Irish (1940)

City for Conquest (1940) — as New York

Strawberry Blonde (1941) — Nick's barber shop

You Can't Escape Forever (1942)

All through the Night (1942) — as New York

Gentleman Jim (1942) — as San Francisco

To Have and Have Not (1944) — as Martinique

Shine on, Harvest Moon (1944)

Saratoga Trunk (1945; shot in 1943) — "Beuge's Restaurant"

Rhapsody in Blue (1945) — "Gershwin flat" and "penny arcade"

The Big Sleep (1946; shot in 1945) — Marlowe's Office on set's western wall

Humoresque (1946)

My Wild Irish Rose (1946)

Three Strangers (1946) — Peter Lorre

Dark Passage (1947) — "alley"

Escape Me Never (1947) — "shabby street"

Whiplash (1948)

One Sunday Afternoon (1948) — as 1910

Beyond the Forest (1949)

Two Million Dollar Bank Robbery (aka *Highway 301*) (1950)

The Enforcer (1951)

I Was a Communist for the FBI (1951)

Come Fill the Cup (1951) — "Charlie's Apartment" and "Maria's Apartment"

The Eddie Cantor Story (1953) — New York opening scenes

Calamity Jane (1953)

House of Wax (1953) — as 1890s New York

Pete Kelly's Blues (1955)

Helen Morgan Story (1957)

Onionhead (1958)

The FBI Story (1959)

The Rise and Fall of Legs Diamond (1960)

Portrait of a Mobster (1961) — as New York

Fever in the Blood (1961)

Gypsy (1962)

Days of Wine and Roses (1963) — as San Francisco

My Fair Lady (1964) — "With a Little Bit" number

Cheyenne Autumn (1964) — "montage"

The Incredible Mr. Limpet (1964) — Limpet's apartment building

The Great Race (1965) — car crashes into storefront on northwest corner

Portnoy's Complaint (1972)

Cleopatra Jones (1973)

Mame (1974)

Police Woman (television, 1974–1978) — assorted

The Ultimate Warrior (1975)

A 1970's Fairy Tale (1975) — short subject by director Paul D. Marks

Harry and Walter Go to New York (1976) — nineteenth-century New York

Wonder Woman (television, 1976–1979) — assorted

Hooper (1978) — as studio backlot

Time after Time (1979) — as London, for Jack the Ripper scenes

Altered States (1979) — as Roxbury Park, Boston

Roots: The Next Generation (television, 1979) — race riots

Falcon Crest (television, 1981–1990) — "Above Suspicion"

Annie (1982) — rental/Columbia — built orphanage façade

Hey Good Lookin' (1982) — live action scenes

T.J. Hooker (television, 1982–1986) — assorted

Bring 'Em Back Alive (television, 1982–1983) — as Singapore

Scarecrow and Mrs. King (television, 1983–1987) — assorted

City Heat (1984) — as Kansas City

Michael Jackson "Pepsi" commercial (1984)

Mike Hammer (television, 1984–1987) — Stacy Keach

Club Paradise (1986) — retakes

Karate Kid II (1986) — rental/Columbia — as Tokyo, Japan

Bird (1988)

Beaches (1998) — rental/Disney — as restaurant

Lethal Weapon II (1989) — as Los Angeles

Harlem Nights (1989) — rental/Paramount — as New York

Family Matters (television, 1989–1998) — assorted

Bukharin: Enemy of the People (1990) — rental

Dick Tracy (1990) — rental/Disney

Gremlins II: The New Batch (1990) — as New York

Bugsy (1991) — rental/Columbia

Mobsters (1991) — rental/Universal

The Butcher's Wife (1991) — rental/Paramount — as New York

Sisters (television, 1991–1996) — assorted

Newsies (1992) — rental/Disney — as New York

Batman Returns (1992) — as Gotham City

The Mambo Kings (1992) — New York

Point of No Return (1993) — Bridget Fonda

Adventures of Brisco County Jr. (television, 1993–1994) — used once

Swing Kids (1993) — rental/Disney

The Shadow (1993) — rental/Universal

Lois and Clark: The New Adventures of Superman (television, 1993–1997) — assorted

NYPD Blue (television, 1993–2005) — used several times

A Little Princess (1994) — as 1918 New York

ER (television, 1994–2009) — assorted

Friends (television, 1994–2004) — assorted

The Mask (1994) — rental/New Line Cinema

The Client (television, 1995–1996) — assorted

Batman Forever (1995) — as Gotham City

Sliders (television, 1995–2000) — used once

Barb Wire (1996) — rental/Polygram

Dark Skies (television, 1996–1997)

Herbie The Love Bug (television, 1996) — rental/Disney — TV remake

Wolf Pack (television, 1996) — unsold pilot with Dennis Weaver

Prey (television, 1997)

Batman and Robin (1997) — as Gotham City

Paulie: A Parrot's Tale (1997) — rental/Dreamworks

The Dukes of Hazzard Reunion! (television, 1997)

"Subaru" commercial (television, 1997) — Mel Gibson (seen in Japan only)

Fallen (1998) — Denzel Washington

Blade Squad (television, 1998)

Brimstone (television, 1998)

Why Do Fools Fall in Love? (1998) — as New York

Hyperion Bay (television, 1998) — assorted

Sex and the City (television, 1998–2003) — third season Hollywood episode

Payback (1999) — rental/Paramount

Angel (television, 1999) — used once

Annie (television, 1999) — rental/Disney — remake of above

Lansky (television, 1999) — Richard Dreyfus

Jack and Jill (television, 1999–2001) — assorted

Opposite Sex (television, 1999)

Everybody Loves Raymond (television, 1999–2005) — occasional

Tuesdays with Morrie (television, 1999) — rental/Hallmark — Jack Lemmon's last role

Suddenly Susan (television, 1996–2000) — once, 1999 episode

The West Wing (television, 1999–2006) — used December 2, 2004

Batman commercials (2000–2002) — "OnStar" — a series of six

A.I. Artificial Intelligence (2000) — as Rouge City

The Dukes of Hazard: Hazzard in Hollywood (television, 2000) — as Los Angeles

Swordfish (2000)

That's Life (television, 2000–2002) — rental/Paramount — used once

Bull (television, 2000) — assorted

What Women Want (2000) — rental/Paramount — as New York

Rock Star (2000)

Spiderman (2001) — rental/Columbia — alley used for upside-down kiss

Minority Report (2001) — rental/Fox/Dreamworks — jet pack fight along eastern wall

Sweet November (2001) — as San Francisco

Road to Perdition (2001) — rental/Dreamworks — Tom Hanks–Paul Newman shootout

Gilmore Girls (television, 2001–2007) — assorted

Off Centre (television, 2001–2002) — as New York

Thieves (television, 2001)

Dead Last (television, 2001)

Vengeance Unlimited (television, 2001)

Daredevil (2002) — rental/20th Century Fox — Ben Affleck's apartment on southern wall

Bloodwork (2002) — Clint Eastwood — chase scene in alley

The Court (television, 2002) — used once

Birds of Prey (television, 2002) — pilot and subsequent episodes, as Gotham City

Without a Trace (2002–2009) — assorted

Anger Management (2003) — rental/Columbia

Starsky and Hutch (2003)

Cold Case (television, 2003–2010) — used November 2003

The Practice (television, 1997–2004) — rental/20th Century Fox — used once, for 2003 season

The Last Samurai (2003) — as 1800s San Francisco

Something's Gotta Give (2003) — Columbia co-production — Nicholson and Keaton flirted on east sidewalk

Skipping Christmas (2004) — rental/Columbia

Flashlight (2004) — unsold pilot

Taking Lives (2004)

Rent (2005) — rental/Columbia — as New York

You Don't Mess with the Zohan (2008) — rental/Columbia

"Pepsi" commercial (television, December 30, 2008)

Entourage (2004–2011) — HBO — used 2008 season

Mad Men (television, 2007–2014) — used once, 2012 season

Cloverfield (2008) — rental/Paramount — as New York

Valentine's Day (2009)

J. Edgar (2011)

Argo (2012) — John Goodman is stopped on his way to his studio office on this set

Wimpole Street

My Fair Lady (1964) — sets used on stage, moved here
Harper (1966) — as Los Angeles
Mame (1974)

Hank's School

The Music Man (1962) — River City High for "76 Trombones"
Critic's Choice (1963) — "Public School #32"
Robin and the 7 Hoods (1964) — police station
Hank (television, 1965–1966)
Village of the Giants (1965) — rental/Embassy
The Waltons (1971–1981) — "Boatwright University"
The Jimmy Stewart Show (television, 1971–1972) — "Josiah Kessel College"

Midwest Street

Smart Money (1931) — original Midvale Street
Cabin in the Cotton (1932) — original Midvale Street
Dr. Socrates (1935) — original Midvale Street, Big Bend, Indiana
White Banners (1938) — original Midvale Street
Four Wives (1939) — current set built for this film
Invisible Stripes (1939)
Four Mothers (1941) — as "Briarwood," "Lemp house"
Meet John Doe (1941)
The Maltese Falcon (1941) — "Suburban Street — C. Wm. Frank mailbox"
King's Row (1942) — (re)built houses
The Male Animal (1942)
Edge of Darkness (1942)
Yankee Doodle Dandy (1942) — as Providence, Rhode Island
The Hard Way (1943) — courthouse as "Green Hill High School"
Proudly We Serve (1944) — short subject
Saratoga Trunk (1945; shot in 1943) — as New Orleans
Danger Signal (1945)
A Stolen Life (1946) — as a New England village
Always Together (1947) — as Reno, Nevada
My Wild Irish Rose (1947)
Johnny Belinda (1948) — Dr. Gray's office, street
Two Guys from Texas (1948)
Flamingo Road (1949) — as town of Bolden
The House across the Street (1949)
It's a Great Feeling (1949) — as Gurkins Corners, Wisconsin

Young Man with a Horn (1950) — car accident on residential street
Dallas (1950)
Storm Warning (1950) — "residential street"
I Was a Communist for the FBI (1951)
The Enforcer (1951) — courthouse
On Moonlight Bay (1951)
I'll See You in My Dreams (1951)
Painting the Clouds with Sunshine (1951)
Strangers on a Train (1951) — "residential street"
No Pets Allowed (1952) — short subject
She's Working Her Way through College (1952)
Retreat? Hell! (1952)
The Big Trees (1952)
Springfield Rifle (1952)
Our Miss Brooks (television, 1952–1956) — assorted
Room for One More (1952) — Cary Grant
By the Light of the Silvery Moon (1953)
Walking My Baby Back Home (1953) — rental/ Universal
House of Wax (1953) — street alley
East of Eden (1954) — as Salinas, California
Lucky Me (1954)
Young at Heart (1954) — as Connecticut
Rebel without a Cause (1955) — Plato's house
King's Row (television, 1955–1956)
I Died a Thousand Times (1955) — "Velma's house"
The McConnell Story (1955) — Alan Ladd
Our Miss Brooks (1956) — feature based on TV show
So You Want to Be Pretty (1956) — short subject
The Pajama Game (1957) — Doris Day in Cedar Rapids, Iowa
Sugarfoot (television, 1957–1961) — played San Francisco twice: "Highbinder" and "Fernando"
Damn Yankees (1958) — the Boyd house
The Missouri Traveler (1958)
Lafayette Escandrille (1958) — car crash at beginning of film
The Left-Handed Gun (1958)
No Time for Sergeants (1958) — service station, etc.
Rock-a-Bye Baby (1958) — rental/Paramount — Jerry Lewis
Onionhead (1958)
The FBI Story (1959) — James Stewart married in church
A Summer Place (1959) — as Pine Island, Maine
Ice Palace (1960) — as Seattle, Washington
Pollyanna (1960) — rental/Disney — as Beldingsville, Vermont
Guns of the Timberland (1960) — Alan Ladd in town of "Deep Wells"

Ocean's Eleven (1960) — climax is set in church

The Dark at the Top of the Stairs (1960) — as Oklahoma

The Bramble Bush (1960) — as New England

Gypsy (1962) — "Hovick House" next to church

The Music Man (1962) — as River City, Iowa

Papa's Delicate Condition (1963) — rental/Paramount — Jackie Gleason in "Texarkana"

Island of Love (1963) — courthouse as New York Public library

4 for Texas (1963)

The Man from Galveston (1963)

Days of Wine and Roses (1963) — church entranceway

Critic's Choice (1963)

Cheyenne Autumn (1964)

Two on a Guillotine (1964) — a southern California town

Robin and the 7 Hoods (1964) — Bing Crosby's "home," also church, in Chicago

The Third Day (1965)

The Chase (1966) — Robert Redford gets shot on courthouse steps

Bonnie and Clyde (1967) — inserts of bank exteriors

The Invaders (television, 1967) — rental/ABC — used several times, including "Valley of the Shadow"

Cool Hand Luke (1967) — Paul Newman cut heads off parking meters here

A Covenant with Death (1967)

First to Fight (1967)

The Good Guys and the Bad Guys (1968) — boardinghouse Robert Mitchum stays at

Mayberry R.F.D. (television, 1968–1971) — used 1970–1971 seasons only

The Arrangement (1969)

More Dead than Alive (1969) — rental/UA

The Learning Tree (1969) — as Kansas

Butch Cassidy and the Sundance Kid (1969) — rental/Fox

The Bill Cosby Show (television, 1969–1971)

Suppose They Gave a War and Nobody Came? (1970) — rental/ABC

The Phynx (1970)

The Skin Game (1971)

The Jimmy Stewart Show (television, 1971–1972)

The Waltons (television, 1972–1981) — as Charlottesville, Virginia

Oklahoma Crude (1973) — rental/Columbia

Mame (1974)

Blazing Saddles (1974) — as Rock Ridge

North and South (television, 1985) — miniseries

The Shootist (1976) — rental/Paramount — John Wayne in Carson City, Nevada

Nickelodeon (1976) — rental/Columbia

Wonder Woman (television, 1976–1979) — assorted

It Happened One Christmas (television, 1977) — remake of *It's a Wonderful Life*

Carter Country (television, 1977–1979) — as Georgia

On Our Own (television, 1977–1978) — used once

Starsky and Hutch — (television, 1975–1979) — used once, 1977

The Swarm (1978) — killer bees in Marysville, Texas

Fantasy Island (television, 1978–1984) — assorted

Hooper (1978)

The Bastard (television, 1978) — miniseries

'Salem's Lot (television, 1979) — miniseries

Roots: The Next Generation (television, 1979) — as Elizabeth City, North Carolina, 1939

The Dukes of Hazzard (television, 1979–1985)

Altered States (1980) — as Boston

Moviola: The Scarlett O'Hara War (television, 1980)

"Dr. Pepper" commercial (television, 1980) — as southern town

Code Red (television, 1981–1982) — Lorne Greene, as Los Angeles

East of Eden (television, 1981) — miniseries remake

Falcon Crest (television, 1981–1990) — "Divided We Fall" episode

Gremlins (1984) — as Kingston Falls

Police Academy 2 (1985)

Growing Pains (television, 1985–1992) — the Seaver house in Long Island, New York

Fright Night (1985) — rental/Columbia

Lethal Weapon (1987) — as Los Angeles

Over the Top (1987) — Sylvester Stallone

The Monster Squad (1987) — rental/Tri-Star

Elvira: Mistress of The Dark (1988) — rental/New World — as town of "Falwell"

Life Goes On (television, 1989–1993) — used at least once

Quantum Leap (television, 1989–1993) — rental/Universal — used once

Postcards from the Edge (1990) — rental/Columbia — as a studio lot

Delirious (1991) — rental/MGM — John Candy in Ashford Falls

Naked Gun 2½ (1991) — rental/Paramount

Homefront (television, 1991)

Sisters (television, 1991–1996) — as Winnetka, Illinois

Love and Bullets (television, 1991) — Susan Dey

Sleepwalkers (1992) — rental/Columbia — as Travis, Indiana

Point of No Return (1993) — as New Orleans, LA

Lois and Clark: The New Adventures of Superman (television, 1993–1997) — as Smallville, Kansas

Stuart Saves His Family (1994) — rental/Paramount
Friends (television, 1994–2004) — assorted, including
    Monica's childhood home
ER (television, 1994–2009) — assorted
Family Album (1994) — miniseries — Jaclyn Smith
Outbreak (1995) — Dustin Hoffman helicopter landing
Grumpier Old Men (1995) — reshoots, as Wabasha,
    Minnesota
The Judds (aka *Bridge over Troubled Waters*) (television,
    1995) — rental — miniseries
The Client (television, 1995–1996)
The Drew Carey Show (television, 1995–2004) —
    assorted, including "Drew and the Batmobile"
    episode
Charlie Grace (television, 1995) — Mark Harmon's
    home near film vault
A Walton Wedding (television, 1995) — as Charlottes-
    ville, Virginia
Houdini (television, 1996) — rental/TNT Movie
Suddenly Susan (television, 1996–2000) — premiere
    episode
Space Jam (1997) — Michael Jordan's yard
Goosebumps (television, 1997) — Jeff Goldblum
Girls across the Lake (television, 1997) — Cindy
    Williams
The Dukes of Hazzard Reunion! (television, 1997) — as
    Hazzard County
Casper: A Spirited Beginning (direct to video, 1997)
Skeletons (1998) — rental/HBO Pictures
Jack Frost (1998) — as Medford, Colorado
Batman and Robin (1998) — Gazebo for Mr. Freeze's
    wedding
Vengeance Unlimited (television, 1998) — assorted
George Wallace Story (television, 1998) — Gary Sinese
Blade Squad (television, 1998) — assorted
Brimstone (television, 1998) — used once
Prey (television, 1998) — assorted
Seinfeld (television, 1990–1998) — as Massachusetts,
    1998 episode, "The Finale"
Dennis the Menace II (direct to video, 1998) — Don
    Rickles
Hyperion Bay (television, 1998) — as Hyperion Bay,
    California
Being Dunbar (television, 1999) — rental/Touch-
    stone
Inherit the Wind (television, 1999) — rental/ MGM —
    as 1925 Tennessee
The West Wing (television, 1999–2006) — occasional
Being Dunbar (television, 1999) — rental/Touch-
    stone
Jesse (television, 1999) — assorted

The Trial of Old Drum (television, 1999)
Jack and Jill (television, 1999–2001) — assorted
Opposite Sex (television, 1999) — used once
Season of Miracles (television, 1999) — rental/
    Hallmark
The Dukes of Hazzard: Hazzard in Hollywood (televi-
    sion, 2000)
Gilmore Girls (television, 2000–2007) — as Stars Hol-
    low, Connecticut
Bull (television, 2000) — used at least once
O Brother, Where Art Thou? (2000) — rental/Disney
The Yellow Bird (2001) — rental/Faye Dunaway short
Cats and Dogs (2001)
Nikki (television, 2001) — dance sequence
Dead Last (television, 2001)
Maybe It's Me (television, 2001–2002) — assorted
Ellen Again (television, 2001) — rental/CBS — pilot
Romeo Fire (television, 2002) — pilot
Cold Case (television, 2003–2010) — used March 11,
    2005
Maniac Magee (television, 2003) — Nickelodeon movie
National Lampoon's Cousin Eddie's Christmas Vacation
    (television, 2003)
Norbit (2006) — rental/Paramount — Eddie Murphy
    in Tennessee
Just For Laughs (2007) — rental/Dakota Films
    — Sinbad
Batman: The Dark Knight (2007) — shot pickups on
    December 13, 2007
"Lincoln Mercury" commercial (2008)
Mirrors (2008) — rental/Fox — Kiefer Sutherland
Yes Man (2008)
The Ghost Whisperer (television, 2008) — rental/ABC
    — 2008 season after fire on Universal sets
Opposite Day (2008)
Eastwick (television, 2009)
J. Edgar (2011) — as Centralia, Washington
Heart of Dixie (television, 2011–) — as Bluebell,
    Alabama
The Muppets (2011) — rental/Disney — as Smalltown

Western Street

Cheyenne (television, 1955–1963) — assorted
Shootout at Medicine Bend (1957) — "saloon" and street
Colt .45 (television, 1957–1960) — assorted
Sugarfoot (television, 1957–1961) — assorted
Maverick (1957–1962) — assorted
Fort Dobbs (1958) — opening scenes "Largo"
No Time for Sergeants (1958)
Bronco (television, 1958–1962) — assorted

The Naked and the Dead (1958) — rental/RKO
The FBI Story (1959) — bank in Oklahoma oil town
Guns of the Timberland (1960) — Alan Ladd in town of "Deep Wells"
Ice Palace (1960)
The Music Man (1962) — River City rail depot
Lad: A Dog (1962)
Black Gold (1963)
Temple Huston (1963–1964) — assorted
The Great Race (1965) — as "Boracho"
A Big Hand for the Little Lady (1966)
The High Chaparral (television, 1967–1971) — assorted
Hotel (1967) — "Beauvoir lobby"
A Covenant with Death (1967)
The Good Guys and the Bad Guys (1968) — as town of "Progress"
Bonanza (television, 1959–1973; used 1969–1972 only)
The Skin Game (1971)
Kung Fu (television, 1972–1975) — assorted
Get to Know Your Rabbit (1972)
Westworld (1973) — rental/MGM — as Westworld
The Cowboys (television, 1974) — as New Mexico, based on movie
Blazing Saddles (1974) — as Rock Ridge

Mexican Street

Cheyenne (television, 1955–1963) — episodes: "Wedding Ring" and others
Sugarfoot (television, 1957–1961) — assorted
Maverick (1957–1962) — assorted
Bronco (television, 1958–1962) — assorted
Lawman (television, 1958–1962) — assorted
The FBI Story (1959)
The Sins of Rachel Cade (1961)
Gold of the Seven Saints (1961)
The Gallant Men (television, 1962–1963) — World War II Italy
Temple Huston (1963–1964) — assorted
America, America (1963) — played a Greek village
Marriage on the Rocks (1965)
The F.B.I. (television, 1965–1974) — assorted
A Big Hand for the Little Lady (1966)
Not with My Wife You Don't (1966)
Camelot (1967) — medieval village
A Covenant with Death (1967
High Chaparral (television, 1967–1971) — assorted
More Dead than Alive (1969)
13 Clocks (1969; uncompleted?) — medieval village
The Great Bank Robbery (1969) — as the village Clint Walker kills a gang of outlaws in

Bonanza (television, 1969–1972 only) — including 1971's "The Customs of the Country" and 1972's "Day of Disaster"
Which Way to the Front (1970) — World War II Allied headquarters
Mrs. Pollifax—Spy (1971) — rental/UA — as Albania
The Skin Game (1971)
Search (television 1972–1973) — used once
Kung Fu (television, 1972–1975) — assorted, including "My Brother Executioner" (1974)

Laramie Street

Cheyenne (television, 1955–1963) — assorted
Sugarfoot (television, 1957–1961) — assorted
Colt .45 (television, 1957–1960) — assorted
Maverick (television, 1957–1962) — assorted
Lawman (television, 1958–1962) — as "Laramie"
Bronco (television, 1958–1962) — assorted
The Left Handed Gun (1958) — Paul Newman as Billy the Kid in Lincoln County, New Mexico
Westbound (1959) — as Colorado
Guns of the Timberland (1959) — Alan Ladd in town of "Deep Wells"
Claudelle Inglish (1961) — a contemporary rural setting
The Dakotas (television, 1963) — assorted
Temple Houston (television, 1963–1964) — assorted
F Troop (television, 1965–1967) — as Fort Courage
The Great Race (1965) — as "Boracho"
High Chaparral (television, 1967–1971) — assorted
Firecreek (1968) — James Stewart and Henry Fonda (pickups)
The Good Guys and the Bad Guys (1968) — as town of "Progress"
More Dead than Alive (1969)
Sam Whiskey (1969) — Burt Reynolds
The Great Bank Robbery (1969) — street extensively rebuilt to portray Friendly, Texas
Bonanza (television, 1959–1973; 1970–1973 seasons only) — as Virginia City
There Was a Crooked Man (1970) — Henry Fonda
The Skin Game (1971) — James Garner
Kung Fu (television, 1972–1975) — assorted
The Cowboys (1972) — John Wayne (pickups)
Westworld (1973) — rental/MGM — Yul Brynner's fall from saloon window
A Dream for Christmas (television, 1973) — as Sweet Clover, Arkansas
The Cowboys (television, 1974) — as New Mexico, based on movie

Blazing Saddles (1974) — the famous "horse-punching" scene

Little House on the Prairie (television, 1974–1983) — town of "Sleepy Eye"

A 1970's Fairy Tale (1975) — short subject by director Paul D. Marks

From Noon till Three (1976) — as "Gladstone City"

Roots (television, 1977) — miniseries — episode 8 (shot September 21–22, 1976): as Company Shop, North Carolina

Fantasy Island (1978–1984) — occasional

Hooper (1978) — as a studio lot

The New Maverick (television, 1978)

The Frisco Kid (1979) — Harrison Ford

The Muppet Movie (1979) — far eastern row of buildings passed by Kermit on bike

Hart to Hart (television, 1979–1984) — used once

The Dukes of Hazzard (television, 1979–1985) — occasional

Young Maverick (television, 1979–1980)

Bret Maverick (television, 1981–1982) — as Sweetwater, Arizona

The Fall Guy (television, 1981–1986) — occasional, as a Hollywood set

National Lampoon's Vacation (1983) — as (modern) Dodge City, Kansas

North and South (1985) — miniseries

Star Trek: The Next Generation (television, 1987–1994) — used once

Postcards from the Edge (1990) — as movie backlot

The Adventures of Brisco County Jr. (television, 1993–1994) — assorted

Dr. Quinn: Medicine Woman (television, 1993–1998) — used once

Little Giants (1994) — open area in back of courthouse for ballgames

Maverick (1994) — incidental footage only

Wyatt Earp (1994) — incidental footage only

Wild Bill (1995) — rental/MGM — as Deadwood, South Carolina

Twister (1996) — used open area in back of courthouse

Suddenly Susan (television, 1996–2000) — used once

The Jamie Foxx Show (television, 1996–2002) — used once

The Cherokee Kid (television, 1996) — HBO movie

Big Guns Talk: The Story of the Western (television, 1997) — James Garner (host)

The Dukes of Hazzard Reunion (television, 1997)

Sobbin' Women: The Making of 7 Brides for 7 Women (made for video, 1997) — Howard Keel

Soldier (1998) — Kurt Russell, inserts

Ransom of Red Chief (television, 1998) — rental/Hallmark — Christopher Lloyd

Houdini (television, 1998) — rental/ TNT

Sunset Strip (1998) — rental/20th Century Fox

Purgatory (television, 1999) — rental/TNT movie — as town of "Refuge"

"Wild Wild West" music video (1999) — Will Smith

"Bulls-Eye Barbecue Sauce" commercial (television, 1999)

The Last Samurai (2003) — "Oriental" tile put on rooftops to play Japan

Note that the set was also used for David Carradine's wedding (1998) — not a movie, his actual wedding! And for photo shoots involving Sharon Stone, Kevin Costner, Clint Eastwood, and TV's western stars for *Vanity Fair*, with Annie Leibovitz as photographer.

Tatum Ranch/Fort Courage

Cheyenne (television, 1955–1963) — assorted

Sugarfoot (television, 1957–1961) — assorted

Colt .45 (television, 1957–1960) — assorted

Maverick (television, 1957–1962) — assorted

Lawman (television, 1958–1962) — assorted

Bronco (television, 1958–1962) — assorted

The Dakotas (television, 1963) — assorted

Temple Houston (television, 1963–1964) — assorted

F Troop (television, 1965–1967) — Fort Courage

Jungle

Santiago (1956) — first film on current set

Bombers B-52 (1957)

Colt .45 (television, 1957–1960) — episodes: 1959: "Devil's Godson" and others

Sugarfoot (1957–1961) — assorted

Shootout at Medicine Bend (1957) — "riverbank"

Band of Angels (1957) — Clark Gable, "Taylor's Glen"

Frankenstein 1970 (1958) — rental/Allied Artists — opening scene

No Time for Sergeants (1958)

Onionhead (1958)

The Deep Six (1958) — Alan Ladd, lake

Darby's Rangers (1958)

Fort Dobbs (1958) — "Indian Ambush" at "Doonevan Flats"

The Miracle (1959) — as Spain

Island of Lost Women (1959) — as a Pacific Island

Up Periscope (1959) — James Garner

Bronco (television, 1958–1962) — 1959 episodes: "Bodyguard," and others

Yellowstone Kelly (1959)

Cash McCall (1960) — as upstate New York

Ice Palace (1960) — as Alaska

The Rise and Fall of Legs Diamond (1960)

The Sins of Rachel Cade (1961)

A Fever in the Blood (1961)

Gypsy (1962)

PT 109 (1963) — as a Pacific island

Days of Wine and Roses (1963) — as California

Mary, Mary (1963)

Rampage (1963) — as Malaysia

Island of Love (1963) — Robert Preston on a Greek island

None But the Brave (1965) — as a Pacific island

F Troop (television, 1965–1967) — assorted

The Great Race (1965) — Natalie Wood's swim

The F.B.I (television, 1965–1974) — assorted

Mister Roberts (television, 1965) — assorted

Not With My Wife You Don't (1966) — Tony Curtis

A Fine Madness (1966) — "B-52 Rocks"

Lt. Robin Crusoe, U.S.N. (1966) — rental/Disney — as a South Seas island

Camelot (1967) — "The Lusty Month of May" number

A Covenant with Death (1967)

The Green Berets (1968) — as Viet Nam

Finian's Rainbow (1968) — as the Deep South

The Big Bounce (1968) — "Mexican graveyard"

Bonanza (television, 1959–1973) — assorted, last three seasons only

The Good Guys and the Bad Guys (1969) — "Doonevan Flats"

The Learning Tree (1969) — as Kansas

The Arrangement (1969)

More Dead than Alive (1969)

Rabbit Run (1970) — James Caan

Suppose They Gave a War and Nobody Came? (1970) — rental/ABC

There Was a Crooked Man (1970) — Henry Fonda

Which Way to the Front? (1970)

The Omega Man (1971) — Charlton Heston in deserted park

The Skin Game (1971) — James Garner

The Waltons (television, 1972–1981) — farmhouse was where parking lot is now

Kung Fu (television, 1972–1975) — David Carradine claimed to have planted bamboo near pond!

Fantasy Island (1978–1984) — assorted

The Muppet Movie (1979) — "The Rainbow Connection" number

The Dukes of Hazzard (television, 1979–1985) — assorted

Hart to Hart (television, 1979–1984) — used at least once

Altered States (1979) — "Franklin Park Zoo"

1941 (1979) — rental/Universal — pond played La Brea Tar Pits

Private Benjamin (1980) — Goldie Hawn training maneuvers

When Time Ran Out (1980) — as a Pacific island

First Family (1980) — Bob Newhart, lagoon

Moviola: The Scarlett O'Hara War (television, 1980) — Clark Gable's duck blind

Club Paradise (1982) — Robin Williams reshoots

Bring 'Em Back Alive (television, 1982–1983) — assorted

Sudden Impact (1983) — "clearing in woods"

Wizards and Warriors (television, 1983)

Falcon Crest (television, 1981–1990) — 1983 episode: "Above Suspicion"

The Goonies (1985) — "cave entrance"

Pee Wee's Big Adventure (1985) — Pee Wee flies over lake on bike!

Tour of Duty (television, 1987–1990) — assorted, as Viet Nam

China Beach (television, 1988–1991) — assorted, as Viet Nam

Sisters (television, 1991–1996) — assorted, as Illinois

Sleepwalkers (1992) — rental/Columbia — Walton farmhouse

The Little Rascals (1993) — rental/Universal — lake

Hot Shots: Part Deux (1993) — rental/Paramount — as Viet Nam (usually)

The Adventures of Brisco County Jr. (television, 1993–1994) — assorted

Lois and Clark: The New Adventures of Superman (television, 1993–1997) — assorted

The Specialist (1994) — James Woods in Los Angeles fought Sylvester Stallone in Miami!

On Deadly Ground (1994) — Steven Seagal in "Alaska"

Little Giants (1994)

Family Album (television, 1994) — miniseries — Jaclyn Smith directs a lake creature

A Little Princess (1994) — as India

ER (television, 1994–2009) — 1995's "Hell and High Water" with George Clooney

Outbreak (1995)

Free Willy II (1995) — used pond for special effects

"Budweiser" frog commercials (television, 1995–1998) — lake

Star Trek: Voyager (television, 1995–2001) — used once only

Congo (1995) — rental/Paramount — jungle scenes with gorillas (men in suits)

Batman Forever (1995)

Twister (1996) — storm devastation scenes

Eraser (1996) — Arnold Schwarzenegger

Midnight in the Garden of Good and Evil (1997) — as Louisiana

Girls across the Lake (television, 1997) — lake and Cindy Williams

The Army Show (television, 1998) — used once

Prey (television, 1998) — assorted

Houdini (television, 1998) — rental/TNT Movie

Six Days Seven Nights (1998) — rental/Disney — Harrison Ford on an island with Anne Heche

Vengeance Unlimited (television, 1998) — assorted

Dennis the Menace II (direct to video, 1998) — Don Rickles

Hyperion Bay (television, 1998) — assorted

The Cell (1999) — rental/New Line Cinema

The Green Mile (1999) — rental/Castle Rock — Tom Hanks

Jack and Jill (television, 1999–2001) — assorted

Gilmore Girls (television, 1999–2007) — assorted

Rules of Engagement (2000) — rental/Paramount

Bubble Boy (2000) — rental/Disney

The Elian Gonzalez Story (television, 2000) — rental/Fox

Malcolm in the Middle (television, 2000) — rental/Fox — used once

The Dukes of Hazzard: Hazzard in Hollywood (2000)

Dead Last (television, 2001) — used once

Collateral Damage (2001) — Arnold Schwarzenegger

Thieves (television, 2001)

Maybe It's Me (television, 2001)

Bull (television, 2001) — assorted

Adaptation (2002) — rental/Columbia — Meryl Streep looks for orchids

Without a Trace (television, 2002–2009) — second and third seasons

National Lampoon's Cousin Eddie's Christmas Vacation (television, 2003) — small jungle pond

Jag (television, 1995–2005) — rental/Paramount — used once, 2003 season

The Last Samurai (2003) — Japanese house built on lake

Looney Tunes: Back in Action (2003)

Million Dollar Baby (2004) — very last shot in film at lake cabin

Ocean's Twelve (2004)

Invasion (television, 2005) — built cabin and barn on western side of set

True Blood (television, 2007–) — HBO — "Merlotte's Bar"

Terminator: Sarah Connor Chronicles (television, 2008–2009) — assorted

Get Smart (2008)

Pretty Little Liars (television, 2010–) — built house on eastern end of set

Camelot Castle

Camelot (1967)

The Illustrated Man (1969)

The Phynx (1970)

Which Way to the Front? (1970)

Mrs. Pollifax—Spy (1971) — rental/UA — as Albania

Kung Fu (television, 1972–1975) — Shaolin temple

Lost Horizon (1973) — rental/Columbia — Shangri La

A 1970's Fairy Tale (1975) — short subject

Notes

Chapter 1: Breaking Ground

1. From an interview with Cass Warner Sperling.

Chapter 2: Burbank

1. Leith Adams, "From the Archive," *WB Highlights*, vol. 7, 1997.
2. "Films Go on Despite Fire," *Los Angeles Times*, December 6, 1934.
3. Jack Warner, *My First Hundred Years in Hollywood* (New York: Random House, 1964).
4. "Arson Probers Looking for 'Fire Happy' Person," *Los Angeles Times*, July 10, 1952.
5. "Warner Bros. to 'Taper off' Film Production," *Los Angeles Times*, March 5, 1953.

Chapter 3: Front Lot Studio Tour

1. From the documentary *Here's Looking at You, Warner Bros.*, directed by Robert Guenette (Los Angeles: Warner Home Video, 1991).
2. From a 1939 studio press release.
3. From a 1947 press release for the film *Always Together*.
4. From a 1973 studio press release.
5. From an undated studio press release.
6. R. R. O'Neal, "I Want a Laborer," *Warner Club News*, May 1941.
7. Quotes from a 1939 studio press release.
8. Nat Segaloff, *Hurricane Billy: The Stormy Life and Films of William Friedkin* (New York: William Morrow and Company, 1990).
9. Irene Lacher, "A Friedkin Connection," *Los Angeles Times*, May 12, 2013.
10. Joe Adamson, *Byron Haskin: Director's Guild of America Series 1* (New York: Scarecrow Press, 1995).

11. From Fredd Wayne's unpublished autobiography.

12. Don Siegel, *A Siegel Film: An Autobiography* (London: Faber and Faber, 1993).

13. "Burbank Library Gets Warner Research Services," *Daily Variety*, August 11, 1975.

14. Dick Rawlings, as told to Carlisle Jones, "It's a Picture," *Warner Club News*, January 1940.

15. From an interview with Dick Mason.

16. Stuart Jerome, *Those Crazy Wonderful Years When We Ran Warner Bros.* (Secaucus, NJ: Lyle Stuart Inc., 1983).

17. Ronald L. Davis, *Just Making Movies: Company Directors on the Studio System* (Oxford: University Press of Mississippi, 2005).

18. Jerome, *Those Crazy Wonderful Years When We Ran Warner Bros.*

19. From a Joe Musso interview.

20. Sophie Rosenstein, "Talent and Agriculture," *Warner Club News*, June 1943.

21. From a Dick Mason interview.

22. Jack Warner, *My First Hundred Years in Hollywood* (New York: Random House, 1964).

23. From a Dick Mason interview.

24. "The Green Room," *Warner Bros. Studio National Magazine*, August 29, 1947.

25. Debbie Reynolds and David Patrick Columbia, *Debbie: My Life* (New York: William Morrow and Company, 1988).

26. From a Dick Mason interview.

27. Don Winters, "The Dream Factory," *Los Angeles*, August 2012.

28. Interview with Tom Ray.

29. A quote from Williams at the 1996 Academy Awards show.

Chapter 4: The World on a Soundstage

1. From an interview with Dean Ricca.

2. Ronald Reagan and Richard C. Hubler, *Where's the Rest of Me?* (New York: Hawthorn, 1965).

3. Interview by Bill Shaefer of Champ Milaman.

4. From a 1941 press release.

5. From a 1948 publicity release.

6. Warren Littlefield, "With *Friends* like These," *Vanity Fair*, May 2012.

7. Bosley Crowther, "A Star Is Born Bows; Judy Garland, James Mason in Top Roles," *New York Times*, October 12, 1954.

8. Kenneth Crist, "Indoor Ocean," *Los Angeles Times Sunday Magazine*, March 17, 1940.

9. Bob Thomas, *Clown Prince of Hollywood* (New York: McGraw-Hill Publishing, 1990).

Chapter 5: The Backlot—30 Acres of Fairyland

1. Earl Hamner and Ralph Giffin, *Goodnight John Boy* (Nashville, TN: Cumberland House Publishing, 2002).

2. F. Scott Fitzgerald, *The Last Tycoon* (New York: Charles Schribner's Sons, 1941).

3. Nathaniel West, *The Day of the Locust* (New York: New Directions, 1939).

4. Cass Warner Sperling and Cork Miller, with Jack Warner Jr., *Hollywood Be Thy Name: The Warner Bros. Story* (Rocklin, CA: Prima Publishing, 1994).

5. From an interview with Clint Walker.

6. From an interview with Joan Leslie.

7. Chet Alters and Bud Weeks, "Prop Shoppers," *Warner Club News*, September 1957.

8. Will Hutchins, "A Touch of Hutch," *Western Clippings*, January 2009.

9. David Walstad, "For Years, This Was How the West Was Done," *Los Angeles Times*, August 13, 2003.

10. Walstad, "For Years, This Was How the West Was Done."

11. From an interview with James Hampton.

12. "Man Made Jungle," *Warner Club News*, January 1956.

13. Will Hutchins, "A Touch of Hutch," *Western Clippings*, March 2010.

14. Ann Louis Hamilton, *Eugene Lourie: A Directors Guild of America Oral History* (Los Angeles: DGA Press, 1983).

Chapter 6: Into Hollywood's Future

1. Bob Thomas, *Clown Prince of Hollywood* (New York: McGraw-Hill, 1990).

2. "The Day the Dream Factory Woke Up," *Life*, February 27, 1970.

3. Gene Fernett, *American Film Studios: An Historic Encyclopedia* (Jefferson, NC: McFarland & Company, 1988).

4. Charles Champlin, "Jack L. Warner Ends Association with Studio," *Los Angeles Times*, September 29, 1969.

5. Robert E. Wood, "Warner's, Columbia to Merge Studio Facilities," *Los Angeles Times*, June 4, 1971.

6. From my interview with an anonymous employee.

7. From the same anonymous interviewee cited in note 6.

Chapter 7: Shadow Lots

1. "Workmen Razing Home of Talkies," *Los Angeles Times*, March 20, 1955.

2. Bernard Rosenberg and Harry Silverstein, *The Real Tinsel* (New York: Macmillan Company, 1970).

3. From an interview with Lara Scheunemann.

4. "Jack Warner on His Quota Plans," *The Daily Film Renter Express*, October 26, 1937.

5. Quoted from Jerry L. Schneider's website, http://www.movielocationsplus.com.

6. Robert Lloyd, "The Unvarnished Pryor," *Los Angeles Times*, May 31, 2013.

7. Tinsley E. Yarbrough, *Those Great Western Movie Locations* (Greenville, NC: Tumbleweed Press, 2008).

Bibliography

Books

Adamson, Joe. *Byron Haskin: Director's Guild of America Series 1*. New York: Scarecrow Press, 1995.

Affron, Charles, and Affron, Mirella Jona. *Sets in Motion: Art Direction and Film Narrative*. New Brunswick, NJ: Rutgers University Press, 1995.

Behlmer, Rudy. *Inside Warner Brothers*. New York: Viking Press, 1985.

Bingen, Steven, Sylvester, Stephen X., and Troyan, Michael. *M-G-M: Hollywood's Greatest Backlot*. Solana Beach, CA: Santa Monica Press, 2011.

Davis, Ronald, L. *The Glamour Factory: Inside Hollywood's Big Studio System*. Dallas, TX: Southern Methodist University Press, 1993.

———. *Just Making Movies: Company Directors on the Studio System*. Oxford: University Press of Mississippi, 2005.

Eyman, Scott. *The Speed of Sound: Hollywood and the Talkie Revolution 1926–1930*. New York: Simon & Schuster, 1997.

Fernett, Gene. *American Film Studios: An Historic Encyclopedia*. Jefferson, NC: McFarland & Company, 1988.

Fitzgerald, F. Scott. *The Last Tycoon*. New York: Charles Scribner's Sons, 1941.

Friedrich, Otto. *City of Nets*. New York: Harper & Row, 1986.

Gabler, Neil. *An Empire of Their Own: How the Jews Invented Hollywood*. New York: Doubleday, 1988.

Hamilton, Ann Louis. *Eugene Lourie: A Directors Guild of America Oral History*. Los Angeles: DGA Press, 1983.

Hamner, Earl, and Giffin, Ralph. *Goodnight John Boy*. Nashville, TN: Cumberland House Publishing, 2002.

Harmetz, Aljean. *The Making of Casablanca: Bogart, Bergman, and World War II*. New York: Hyperion, 2002.

Hirschhorn, Clive. *The Warner Bros. Story*. New York: Crown Publishers, 1979.

A *History of Warner Bros Studio*. Burbank, CA: Warner Bros. Studio Facilities, 1995.

Jerome, Stuart. *Those Crazy Wonderful Years When We Ran Warner Bros.* Secaucus, NJ: Lyle Stuart Inc., 1983.

Jones, Chuck. *Chuck Amuck: The Life and Times of an Animated Cartoonist.* New York: Farrar, Straus and Giroux, 1989.

Medved, Harry, and Medved, Michael. *The Hollywood Hall of Shame.* New York: Perigee, 1984.

Pauley, Jim. *The Three Stooges: Hollywood Filming Locations.* Solana Beach, CA: Santa Monica Press, 2012.

Peerless, Grant, and Riding, Richard. *Leavesden Aerodrome: From Halifaxes to Hogwarts.* Gloucestershire, UK: Amberley, 2011.

Reagan, Ronald, and Hubler, Richard C. *Where's the Rest of Me?* New York: Hawthorn, 1965.

Reynolds, Debbie, and Columbia, David Patrick. *Debbie: My Life.* New York: William Morrow and Company, 1988.

Rosenberg, Bernard, and Silverstein, Harry. *The Real Tinsel.* New York: Macmillan Company, 1970.

Sanders, James. *Celluloid Skyline: New York and the Movies.* New York: Alfred A. Knopf, 2003.

Schickel, Richard, and Perry, George. *You Must Remember This: The Warner Bros. Story.* Philadelphia: Running Press, 2008.

Segaloff, Nat. *Hurricane Billy: The Stormy Life and Films of William Friedkin.* New York: William Morrow and Company, 1990.

Siegel, Don. *A Siegel Film: An Autobiography.* London: Faber and Faber, 1993.

Stephens, E. J., and Wanamaker, Marc. *Images of America: Early Warner Bros. Studios.* Charleston, SC: Arcadia Publishing, 2010.

Thomas, Bob. *Clown Prince of Hollywood: The Antic Life and Times of Jack L. Warner.* New York: McGraw-Hill Publishing, 1990.

Warner, Jack. *My First Hundred Years in Hollywood.* New York: Random House, 1964.

Warner Bros.: The Stuff That Dreams Are Made Of. Burbank, CA: Warner Bros. Entertainment Inc., 2005.

Warner Sperling, Cass, and Miller, Cork, with Warner, Jack, Jr. *Hollywood Be Thy Name: The Warner Bros. Story.* Rocklin, CA: Prima Publishing, 1994.

West, Nathaniel. *The Day of the Locust.* New York: New Directions, 1939.

Yarbrough, Tinsley E. *Those Great Western Movie Locations.* Greenville, NC: Tumbleweed Press, 2008.

Periodicals

Adams, Leith. "From The Archive." *WB Highlights*, vol. 7, 1997.

Alters, Chet, and Ramsay, Fred. "A Street Is Born." *Warner Club News*, December 1956.

————, and Weeks, Bud. "Prop Shoppers." *Warner Club News*, September 1957.

Anselm, Harvey. "New Mid-West Street." *Warner Club News*, September 1939.

"Arson Probers Looking for 'Fire Happy' Person." *Los Angeles Times*, July 10, 1952.

Auerback, Peter. "Casting." *Warner Club News*, November 1942.

Avery, John J. "Push It . . ." *Warner Club News*, May 1955.

"Blayney Matthews Writes Sabotage." *Warner Club News*, January 1942.

"Burbank Library Gets Warner Research Services." *Daily Variety*, August 11, 1975.

Champlin, Charles. "Jack L. Warner Ends Association with Studio." *Los Angeles Times*, September 29, 1969.

Clark, Vern, and Stoica, George. "Set Builders." *Warner Club News*, April 1942.

Crist, Kenneth. "Indoor Ocean." *Los Angeles Times Sunday Magazine*, March 17, 1940.

Crowther, Bosley. "'A Star Is Born' Bows; Judy Garland, James Mason in Top Roles." *New York Times*, October 12, 1954.

Dawes, Amy. "Fire on Walton Mountain." *Daily Variety*, November 25, 1991.

"The Day the Dream Factory Woke Up." *Life*, February 27, 1970.

Ditzel, Paul. "On the Job: Hollywood." *Firehouse*, October 1983.

"Films Go on Despite Fire." *Los Angeles Times*, December 6, 1934.

"Fire Hits Film Studio Sets." *Los Angeles Times*, July 21, 1983.

Forker, Jack. "Scoring a Picture." *Warner Club News*, November 1939.

Goedeck, Eddie. "MacWilliams Originated First Aid in Pics." *Warner Club News*, December 1940.

Granroth, Florence. "Research Department." *Warner Club News*, April 1955.

"The Green Room." *Warner Bros. Studio National Magazine*, August 29, 1947.

Hutchins, Will. "A Touch of Hutch." *Western Clippings*, January 2009.

———. "A Touch of Hutch." *Western Clippings*, March 2010.

"Jack Warner on His Quota Plans." *Daily Film Renter Express*, October 26, 1937.

Jones, Carlisle. "Pass the Aspirin." *Warner Club News*, December 1943.

Kuter, K. "Works of Art." *Warner Club News*, September 1941.

Lacher, Irene. "The Friedkin Connection." *Los Angeles Times*, May 12, 2013.

Landsberg, Klaus. "Workmen Razing Home of Talkies." *Los Angeles Times*, March 20, 1955.

Littlefield, Warren. "With *Friends* like These." *Vanity Fair*, May 2012.

Lloyd, Robert. "The Unvarnished Pryor." *Los Angeles Times*, May 31, 2013.

"Man Made Jungle." *Warner Club News*, January 1956.

Markovitz, Adam. "Casting the Spell." *Entertainment Weekly*, July 8–15, 2011.

Milliken, Carl. "Information Please." *Warner Club News*, June 1940.

"Montage." *Warner Club News*, August 1943.

"Murder Mystery to Be Filmed at Former Ranch." *Toledo Blade*, September 8, 1968.

"New Owner of Goldwyn Studio." *Daily Variety*, April 9, 1980.

O'Neal, R. R. "I Want a Laborer." *Warner Club News*, May 1941.

"Our Working Studio: Costume Department." *Warner Bros. Studios: Burbank Community Newsletter*, January 2010.

"Our Working Studio: Drapery Department." *Warner Bros. Studios: Burbank Community Newsletter*, July 2011.

"Our Working Studio: Property Department." *Warner Bros. Studios: Burbank Community Newsletter*, July 2010.

"Our Working Studio: Scenic Art." *Warner Bros. Studios: Burbank Community Newsletter*, July 2009.

"Pat Reagan (Daniel Boone)." *Warner Club News*, June 1955.

"Public Library Access to WB's 42 Years of Historic Film Data." *Daily Variety*, August 13, 1975.

Rawlings, Dick, as told to Jones, Carlisle. "It's a Picture." *Warner Club News*, January 1940.

Roop, Marshall. "Print It." *Warner Club News*, July 1943.

Rosenstein, Sophie. "Talent and Agriculture." *Warner Club News*, June 1943.

Ryan, Lee. "Plant Protection and Personnel." *Warner Club News*, November 1944.

Strong, Tom. "We Roll—Day and Night." *Warner Club News*, July 1941.

"The Studios of Hollywood Call the Roll of Honor." *Motion Picture Herald*, March 25, 1944.

Tomany, M. "Hit the Switches." *Warner Club News*, April 1940.

Vanden, Ruby. "Come and Get It." *Warner Club News*, December 1941.

Walstad, David. "For Years, This Was How the West Was Done." *Los Angeles Times*, August 13, 2003.

Wanamaker, Marc. "Historic Hollywood Movie Studios," part 1. *American Cinematographer*, March 1976.

———. "Historic Hollywood Movie Studios," part 2. *American Cinematographer*, April 1976.

———. "Historic Hollywood Movie Studios," part 3. *American Cinematographer*, May 1976.

"Warner Bros. to 'Taper off' Film Production." *Los Angeles Times*, March 5, 1953.

"Warner Brothers' Inferno." *Life*, June 9, 1952.

"Warners Regroups Research Dept. under Carl Milliken Jr." *Hollywood Reporter*, January 16, 1975.

"WB Back Lot Newest Addition." *Location Update*, December 2000.

Williams, Al G. "Meet Bob Martin." *Warner Club News*, June 1940.

Williams, Harry. "The Mailing Department." *Warner Club News*, December 1940.

Winters, Don. "The Dream Factory." *Los Angeles*, August 2012.

Wood, Robert E. "Warner's, Columbia to Merge Studio Facilities." *Los Angeles Times*, June 4, 1971.

Websites

http://www.tvstudiohistory.co.uk/studio%20history.htm#teddington early
    —Teddington Studios
http://nzpetesmatteshot.blogspot.com/2010/08/warner-bros-presents-sulute-to.html
    —Article about Stage 5 departments
http://www.movielocationsplus.com
    —General history of specific studio lots
http://groups.yahoo.com/group/StudioBacklots/
    —Lively studio backlot discussion site
http://www.bisonarchives.com
    —Bison Archives website
http://dearoldhollywood.blogspot.com
    —Blog with much invaluable location and backlot information
http://silentlocations.wordpress.com
    —John Bengtson's groundbreaking location site

Video

The Brothers Warner. Directed by Cass Warner Sperling. Los Angeles: Warner Home Video, 2010.

Here's Looking at You, Warner Bros. Directed by Robert Guenette. Los Angeles: Warner Home Video, 1991.

You Must Remember This: The Warner Bros. Story. Directed by Richard Schickel. Los Angeles: Warner Home Video, 2008.

Index

·············

About the Author

STEVEN BINGEN is an author, archivist, and nearly twenty-year Warner Bros. veteran who has contributed to numerous Hollywood-related books, magazine articles, and documentaries. He coauthored (with Stephen X. Sylvester and Michael Troyan) the bestselling MGM: *Hollywood's Greatest Backlot*, and wrote the text for the studio-published *Warner Bros: The Stuff That Dreams Are Made Of.* His screenplays include *The Ghastly Love of Johnny X* (2012) and *The Eleven* (scheduled for release in 2015). He lives in the world's largest backlot, also known as Los Angeles, CA, with his wife, Beth, and his daughter, Zoe.